Palgrave Studies in Classical Liberalism

Series Editors
David Hardwick
Vancouver, BC, Canada

Leslie Marsh
Department of Pathology and Laboratory
Medicine, Faculty of Medicine
University of British Columbia
Vancouver, BC, Canada

This series offers a forum to writers concerned that the central presuppositions of the liberal tradition have been severely corroded, neglected, or misappropriated by overly rationalistic and constructivist approaches. The hardest-won achievement of the liberal tradition has been the wrestling of epistemic independence from overwhelming concentrations of power, monopolies and capricious zealotries. The very precondition of knowledge is the exploitation of the epistemic virtues accorded by society's situated and distributed manifold of spontaneous orders, the DNA of the modern civil condition. With the confluence of interest in situated and distributed liberalism emanating from the Scottish tradition, Austrian and behavioral economics, non-Cartesian philosophy and moral psychology, the editors are soliciting proposals that speak to this multidisciplinary constituency. Sole or joint authorship submissions are welcome as are edited collections, broadly theoretical or topical in nature.

More information about this series at
http://www.palgrave.com/gp/series/15722

Eric S. Kos
Editor

Michael Oakeshott on Authority, Governance, and the State

Editor
Eric S. Kos
Department of Political Science
Siena Heights University
Adrian, MI, USA

Palgrave Studies in Classical Liberalism
ISBN 978-3-030-17454-5   ISBN 978-3-030-17455-2   (eBook)
https://doi.org/10.1007/978-3-030-17455-2

This Palgrave Macmillan imprint is published by the registered company Springer Nature
Switzerland AG
The registered company address is: Gewerbestrasse 11, 6330 Cham, Switzerland

ACKNOWLEDGEMENTS

For their help and support in preparing this collection, I would like to acknowledge Leslie Marsh, Joseph Raab, Shannon Kos, my editors at Palgrave Macmillan John Stegner and Michelle Chen, and all of the authors of this volume.

CONTENTS

LIST OF CONTRIBUTORS

James Alexander Department of Political Science, Bilkent University, Ankara, Turkey

Gary Browning Oxford Brookes University, Oxford, UK

Agostino Carrino University of Naples Federico II, Naples, Italy

David D. Corey Honors Program, Baylor University, Waco, TX, USA

Timothy Fuller Colorado College, Colorado Springs, CO, USA

Ferenc Hörcher Research Institute of Politics and Government, National University of Public Service, Budapest, Hungary;
Institute of Philosophy, Hungarian Academy of Sciences, Budapest, Hungary

Eric S. Kos Department of Political Science, Siena Heights University, Adrian, MI, USA

Carlos Marques de Almeida Institute for Political Studies, Catholic University of Portugal, Lisboa, Portugal

Jordan Rudinsky Department of Government, Harvard University, Cambridge, MA, USA

Gülşen Seven Department of Political Science and International Relations, TED University, Ankara, Turkey

Shekhar Singh Department of International Relations and Governance Studies, School of the Humanities and Social Sciences, Shiv Nadar University, Greater Noida, India

CHAPTER 1

Introduction

Eric S. Kos

One can fairly say, interest and scholarship on Michael Oakeshott has become a global phenomenon. In the decades since his death, Oakeshott's work has been translated into Italian, French, Spanish, Portuguese, Chinese, Japanese, Korean, and I am aware of one attempt to publish an essay in Serbian. Scholarship is also conducted all over the world, as the most recent volumes on Oakeshott attest,[1] and is conducted in many languages. What remains more elusive is explaining these phenomena. A recent commentator has noted how value in philosophy, as in art, is very personal; "always a matter of inner conviction, of immediate and sincere acknowledgement of the quality of thought displayed."[2] I suspect many first-time readers find in Oakeshott's writings what Oakeshott himself thought was a product of liberal learning: "the ability to detect the individual intelligence which is at work in every utterance."[3] That is, many find Oakeshott's writings irresistibly profound and erudite without sacrificing accessibility, eloquence, and style. Yet, his work did not initially meet a uniform and positive reception. Part of the reason may be his approach was not in step (deliberately I suspect) with

E. S. Kos (✉)
Department of Political Science, Siena Heights University,
Adrian, MI, USA
e-mail: ekos@sienaheights.edu

© The Author(s) 2019
E. S. Kos (ed.), *Michael Oakeshott on Authority, Governance, and the State*, Palgrave Studies in Classical Liberalism,
https://doi.org/10.1007/978-3-030-17455-2_1

1

his contemporaries, as many commentators have noticed. His approach to political philosophy clearly made his originally published readings confusing and misunderstood to some. The attraction continues, however, to new students far beyond Anglo-American circles, which is striking for a thinker who is in so many ways quintessentially English. The essays here help explain this broadening interest, for they explore new materials available to students of Oakeshott, they engage many of the perennial but universal themes in political philosophy that Oakeshott himself found of interest, and they contribute to both contemporary academic debates and to more practical political concerns.

Many of these essays draw on newly accessible materials. Oakeshott's early lectures at Cambridge, the lectures he developed at the London School of Economics in the 1950s that became a long-running seminar, the many unpublished works (essays and notebooks), and hard to access publications and book reviews have become more readily available due largely to the energies of Luke O'Sullivan.[4] These works are important not only because they often contain different iterations of Oakeshott's ideas in his originally published work, but also because they allow one to follow the development of Oakeshott's thought both in terms of what interested and concerned him, and how his thinking on particular matters evolved. A number of authors below have taken up these early materials to show Oakeshott's continuing and evolving interest in particular ideas.

The ideas taken up here (authority, governance, the state) have been an inextricable part of the study of politics since the earliest of times and have remained a source of controversy and learning. Their centrality to the field makes clarity in these matters essential, and Oakeshott's contribution to this ongoing study has been significant for its unconventional perspective and its historical sensitivity. Oakeshott is unique in concluding the state is not a static structure to behold, but is historically emergent and, as such, dynamic and evolving. Oakeshott, as many of the essays below explore, understands the modern state as a tension between two different visions, each rooted in a particular moral practice and set of ideas. The implications of this idea of the state ripple out into other areas. Oakeshott's views on governance and authority are nuanced and depend on his focus. When theorizing civil association, for example, governance is about attending to non-instrumental rules that sustain conditions of civility, and authority is rooted in acknowledged procedures to promulgate law. When theorizing the modern European state, he recognizes governance and authority are a messier mixture of policy goals and procedures, of power and legitimacy. His views here offer novel, refreshing, controversial, and fruitful perspectives on these important political concepts.

Controversy continues in contemporary debates in political theory. One such issue involves the authority of the state in the modern world—a world increasingly characterized by plurality and individualism. David Boucher has characterized the issue variously as the "depoliticization of politics" and "the crisis of our times."[5] The question here is to what extent a state's authority rests on compatriots united in common cause, a position identified with Carl Schmitt, and to what extent can non-coerced adherence of citizens rest on a *process* of decision-making, a position attached to Oakeshott. For Oakeshott, the state reveals itself historically as an unresolved tension between the two, but theoretically as an ideal of civil association. A related issue involves the character of the rule of law. If the rule of law is a primary function of the state and is valued in part for its non-instrumental character (that it helps solve disputes through set procedures and practices, when it is recognized substantive appeals cannot be universalized) is and can the rule of law be neutral, or does it necessarily promote a substantive end? That is, how does one understand the seeming non-instrumental nature of the rule of law and the challenge liberal realism poses that the rule of law can never be neutral? Readers will need to decide themselves, but the essays here help readers clarify the questions and the possible responses. These are not just academic questions.

The theoretical questions raised here have immediate bearing on our contemporary situation. As I write, the world seems to be experiencing the resurgence of a particular form of statism, where increasingly the exercise of state power is justified and consolidated, in populist fashion, on the basis of achieving particular policy outcomes. Politically, citizens' allegiance is pinned to satisfying citizens' desires; and the state becomes merely an instrument to achieving those desires, authority slowly evaporates, governance becomes management of resources and people, and long-standing institutions (like the rule of law, constitutional provisions, and political norms), that have given structure and pattern to how the arrangements of society are attended to historically, have become casualties to putative progress. The questions here have existential importance, as our understandings of authority, governance, and the state influence their functioning in the world.

Each of the essays below addresses these questions, sometimes explicitly, sometimes implicitly, with new and interesting answers. Arguing that references to "*the* state" are an attempt to strip metaphor out of politics, Alexander convincingly shows that the adoption of the term "the state" amounts to a triumph of vacuous neutrality. In tracing various definitions of the state, Alexander not only clarifies the ways Oakeshott himself used the term and how that usage changed over time, but also highlights the more fruitful approach Oakeshott takes in "theorizing" and describing the modern European state—a task made easier with the newly accessible Oakeshott materials. The approach is to see the state and its authority as historically emergent; an approach that puts flesh back on the stripped-down state and allows Oakeshott to more successfully bridge the modern gap between freedom and authority with history and tradition.

Browning addresses the philosophical and historical approaches Oakeshott uses, especially in *On Human Conduct*, to argue the image of conversation Oakeshott invokes to characterize the relationship between these two explanatory modes imagines them more separated than in fact they are. The separation, and even irrelevance to one another, implied by conversation cannot be sustained even in Oakeshott's own work. The Lectures are examined as an example of how history and philosophy are intertwined. Philosophers' questions grow out of historical contexts, the history of political philosophy requires philosophical expertise to be told, and philosophy itself is a historically emergent and changing practice.

Taking up the question of what grounds the authority of the state, and as a partial answer to the question of how political the state is, Corey investigates modern theories of the character of the liberal political order and finds that legitimating theories of the liberal state fall into consent theories, benefits theories, and theories of procedural fairness. He shows them all to be philosophically wanting. The problem, as Corey sees it, is some theoretical justifications work, however philosophically flawed, as long as citizens don't push too hard for their political demands. The concern is that when modern pluralism and intense partisan conflict confront an increasingly powerful state, it becomes more apparent to citizens that there are winners and losers in the political process. This undermines the philosophically shaky, de facto legitimacy the modern state rests upon. The Oakeshottian formulation of that state as a civil association, with its more limited scope and power, is more compatible with these contemporary conditions and the continuing necessity for obedience and some form of legitimacy. A certain abandonment of authority, in recognition that politics will necessarily involve illegitimate exercises of power, compels the deliberate limiting of centralized power. An interesting question this essay raises is whether Oakeshott's concern was over the lack of an adequate philosophical justification of the exercise of power or whether he was more worried about the implications of mistaking questions of legitimacy with questions of policy.

The relationship between the rule of law, which a state as a civil association requires, and our other liberal commitments, like taking rights seriously, is the central concern of Fuller's essay. Three theorists of law (Ronald Dworkin, Michael Oakeshott, and John Finnis) exemplify different understandings of this relationship. Dworkin's attempt to defend both trans-political rights and the general community welfare is imagined to transform "the political into the consensual, without resort to significant coercion," through the agency of the ideal judge. Dworkin's ideal judge is seen by him to be in a better position to determine the fundamental principles in the existing legal arrangements and either protecting rights or "evolving" those rights in light of progress toward the general, communal welfare. Here the aim of social progress and taking rights seriously takes priority over the rule of law. Oakeshott's view is shown to reverse the priority. The rule of law is a moral relationship, a practice, that doesn't have a specifiable end like protecting rights or making progress toward the just society. Rather, the only ideal association, compatible with free individuals and capable of unanimous subscription to, is not a relationship in terms of an extrinsic goal, but a relationship in terms of a manner or practice of making decisions; of authority; of acknowledging the right of whatever constituted authorities are recognized in a community. John Finnis offers a third perspective that seeks to navigate the arbitrary imposition of one group's preferences and pure proceduralism, by seeing law and rights through the vantage point of the universal desire for human flourishing and identifying the principles and variables that contribute to human flourishing. This is a natural law perspective that recognizes a universal desire for human well-being that prompts individuals to both articulate and make defensible choices in light of shared and acknowledged goods. Individual choice reflects the universal desire to live well. Rights are an expression of the recognition that every individual's well-being must be considered. The rule of law is the technical expression of this respect, a respect which relieves neither the individual nor the community of continual judgment and moral responsibility.

Almeida traces Oakeshott's understanding of the state as a tension through its various iterations, from earlier essays to the one in *On Human Conduct*, with the aim of showing the compatibility of the authority of the state and the freedom of the modern individual. Modern freedom is analyzed in Oakeshott's thought. The absence of concentrations of power, that Oakeshott insists are a necessary condition for freedom, reflect a debt to Burke and to Locke. Oakeshott is drawn to Burke's idea that power is distributed across past, present, and future, and to the elements in Locke's view of limit governmental power, like the division of powers and the rule of law. Almeida sees this combination resulting in a conservative perspective and a liberal outlook for Oakeshott. Civil association and the rule of law are shown to be the most compatible with these conditions of freedom.

Rudinsky examines the points of agreement and divergence between Oakeshott and the Cambridge School, in particular J. G. A. Pocock and Quentin Skinner. Pocock found Oakeshott's writings on tradition useful and developed them as a methodological starting point of his historical inquiries. In particular, Oakeshott's central idea that theorizing was an abstract abridgment of a concrete manner of living was self-consciously adopted by Pocock, as was Oakeshott's critical claim that not all reflection on politics is the same, but there are levels or varieties of reflection on politics. Pocock rejects Oakeshott's claims regarding the non-practical nature of historical inquiry as "antinomian and anarchic"—the reaction of conservatives answering radical historians. Skinner too shares the view that practice precedes theory, as well as the conviction that the modern state was constructed out of the remnants of the medieval world. However, where Skinner relies on a Weberian view of the state, Oakeshott resisted monolithic definitions of the state and, as we have seen, characterized the modern European state as an unresolved tension. Oakeshott's and Pocock's view that there exist many types of reflection on politics, have both rejecting the reduction of all political thought to political ideology, unlike Skinner who concluded there was "nothing but the battle."

In Seven's essay, Oakeshott is initially situated in the objectivist versus relativist framework (placing him in the relativist camp), and in particular he is identified with the realism as reimagined by Bernard Williams—a realism that provides a guide to collective human action, but not from a viewpoint external to the social and political world. The essay is no mere attempt at classification, but rather, is a thoughtful engagement with Oakeshott's unique position that takes the form of an analysis of the ways in which Oakeshott has affinities with and diverges from the framework that dominates analytic schools of political philosophy. A threefold taxonomy of realists (as opposed to moralists) is developed that helps one think through how Oakeshott imagines the task of governing in the contemporary world. Oakeshott's view of the manner of governing in the contemporary world, exhibited most fully in the essay "The Politics of Faith and the Politics of Skepticism,"[6] is argued to be a sober yet optimistic one.

Horcher investigates Oakeshott's early lectures and an under-explored lecture on conservatism to show the connection between his view of the state and his peculiar brand of conservatism. The lectures reveal the significant historical origins of the ideal types Oakeshott laid out in *On Human Conduct*. The distinction between teleocratic and nomocractic views of rule is laid out with historical examples to show Oakeshott's disposition toward a politics of moderation. The particular understanding of human nature in the essay on conservatism is shown to be an important component in Oakeshott favoring a more minimal state in terms of its scope in directing human activity.

Concerned over the growing power of international courts and adjudicative bodies, Carrino analyzes how this particular source of law is moving the international order toward a teleocratic governance, and away from a rule of law. Carrino finds in Oakeshott's distinctions between teleocratic and nomocratic states and between a politics of faith and a politics of skepticism a way to help us unpack this growing shift toward an international order that is envisioned as an enterprise for reshaping the world in its image instead of providing a framework within which states and individuals can pursue their own self-chosen ends. A global *universitas* is emerging, that threatens the very freedom and pluralism the proponents of this universal perspective believe they are advancing but that is in fact corrosive of the very freedom and the rule of law that protects it.

Singh's essay brings into conversation three critics of rationalism (Friedrich Hayek, James Scott, and Michael Oakeshott). Each contributes to a powerful cautionary tale about comprehensive governmental planning and directing of a society's activities. Hayek is skeptical of the ability of human beings to have the kind of panoptic view of complex societies necessary to understand the whole, let alone direct it, and believes attempts at such direction necessitate a concentration of power at odds with democratic rule. The better alternative, according to Hayek, is a regulatory scheme that allows for individuals to plan and direct their own lives. Scott points out, the attempt to rule in this comprehensive manner requires a simplification of highly complex societal processes, puts a heavy premium on administrative and scientific efficiency, looks for crisis opportunities to consolidate the necessary power to achieve its goals, and weakens civil society—all of which work to erode traditional patters of life in favor of planned, universal, and efficient practices that actually work against the goals of efficiency, rationality, and the necessary cooperation needed to make modern states function. Oakeshott's critique is shown to be more philosophical in not abridging the "thick experience of actual practices" into a doctrine, does not prioritize practical activity over other valuable activities, and, in so doing, is better able to theorize the variety of human activities and their relationship to each other.

Cleary Oakeshott's work continues to challenge, prod, and inspire thoughtful responses. Many of these responses recall us back to the earlier question of Oakeshott's appeal beyond the Anglo-American scene. Oakeshott's work as a whole I believe provokes this question. He made a significant contribution to understanding the English theorist Thomas Hobbes and wrote extensively on the rule of law. Yet, the influence of German Idealism and a deep acquaintance with a variety of continental traditions make a clear mark on his thought. His references to Chinese thought invite connections to these other traditions.[7] In many ways Oakeshott was, like Socrates, aware and appreciative of the way of life his particular city afforded him, but remained as a philosopher always on the periphery of the city, as a kind of skeptical cosmopolitan presence, eager to learn from wherever the offer was made.

Chor-yung Cheung has suggested Chinese readers are more drawn to the rationalism and planning of a Frederick Hayek rather than the skepticism of Oakeshott, but Chinese liberals are also drawn to the notion of a limited state.[8] Though, as O'Sullivan notes, this makes the state an "instrumental device for accommodating diversity and promoting liberal reform" more than the kind of state Oakeshott himself imagined in civil association.[9] An informal survey of the authors of these essays has suggested a number of reasons for his wider appeal. His reception in Italy was partly through the translation of *On Human Conduct* by an Italian sociologist of law, but that his thoughts on governing and rationalism have garnered interest (with *Rationalism in Politics*, and *The Politics of Faith and the Politics of Scepticism* in print in Italian). In India, not surprisingly, there has been interest in exploring the idea of the rule of law and civil association, especially in theories that offer alternatives to democratic consent as the basis of legitimacy. Interestingly, some of the attraction has been in Oakeshott offering an alternative to a style of Indian theorizing that is dominated by pragmatism and normative theory. These are, no doubt, only preliminary suggestions for why Oakeshott has continued to find an expanding audience.

What can be said with certainty is that the lasting value of Oakeshott's work will be its continued ability to, as it did with his immediate acquaintances and his initial audience, elicit fresh and lively thinking, and to enrich and extend our continuing conversation.

NOTES

1. See, for example, David Dyzenhaus and Thomas Poole eds., *Law, Liberty and State: Oakeshott, Hayek and Schmitt on the Rule of Law* (Cambridge: Cambridge University Press, 2015); Terry Nardin ed., *Michael Oakeshott's Cold War Liberalism* (New York: Palgrave Macmillan, 2015); and Noël K. O'Sullivan ed., *The Place of Michael Oakeshott in Contemporary Western and Non-Western Thought* (Exeter: Imprint Academic, 2017).
2. Efraim Podoksik ed., *The Cambridge Companion to Oakeshott* (Cambridge: Cambridge University Press, 2012), 1.
3. Michael Oakeshott, "Learning and Teaching," in *The Voice of Liberal Learning: Michael Oakeshott on Education*, ed. Timothy Fuller (New Haven and London: Yale University Press, 1989), 61.
4. A multi-volume set, under the series title *Selected Writings*, is continued to be produced and is published through Imprint Academic.
5. David Boucher, "The Depoliticization of Politics: Crisis and Critique in Oakeshott, Schmitt, and Koselleck," in *The Place of Michael Oakeshott in Contemporary Western and Non-Western Thought*, ed. Noël K. O'Sullivan (Exeter: Imprint Academic, 2017), 107–22; David Boucher, "Schmitt, Oakeshott, and the Hobbesian Legacy in the Crisis of Our Times," in *Law, Liberty and State*, ed. Dyzenhaus, 123–25.
6. Michael Oakeshott, *The Politics of Faith and the Politics of Scepticism*, ed. Timothy Fuller (New Haven and London: Yale University Press, 1996).
7. See Michael Oakeshott, *Rationalism in Politics and Other Essays*, new and expanded edition, ed. Timothy Fuller (Indianapolis: Liberty Press, 1991), 14n7, 41n41, 236n8, 480n2; Oakeshott, *The Politics of Faith*, 121n3.
8. Chor-yung Cheung, "Oakeshott, Hayek and the Conservative Turn of Chinese Liberalism," in *The Place of Michael Oakeshott*, ed. O'Sullivan, 160–80.
9. O'Sullivan, *The Place of Michael Oakeshott*, 16.

CHAPTER 2

The State Is the Attempt to Strip Metaphor Out of Politics

James Alexander

I

In *On Human Conduct* Oakeshott wrote: "The use of the word 'state' to identify the emergent associations of modern Europe may be recognised as a masterpiece of neutrality: it revealed nothing about what might be thought to be the character of the associates or the condition (*l'estat*) they shared."[1]

This is the key to any theory of the state.

A theory of the state is a theory as if written on a blank slate. The state is the attempt to strip metaphor out of politics. It attempts to remove all older and authoritative meanings from politics. It opens up the opportunity to theorise until one has stated decisively what the object of theorisation has to be if it is coherent. It also makes it possible to theorise this object as if it is nothing more than the contestation over its very meaning. What is remarkable about Oakeshott is, in

J. Alexander (✉)
Department of Political Science, Bilkent University, Ankara, Turkey
e-mail: jalexand@bilkent.edu.tr

© The Author(s) 2019
E. S. Kos (ed.), *Michael Oakeshott on Authority, Governance, and the State*, Palgrave Studies in Classical Liberalism,
https://doi.org/10.1007/978-3-030-17455-2_2

the course of a long life, he saw it both ways. I shall say something in this chapter about both of Oakeshott's ways of seeing the state, though not simply for the purpose of exposition or explanation of the structure of Oakeshott's thought or even narrative of the development of this thoughts—though there is some of that here, and it *is* of interest—but also to try to say something decisive about the still vexed subject of the state.

At all times Oakeshott insisted that the state is not government.

Let me say it on my own account.

The state is not government.

We can of course use the word "state" to mean "government" but, if we do, we are emptying everything of interest out of the word state. We are using a part, even if a necessary part, the ruling part, to stand for the whole. And this is a mistake.

In this chapter I shall pay rather more attention to the word "state" than is usual. Oakeshott himself wrote that "the task is one of definition, not the definition of words, but of concepts".[2] But it seems to me that there would be no concept of the state without the word "state". And, significantly, I think that the ambiguities of the word have thrown up conceptual ambiguities which have caused, conditioned and structured much in the theories which have flourished under its banner.

The word refers to a particular condition or "estate". It seems to me that the word "state" has three successive meanings. A "state" may mean a condition, *any* condition: which could be a natural or conventional condition or a particular condition such as the civil condition. The last gives us the second meaning. A "state" may mean the civil condition, and therefore the entity that enjoys a civil condition: the body politic, or commonwealth, or some sort of abstraction that stands for the whole, such as a legal fiction, a moral person, or a mere word. The third meaning is given by what makes a civil condition possible. A "state" may mean the particular thing that makes it possible for the whole to enjoy the civil condition, for instance, a government or law or something else.

The three meanings are, in short:

1. a condition;
2. a civil condition;
3. the sufficient condition of a civil condition.

The state, therefore, *can* mean government, if government is the sufficient condition of the civil condition. This is acceptable in ordinary speech. But there is nothing more exasperating than the tendency of scholars to follow this common habit of speech, and insist, after a few asides about Hobbes or Weber, that the state *only* means government. The equation "state = government" is still common in many textbooks and scholarly works. It should not be. The state *may be* limited to government, but limiting it by definition so it can *only* mean government is to empty out any significance the word "state" could be said to have had in suggesting to us anything at all about the nature of the experience that made anyone consider it worth talking about it in the first place.

Some writers have seen this very clearly. Quentin Skinner has rightly criticised the "reductionist view of the state" by which "*state* and *government*" are "synonymous terms".[3] He blames Laski and Hobhouse for this, in their overreactions to the exalted theories of Bosanquet and Green. Even a scholar as competent as Moses Finley could paraphrase Laski with approval: "There is no meaningful distinction between state and government. Political metaphysicians notwithstanding, the citizens (or subjects) in any regime equate the two."[4] This is simply hopeless: evidence that meanings have been confused is not evidence that they have to be confused. In fact Laski was saying something slightly subtler than this, that "a state is what its government does", which, if one thinks about it, is not quite the same as saying "the state is government".[5] Nevertheless, Laski was obviously insisting on a reduction, even if not an entirely thoughtless one. And it was this tendency in Laski which earned him Oakeshott's undying contempt.[6] Skinner makes much of this point because, against the "reductionist view of the state" he wants to advocate a Hobbesian view of the state as a "fictional" or legal person.[7] But this is not the only possibility, though Skinner seems to suggest that it is the only serious one.

If the state is not the government, what is it? Skinner suggests it is a person, not a natural person, but a legal person, a *persona ficta*, a person who—as Hobbes argued—stands for the incorporation of the multitude of people into one body at the moment when they transfer their own liberty and power to a sovereign, and thereafter personates or represents them. But Skinner's suggestion is not the only one. There are perhaps two other definitions, which do more justice to the meaning of the word "state" than his definition does. That is to say, they make it clear that if one is ever to say that the state is a "person" that one should admit that this is a metaphor, or, better, an analogy, and no more than that.[8] A state is properly a condition. So one suggestion is Kelsen's suggestion that the state is the condition in the sense of being the law, and specifically, that it is the personification of the law. "If law is the will of the state, then the state is the person, which is to say, the personification, of law."[9] (It should be emphasised that "the personification of the law" is rather different from a "legal person": a legal person is only a person within the law whereas the personification of the law though doubtless, for Kelsen, something within law, is also, by definition, something more than within law.) If this is reminiscent of the Old Testament emphasis on law, then the next suggestion is reminiscent of the New Testament claim that Jesus came not to destroy the law but to fulfil it (Matt. 5.17; cf. Rom. 13.10). This is Hegel's suggestion that the state is the condition in the sense of being the highest ordering principle of ethical life. The completion of the law necessarily involves going beyond the law to something else—if we agree with St. Paul, to something like love.

Neither of these two suggestions adequately recognises that the state may not only be a condition for action but also may be a condition that emerges out of and is sustained by action. So there is also the possibility of conjugating the state not in terms of law alone, but also in terms of power, policy or purpose.

Again, what we see is that Oakeshott theorised the state in two ways, the first in Hegelian terms as the condition of all action, and the second in his own terms as something which could be conceived in two ways, as both a relative condition of action and also as an entity constituted by and conditioning itself by its own actions.

This chapter is a study of Oakeshott's two theories of the state. As those familiar with his works will know, his first theory of the state was a singular theory. His second theory of the state was, so to speak, a tension between two theories. Both were remarkable conceptions. The former was bolder; the latter subtler. I shall consider them both as theories of the state, but I shall do so not only in the spirit of exposition, but also to think with and through and beyond Oakeshott in order to try to say something distinctive about the state.

II

The origin of the word "state" is in an Indo-European root "*sta-*", "to stand". The Greek word *stasis* and the Latin word *status* originally meant a place to stand, where one stands, one's standing, hence, of course, one's condition or status. It is very interesting to contrast them. The first thing to observe is that the word *stasis* is more complicated than the word *status*. The word *stasis* was a word with two meanings in ancient Greek. Let me quote Carl Schmitt on the subject: "*Stasis* means in the first place quiescence, tranquility, standpoint, status; its antonym is *linesis*, movement. But *stasis* also means, in the second place, (political) *unrest*, movement, uproar and civil war."[10] It is a classic case of a word that had two opposite meanings—the sort of word Hegel and Heidegger thought was evidence that Greek was the greatest philosophical language (closely followed by German). So *stasis* could mean both a calm state, and its opposite, a turbulent state. Whereas the first implies a steady state, that is, fixity, the norm, a standard, something which ought not to be changed, the second implies crisis or disruption, that is, disordered change, or a continual changeability which itself can also be a settled condition, though not one to be deliberately sought out. For the Greeks *stasis* in the second sense was the worst possible political experience. But the inner dialectic of the Greek term should make it clear why no theory of the state was possible for Plato or Aristotle. In order to stand for a concept, the word "state" had to be one that did not have an inner dialectic but could itself be the condition and culmination of a dialectic. Liddell and Scott's *Greek-English Lexicon* and Lewis and Short's *Latin Dictionary* suggest that the difference between the two terms is that *stasis* appears to be distinguished horizontally, on a plane, whereas *status* appears to be distinguished vertically, in a hierarchy. *Stasis* always referred to a particular condition, *here* rather than *there*, whereas *status*, though it could refer to a particular condition, *higher* rather than *lower*, could also refer to an entire condition.

   In the *Oxford Latin Dictionary*, *status* is related to words that are all concerned with fixity. It tells us that it is "the fact or condition of being in a standing position", "a particular way of standing", "stature", "the position taken up by a person or thing", "any intellectual, moral, political etc, position", "the point... where the defendant makes a stand", "physical state or condition", "the circumstances affecting a person or thing at a given time, state, condition", "a state of affairs, a situation", "the arrangement, constitution, order (of a state or other institution)", "station in life, ranking", "legal position".[11] The dictionary cites one of the most famous lines in Cicero's *De Re Publica*, "the best state of the city", *optimus status civitatis*. This indicates that, even when the word was used in a political context, it was not any "state" but the "city" or something else that made it political. Not "the best state", but "the best state of the city". As several scholars have pointed out in the last half-century, the key shift which announces the arrival of the modern concept of the state—or, to speak more properly, the modern meaning of the word "state"—is the shift

> *from*
> "the state of *x*," where *x* is the substantive
> *to*
> "the state," where "state" is the substantive.

Before the sixteenth century everyone always spoke of "the state of *x*": the state of the city (*status civitatis*), the state of the republic (*status reipublicae*), the state of the church (*status ecclesiae*), the state of the king (*status regis*), the state of the kingdom (*status regni*), the state of the regime (*status regiminis*) or the state of the prince (*status princeps*).[12] The word "state" just meant "condition" or "standing". But after the emergence of the concept of the state, it was possible to speak of "the state" as a substantive, as if "the state" no longer qualified a substantive "*x*" but was itself the substantive "*x*". After this everyone spoke of the state, *lo stato, der Staat, l'état*.

The shift from "the state of *x*" to "the state" was very important. It signalled the emergence of the state as a substantive that denoted the most decisive or significant political entity.

The Oxford English Dictionary indicates that what happened in English—and we know that the same thing happened in French, German, Italian, Spanish and other languages—was that a word which originally stood for *any condition* became a word for *a particular condition*, the condition of a part, an exalted part, and finally, and decisively, became a word for the condition of the entire body politic *such that* the condition of the entire body politic became the name of the entire body politic.[13] Nothing was specified about what sort of condition this was.

It was just a condition. It was not a condition of anything: or, rather, it was nothing other than the condition of itself, the state of itself.

Oakeshott was aware of all this. In his lectures on the history of political thought delivered at the London School of Economics in 1968 and 1969, he observed that the word "state" was "a word for a new political experience". It was "not originally a political word". It "meant a 'condition' of any sort". "When the Romans used the word politically they showed they were doing so by qualifying it by another word."[14] Of course, once the word "state" became a substantive it incorporated into itself meanings which were bestowed on it from older words like community, commonwealth, republic, city, empire. But the etymological enigma remains. The word "state" most simply means "condition" or "standing". It is, simply, "the condition"—the condition in which we all exist—or "the standing"—the standing of someone, our rulers perhaps, or both the rulers and the ruled. Everyone knows that "standing" is a metaphor: how do you stand, where do you stand, what is your status, where is your place in the hierarchy? But the interesting thing is how pale this metaphor is when we consider the distinctively political meaning of state as not meaning only "status" but "most significant political entity". It seems to suggest a circularity. What is the condition? "The condition is *the* condition." Not the condition of this or that particular but of all the entire entity. What is the standing? "The standing is *the* standing." Not the standing of this or that particular but a general standing. The state is a status which stands by itself because it qualifies no substantive but is itself the substantive. The fact that something stands is the only determinate thing about it: we cannot say exactly *what* is standing. We name it by the fact that it *is*. In the same way, the condition is not this or that but simply the condition. We are conditioned by our condition. The standing stands. The state states.[15]

Skinner's history of the concept of the state involves much complication but is at root very simple. First, the state was the state of the ruler. Then, it was the state of the ruled. Finally, it was something in itself: not the state *of* something but simply the state (which Bodin called in a memorable phrase *l'estat en soi*).[16] In other words, when we spoke of the "state of the king", we had a state which was sanctioned from above, *Deo gratia*, by the grace of God; when we spoke of the "state of the people", we had a state which was sanctioned by some modern European variant of the old Roman *lex regia* by which the people conveyed its *imperium* and *potestas* to the emperor; and when we spoke of the "state", we no longer had a state sanctioned by what Walter Ullmann called a "descending" theory or an "ascending" theory[17] but what we could call a "suspended theory". The state of Hobbes and Hegel, theorise it as we will, is something which hangs in the air.

Ankersmit may be right to say that "language in the West wants to erase itself by being transparent with regard to an underlying reality to which it refers and that is represented by it".[18] But what I want to claim here is that the state was a transparent entity on which it would be possible to inscribe theories which would do the greatest justice to reality for the very reason that those theories were far more detached from any reality than any previous political theories had been.

This makes the state into a constitutive *arcanum*, and I am not fully convinced that I understand the meaning of this as well as I would like. All we can do is trace its effects. Almost everyone since Hobbes has been aware of the significance of metaphors in politics, has disliked them and has found it impossible to avoid them. "Hobbes denounced metaphor with Elizabethan metaphorical exuberance."[19] Like Hobbes, everyone who noticed the ambiguity of language wanted to overcome it. Consider George Cornewall Lewis's *Use and Abuse of Political Terms*: even though he was a contemporary of Carlyle, who in *Sartor Resartus* said that there was nothing in language that was not metaphorical, Lewis also wanted to strip metaphor out of politics.[20] In the twentieth century, philosophers became more sensitive to language, though in general this was not the case for philosophers, theorists or scientists who concerned themselves with the base coinage of politics. What makes Oakeshott distinctive in the history of political philosophy was his sensitivity to language. He had no grand theory about the status of language and metaphor in general, of whether all language is metaphorical or whether there is a distinction between literal and metaphorical language.[21] But he considered metaphors of state carefully, discarded them and favoured instead analogies for the state. And, quite remarkably, as we shall see, Oakeshott's favoured analogy for the state was *language*.

It is worth distinguishing metaphor and analogy so we can make some sort of sense of this. The root of both metaphor and analogy is the simile. A simile says "x is like y". Usually the equation is a simple one. Metaphors and analogies complicate the comparison. A metaphor declares that "x is y", which is one form of complication, suggesting identity rather than likeness. An analogy, like a simile, declares that "x is like y", but compares two complex entities, rather than compare a complex one to a simple one. The difference between a metaphor and an analogy is best understood in terms of complexity. In a metaphor we identify something complicated with something simpler, whereas in an analogy we compare two different equally obscure structures.[22] Metaphors are chosen for their suggestiveness, and depend on the association of ideas. But analogies present a greater difficulty since "abstract categories and relationships are transferred from one domain to another in order to organise the latter".[23] This explains Oakeshott's preference for analogy over metaphor. Any metaphor, whether spiritual, organic or mechanical (the state is a tree, a wheel, a body, a machine, a person, etc.), is a narrowing of meaning—a *synecdoche*, in which a partial characteristic is offered as an explanation of the whole. (The most brutal *synecdoche* of all is "state = government"). Metaphors of course abound. "Political theory is replete with them."[24] But they almost always narrow understanding. An analogy, on the other hand, at least suggests that the meaning of the state is a complicated one.

III

Oakeshott did not publish much by the prodigious standards of a later generation. But since his death, or since just before his death, manuscripts have been found which have enabled us to follow the shifts in his thought better than we otherwise could have done. The best way to make sense of his writings on politics and the state is to see it as falling into a stage of early certainty, a stage of confusion, a stage of drafting and redrafting his ideas, and finally a stage of certainty, such as it was. Through all this we find three sorts of definition of the state, two of which are worthy of study.

In making sense of the development in Oakeshott's thought I think it is best if we set aside the essays collected in *Rationalism and Politics* (1962). These point in no very clear direction, though it is obvious that Oakeshott by the 1950s was very confident in both his criticism of other positions and assertion of his own. It is much more instructive to consider Oakeshott's development in relation to the works which form the bookends of his career, *Experience and Its Modes* (1933) and *On Human Conduct* (1975), and by considering the relation of these to the many works he left unpublished at his death but which have now been published. This reveals that there was a high doctrine of the state in the Fellowship dissertation, "A Discussion of Some Matters Preliminary to the Study of Political Philosophy" (1925),[25] the lectures on "The Philosophical Approach to Politics" (1928–1930),[26] the article "The Authority of the State" (1929),[27] and even the manuscript of "The Concept of a Philosophy of Politics" (which has been dated by Fuller to the mid-1940s though Gerencser must be right to date it to the 1930s[28] since phrases like "the standpoint of the totality of experience" are very reminiscent of *Experience and Its Modes*).[29] After this, there is a silent abandonment of this position. The article entitled "The Concept of a Philosophical Jurisprudence" (1938) seems to be transitional.[30] It is an attempt to think through some of the ambiguities of law—it is at this point that "ambiguity" becomes a theme in Oakeshott's writing. Yet he admits: "I do not pretend to have thought out a complete philosophy of politics myself."[31]

What followed was something quite remarkable. As far as his contemporaries were concerned, Oakeshott was the author of *Rationalism in Politics*. It still dominates his reputation. But far more significant was that he wrote at least three successive recensions of the same argument—first, in the manuscript book entitled "The Politics of Faith and the Politics of Scepticism" (which has been dated to around 1952),[32] second, in the lectures on "Morality and Politics in Modern Europe" (delivered at Harvard in 1958),[33] and, third, in the "Lectures on the History of Political Thought" (delivered at the London School of Economics in 1968 and 1969, though of course for many years before that)[34]—an argument which found eventual publication in the book *On Human Conduct* (1975), in the article "The Vocabulary of a Modern European State" (1975),[35] and in the long essay "The Rule of Law" (1983).[36]

I would go so far as to say that had Oakeshott published, say, *The Politics of Faith and the Politics of Scepticism*—under whatever title he would have given it—in the mid-1950s, this would not only have left us with a very different view of Oakeshott's work: it also would have laid down his doctrine of ambiguity in such a way that no one subsequently would have been able to ignore it. The history of political theory in the late twentieth century would have been very different if political theorists had fully understood Oakeshott's recognition of the ambiguity of our political vocabulary.

With that said, it is worth setting out Oakeshott's three major definitions of the state in chronological order.

First, there is the high philosophical definition. In his Fellowship dissertation, written in the mid-1920s, he wrote:

The State is the whole of moral and social experience.[37]

At around the same time he wrote that the state is "self-subsistent: something which carries with it the explanation of itself, and requires to be linked on to no more comprehensive whole in order to be understood".[38] What is interesting about this definition is that it is certainly not a definition of the type we are now familiar with ever since Weber's "legitimate monopoly of violence" became standard. It is not a sharp definition, of modernist type, in terms of a criterion: that is to say, one which says "If there is *this*, then there is a state". For, here, the state is everywhere. This is a definition from the heroic tradition of Hegel, Green and Bosanquet. The state is the central and constitutive concept of politics. It is not possible to define the state because the state defines.

Secondly, and later, there is what looks like a rather standard sort of definition. In lectures delivered at the London School of Economics, he wrote:

[A state is] a well-defined territory, inhabited by a people who have acquired, or are on their way to acquiring, a certain sentiment of solidarity, ruled by a government endowed with sovereign authority and very great power.[39]

This is clearly an *ad hoc* definition: the sort of thing any lecturer might have said in the twentieth century. It is not particularly philosophically pointed. It looks like a loose definition. Whereas the first definition was designed not to be an ordinary definition, or a legal definition, this one could be. But in fact the *Lectures* reveal that Oakeshott was no longer reflecting on an eternal state but reflecting on a historical state: not the "state" which anthropologists and archaeologists found on the Tigris and Euphrates, but the "modern state" or the "modern European state". For Oakeshott, the "novel political experience" for which the word "state" was used was the experience of trying to generate political entities which would be singular or united orders just as the older empires and kingdoms had been, but would also allow their citizens or subjects some significant autonomy, so that the resulting order would not simply be one of solidarity but also one of "an internal variety which qualifies its solidarity".[40]

Thirdly, as a consequence of his historical exploration of idea of the modern state, Oakeshott developed a theory of the state which was articulated in full in *On Human Conduct* in 1975. In its own way, this definition was meant to be as philosophical as the first, but now a definition informed by a proper sense of history:

> A state may perhaps be understood as an unresolved tension between the two irreconcilable dispositions represented by the words *societas* and *universitas*.[41]

Let us compare the three definitions. The first definition treats the state as a substantial and coherent whole, a constituent or cause of concepts. The second and third treat it as if it is a concept or a congeries of concepts. The second is transitional. It treats it as a loosely coherent singular concept that is historical and as such involves many different elements and can be considered a response to a new experience. The third treats it philosophically as if it is an incoherent mixture of two concepts.

The first and third are the most important. The second is nothing other than the work Oakeshott did in order to generate the third. And the third is Oakeshott's distinctive contribution to political philosophy.

IV

Oakeshott's early theory of the state was rendered obsolete as an element in his own thought after he began to study the history of the state, after he became aware of the ambiguity of our political vocabulary, and after he proposed a new, subtler, theory of the state. But it is not obsolete for us, since it is still a meaningful theory even now.

Oakeshott begins by saying that he wants to define the state. To define anything is to experience it as a whole, understand its innermost essence.[42] The state is a particular form of society or association. Humans, he says, cannot live without association: we are born into it. But "we become true members of that association" when "we contemplate its laws, institutions, art, literature, tastes and prejudices". And it is *this*—this contemplation—which is, believe it or not, the state. "To use the word State is to express a belief that there is a whole of social experience."[43] The corollary of this is that the state is *something which has always existed.* "There never was a time in human history when this state did not exist."[44] What Oakeshott is saying is that the state can be understood in two ways, one of which is "concrete" or total and one of which is "abstract" or partial.

The abstract or partial state, as far as Oakeshott is concerned, is an actual state as defined in law or the state as government. But this is not the philosophical state. "'To theorize' means", he says, "to see as a whole. The actual is a small part of the whole, or a single aspect of it, which, when taken by itself, is, by reason of its incompleteness, both meaningless and comparatively unreal."[45] As I have already said, Oakeshott had no time for the view that "state" is "government" and indeed was quite vituperative about it. If the claim "the state is the government" meant a proposition like "*a* is *a*" then it was, as far as he was concerned, "devoid of significance". It was trivial. It meant only that the word "state" was unnecessary, just a synonym of government, and perhaps a confusing one at that. If on the other hand it meant that the government is the social whole, a conception of life, then the argument was absurd.[46] As far as Oakeshott was concerned, government was simply "that part of state action which makes use of force".[47]

What we have to observe is that Oakeshott insists the state properly understood is not an object that has to be likened to anything else in order to be understood. So it is beyond metaphor. "Every association of minds, as such, is a reaching out, be it of ever so small an extent, towards a perfect State".[48] "The state is not a fact, as many say": or, "it is a conception which we may permit ourselves to call a fact only when we have made it clear to ourselves and complete in itself". Why is this? It is because "a complete conception of the state is one which supersedes all others and beside which they appear neither as possible alternatives, nor as contradictions nor as contributions, but as abstractions to be supplanted".[49] Here is the clearest short statement of what Oakeshott meant by the state:

> If it is a concrete fact, the state must be self-subsistent, something which carries with it the explanation of itself and requires to be linked on to no more comprehensive whole in order to be understood. And it appears to me that nothing fulfils these conditions save the social whole which is correlative to individuals who are complete and living persons; or, in other words, the totality in an actual community which satisfies the whole mind of the individuals who comprise it. All that falls short of this is an abstraction which requires this to explain it.[50]

Simply put, he says: "The state is not the government, it is the social whole which government implies and requires for its explanation."[51] It followed that the state could not be government, because government could not explain itself, but needed to be explained in terms of something greater. "In a true philosophy of politics, the word 'state' will not be used as a name for this or that *thing*.... but is a name for some unifying principle in political life."[52] The state is *required* for explanation. "The State, for philosophy, is not a thing in the phenomenal world, it is a principle which explains all phenomena."[53]

Oakeshott abandoned this theory of the state. But it is not yet dead. It is evident in Bartelson's *Critique of the State* of 2001 and Steinberger's *Idea of the State* of 2004. For Bartelson, there is "an underlying tension between the state conceived as an object of theoretical and empirical knowledge and the state conceived as a transcendental condition of that knowledge".[54] And for Steinberger, the state is a "structure of intelligibility", "an institution composed of propositions", "a systematic structure of ideas on the basis of which the individuals of a society seek jointly to control the physical objects that surround them".[55]

V

The transition between Oakeshott's early and late theories of the state is a very interesting one, and has to be understood not only to understand his late theory, but also, and perhaps more importantly, because *it remains significant for our understanding of the state even if we disagree with Oakeshott's own later theory of the state.* His later theory depends on three major insights.

The first was that the state is historical. Oakeshott shifted from seeing the state as absolutely constitutive to seeing it as only relatively constitutive and itself constituted out of a distinctive historical experience. There are three main views that anyone can take about how long the state has existed in history. Some writers say that there has always been a state.[56] Some say that it is a five thousand-year-old fact.[57] Some say that it is a five hundred-year-old concept.[58] In his early writings, Oakeshott adopted the first of these views and in his later writings he adopted the third. In 1933, he could write: "'The State' has no history".[59] After 1945, and probably after some date much earlier than that, he could no longer have written such a thing.

The second insight was that any theory of politics should begin with the recognition that our language of politics is ambiguous. I have already mentioned that Oakeshott was becoming concerned with ambiguity in the late 1930s. But he did not formulate his views on this subject in full until the 1950s. He expressed it in some reviews and articles, but the fullest statement of this insight was made in the unpublished book manuscript *The Politics of Faith and the Politics of Scepticism* where he wrote: "Our starting point is the evident ambiguity of our political vocabulary."[60] He found ambivalence in our political activity; he found ambiguity in our political language[61]: and he related the two, turning to history in order to understand why ambiguity and ambivalence might be constitutive of our politics.

The third insight was an older one, retained from his earliest philosophical writing. This was that no matter what sort of confusion we find in our activity or our vocabulary or our world we should not replicate that confusion in our theories. There may be compromise in practice, but there should be no compromise in theory. In 1934 he had written: "It is to be doubted whether any theory can be satisfactory which is a compromise."[62] And in 1938 he had written: "Compromise … is always unsatisfactory in philosophy".[63] I think that the shape of Oakeshott's thought from the 1950s onwards, in every statement of his argument, was dominated by these two recognitions, one about ambiguity, one about compromise. The argument ran as follows. On the one hand, our understanding of politics is troubled by ambiguity, but on the other hand, our understanding of *this* (that our understanding of politics is troubled by ambiguity) is not to be confused by the same ambiguity: and so, rather than come up with singular theories which attempt to replicate the confused compromises of our practice, we should come up with dyadic theories which enable us to see clearly the causes of our confusion. A dyad is an antinomy, an opposition, a *yin* and *yang*: that is to say, not necessarily a symmetrical or mirror opposition, but, as he put it in *On Human Conduct*, an "oblique" opposition, like Hegel's "being" and "nothing", or like male and female, with much shared despite radical difference. If Hegel was a philosopher of triads, Oakeshott in his mature writings was a philosopher of dyads. He thought that since the ambiguity in our language is fundamental there could be no single theory of the state. So he sought a theory that took the form of an unresolved tension between two theoretical opposites. The state was now to be seen as what he called a *concordia discors*, a discordant harmony.[64]

This structure of this argument, often misunderstood, is remarkable. It is not often enough recognised that Oakeshott erected his entire mature theoretical structure on the foundational claim that our modern political vocabulary is an ambiguous one.[65] He thought it is very important to recognise ambiguity in our theories without allowing our theories to perpetuate the same ambiguity. Politics requires us to recognise ambiguity in an unambiguous manner. This is, I would claim, the most original line of thought to be found in any political thinker of the twentieth century. It took Oakeshott around twenty years to work out its principles and another twenty years to write it out to a conclusion.

The early Oakeshott had been in some manner Hegelian. In Hegel, the state was supposedly one thing. After Hegel, theorists like Bluntschli and Jellinek had tended to write about the state on two sides, contrasting *Staatsrecht*, the law of the state, which required legal consideration, with *Politik* or *Staatszweck*, the purpose or policy of the state, which required sociological consideration.[66] It is not often recognised that Weber retained this distinction, though he wrote mostly on the sociological rather than on the legal side.[67] But after Weber, the two-sided theory of the state was divided into two antithetical theories of the state. On one side, there was Kelsen who insisted on "a purely juristic point of view" of the state.[68] On the other side, there was Schmitt, bitterly opposed to Kelsen, who went behind the concept of the state to propose his theory of "the political".[69] He thought that "will" could not be attributed to any personification of the law. On the contrary, there had to be an actual "will", the will of a sovereign which would not so much make law as have the capacity to act when the law could not. Even now the division between Kelsen and Schmitt is paradigmatic. Contemporary legal theorists like David Dyzenhaus and Lars Vinx follow Kelsen, while contemporary political theorists, like Chantal Mouffe and Hans Sluga, have found reason to follow Schmitt.[70] The question here is whether the state should be constructed in terms of the "norm" or the "exception", or both. Sluga has commented that "exceptions are the norm in politics".[71] Anyone who agrees follows Schmitt. Anyone who disagrees, or who limits themselves to the legislative rather than to the purposive side of politics, follows Kelsen. No one would deny that this is a disagreement. But I would argue that it is more than a disagreement. It is an antinomy.

Oakeshott did more than anyone else to make sense of the antinomial nature of the state. What he tried to do was restore unity to the state, neither by suggesting that the state was a coherent entity which could be theorised as such, nor by suggesting that it was a coherent entity which could only be theorised on two sides because of the limits of our theories, but by suggesting that the state was fundamentally an incoherent entity for the very reason that it had been built over the centuries out of two coherent theories of association, one legislative and the other purposive.

It remains to sketch some of Oakeshott's transitional ideas about the historical state, and then his final philosophical theory of the state as an unresolved tension.

VI

In his lectures on the history of political thought Oakeshott spoke about different theories of the state through history.[72] He divided theories of the state according to three analogies. He said many thinkers had avoided the question, "What is the state?" in order to ask a far more suggestive question, "What is the state *like*?"[73] Not only was the state a new experience—distinctive to European history around five hundred years ago—but also something obscure which could be brought before consciousness in terms of analogies with other things. He divided these analogies into three types:

> In general, it has been believed that the collectivity of a modern European "state", and the bond which ties its members, is either:
>> natural: a "state" is a "natural community"; or
>> artificial: a "state" is an "artificial association"; or
>> neither natural nor artificial, strictly speaking, but something that partakes of
>>> both: a "historic" bond.[74]

Most metaphors by which the state has been understood were fitted by Oakeshott into the first category. Oakeshott discussed the state as an organism, as a body (the "body politic"), a colony of ants, swarm of bees, a family or household, a nation and (in Montesquieu) "general mental character".[75] The problem with all of these metaphors, according to Oakeshott, was that by calling the state "natural" they seemed to set aside the difficulty of explaining how it emerged and the oddity of its nature. These metaphors were of historical interest but of little philosophical value. Oakeshott did not mention them at all in *On Human Conduct*.

By the time he wrote that book the three categories had been reduced to two, the two categories of Oakeshott's relentless *concordia discors*. Here he described them as artificial and historic. For a time he labelled them telocracy and nomocracy, but by the time of *On Human Conduct* he explained them in terms of analogies to what he called "enterprise associ-ation" and "civil association", or *universitas* and *societas*.

So let us consider what he said about these two categories. The first supposed that the state is an artificial association: "a collection of human beings united, by agreement or choice, in pursuit of a common purpose or enterprise."[76] According to this view, what was natural was not any community itself, but only the individuals who voluntarily come into community through some activity of association. Oakeshott explored the analogies by which this theory was elucidated: that of a joint stock com-pany or religious sect.[77] These associations sought to embody virtue or to exploit nature: to achieve ends which individuals would not be able to achieve alone. The idea here was simply that individuals came together in association in order to form a greater actor, a *persona*, which would be able to achieve the collective good.

The weakness of the artificial view of the state is perhaps what pro-voked Oakeshott to turn to the third, historical, view. If the first the-ory had ignored the contingency of the state in one sense (by suggesting it was natural it also suggested it was inevitable), so the second theory ignored the fact that the state was not something simply made or chosen or constructed but something which had emerged contingently in his-tory. It was not a rational choice: not a choice made rationally in terms of certain conscious ends, but something which was "not designed and made to serve any specific and premeditated purpose".[78]

So we come to the third:

> In short, a "state" is to be understood as a collection of human beings who have no "natural" ties, who are not united by common blood, who cannot be supposed to have entered into an express agreement to associate with one another for the achievement of a specific purpose, but whom chance has brought together, and who have acquired a sentiment of solidarity from having enjoyed, over the years, a common and continuous "historical" experience.[79]

Oakeshott held Calvin, Locke, Bacon, Rousseau, Bentham, Mill and Green responsible for the second theory.[80] For the third, he gave credit to Ferguson, Hume, Burke, Coleridge, Vico, Herder, Savigny and

Hegel.[81] According to them, "It is neither an agreed purpose nor a 'natural' affiliation which unites the members of a 'state', but a common 'historical' experience".[82]

Now, so far Oakeshott had spoken in terms of analogies. The state was "naturally" like a body, or family, or nation; artificially it was like a company or sect: so what was the analogy for the historic theory of the state? The answer was perhaps unexpected. Instead of a metaphor like "body", or an analogy with another, lesser, sort of association, there was the analogy of all analogies, an analogy with the source of all analogy and all metaphor—language itself. Note this well, not something taken from language, but all of language.

> It may be said that if there is one analogy more than another which is appealed to in this interpretation of a "state", it is the analogy of a "language".[83]

His reason for saying this was that a language is neither natural nor artificial in any simple sense but a product of history. And this analogy had a singular merit, which was that, for Oakeshott, it guaranteed that any good theory of the state would never become too decisive. "The collectivity of a 'state' understood in this manner suggests that it is always a matter of degree; it is never absolute as it would be if it were either 'natural' or genuinely 'artificial'. A 'state', like a language, is as stable as it had managed to become."[84]

In his lectures, Oakeshott refused to advocate any one of these theories of the state. "It can't be said that European thought on this matter has reached any single and unmistakeable conclusion".[85] Each theory suggested a different way of behaving politically. This was as far as he went in his lectures.

VII

When we turn to *On Human Conduct* (1975) we see how two of these three historical categories were judged to be the two relevant categories for the philosophical understanding of the state, and how one of them was explicitly, though not formally, favoured. The first of the three categories (the state as natural) was jettisoned because Oakeshott's third chapter was about the character of the "modern European state", not the state as such, and certainly not about the classical state, or *polis*, or any of its rivals, *imperium* or *ecclesia*. It is significant that in this chapter there was no reference to Plato, and only one reference to Aristotle, in relation to constitutions. In this chapter he discussed the character of the modern European state in terms of "several well-worn analogies". He added: "some of which we may neglect, not because they did not enjoy considerable vogue, but because they soon revealed themselves to be inadequate and implausible".[86] Here he was referring to all of the analogies which in his lectures he had discussed when dealing with the theory that the state is "natural"—analogies we would call metaphors. So he now dismissed the view that the state is like a "family" or an "organism". He set all such theories to one side for two analogies which he thought more adequate: "a state understood in the terms of *societas*, and a state understood in the terms of *universitas*".[87]

Oakeshott probably took the words *societas* and *universitas* from Gierke via Maitland. "In clear words", wrote Maitland in his introduction to part of the *Genossenschaftsrecht*, "Innocent IV had apprehended the distinction: the *universitas* is a person; the *societas* is only another name, a collective name, for the *socii*".[88] But Oakeshott endowed them with his own meaning by bringing them together. These words, he commented, "stood for two different modes of human association". They both derived from Roman private law. In short, *universitas* was a corporation aggregate, like a guild, a cathedral chapter or a university, a collection of individuals coming together to achieve some common purpose, while *societas* was an association of individuals coming together in terms of a shared recognition of rules. The former stood for what in his lectures ten years earlier Oakeshott had called "artificial association", the latter stood for what he had called "historic association". These were words for certain types of legal association. But what Oakeshott suggested was that these offered "two useful, but admittedly imperfect, analogies" for the state.[89]

Oakeshott, brilliantly, as it seems to me, decided to "recruit them to serve again the purpose for which they were invented, that of distinguishing and making intelligible the many-in-one of human associations".[90] They captured perfectly the "ambiguous character" of the state. Hence, as we have already seen:

> A state may perhaps be understood as an unresolved tension between the two irreconcilable dispositions represented by the words *societas* and *universitas*.[91]

If the state is an unresolved tension, then it is incoherent. How better to theorise this than to show that the state is torn between two theories, that is to say, between two analogies, neither of which is perfect, and both of which cannot be combined into a coherent whole?

I do not want to go through the next one hundred pages in which Oakeshott explains the analogies. What we can say, very simply, is that the difference between them is that in *universitas*, as in artificial association, humans come together to form a new *persona*, whereas in *societas*, as in historical association, humans remain the only *personae* which matter, and come together only in terms of the recognition of rules by which they shall live together. So *societas* is association in terms of law,[92] whereas *universitas* involves the creation of a new person. It is a "partnership of persons which is itself a Person, or in some important respects like a person". Those in *societas* are united in terms of rules by which they order their practices, or traditions, whereas those in *universitas* are united in terms of a common purpose.[93]

In the previous chapter, "On the Civil Condition", Oakeshott offers, or repeats, his analogy for this sort of association. This is a sort of association which resembles a language. Here, in *On Human Conduct*, the analogy is barely adverted to, but it is there. He calls the rules which persons live by in civil association *lex*, and adds: "*lex* is to be recognised as a vernacular language in which *cives* understand themselves and their mutual relations."[94]

So Oakeshott's preferred analogy for the state—one which he admits is not sufficient by itself—is of an analogy to the legal association of *societas*, that is, an association in which individuals are united in respect of rules, and in respect of the recognition of rules. Then there is a further analogy, by which this association is likened to a language: an association in which one acts in accordance with rules but in which one's actions are not predetermined. In the chapter on the modern European state he refers to this analogy again, when he says that those who are associated in *universitas* "(unlike *socii*) are agreed, not merely to speak the same language, but to say the same thing".[95] This is very interesting. We should distinguish

socii, or those associated in terms of *societas*, who speak the same language, but say different things; and

those who are associated in terms of *universitas* (who, we should note, lack a name like *socii* because they have no independent existence in this respect since they have been incorporated into one person), and who say the same thing.

Both are required because the state, as Oakeshott noticed in his *Lectures*, involves both solidarity and variety.

Oakeshott's last word on the state was an article "The Vocabulary of a Modern European State", also published in 1975. He commented on the word "state", that it was "added to the European vocabulary of association and, after some hesitation began to be used alongside older expressions (such as a 'realm' or 'principality') to denote these emergent associations". Interestingly, he added: "It began as a metaphor." By this he meant that at first "a state was a sort of an 'estate.'" Later it became more than this, as it silently acquired other and older meanings, yet, because of its own ambiguity, did not need to commit itself to them.[96] As he put it most pithily: "The word 'state' identified an unavoidable association of almost unknown character and of a character still in the making."[97] Which, as we might expect, brought Oakeshott to the analogies of *societas* and *universitas* which he thought had been the most suggestive ways of understanding its character. However, and again, as he wrote to those who had "misunderstood" *On Human Conduct*: "Neither [analogy] could be made to fit exactly."[98]

As the metaphor of the state as a particular estate faded, as the new use of the word was established, the entity the word "state" denoted seemed more and more enigmatic, more and more in need of explanation (hence modern political theory since Machiavelli, Bodin and Hobbes). The standing stood. It was Oakeshott's achievement to say, in effect, that modern political theory had to be understood historically because the word "state" had opened up an empty page on which theorists could successively inscribe their theories. The state, seen this way, was a palimpsest.

VIII

Let me return to the distinction between the early and late Oakeshott, in order to make some general points. The difference between these two points of view could not be more radical without abandoning the concept of the state altogether.

First, the state is one and all, is of independent origination, and has always existed. It is not so much an idea as the cause of our ideas.

Second, the state has no independent origination, and so has only existed as a conceptual confusion in the last five hundred years. It is a confusion between two ideas, which are themselves contingent. It is an attempt to see through a glass darkly, and there is no fully coherent way of theorising it. Oakeshott theorises it in terms of a state-for-war and a state-for-peace and, naturally, prefers the latter. "So far from its being the case (as Hegel suggested) that the character of an association in terms of the rule of law is most fully expressed when it is engrossed in the pursuit of policy or when it is at war, these are the occasions when it is least itself."[99] There are many ways to express the antinomy which was the achievement of his later thought. It was *purpose* versus *practice*, *policy* versus *law*, *war* versus *peace*, *solidarity* versus *variety*, or, as he put it in the *Lectures*, "the disposition to generate solidarity by *destroying* diversity, and the disposition to generate solidarity by *containing* diversity".[100]

The first of these theories is beyond metaphor. The state is like language: we cannot think without it. The second theory also beyond metaphor, for metaphors are only poor analogies, imposed without enough hesitation: and, as Oakeshott showed in his lectures on the history of political thought most of the major metaphors for the state were implausible. He ignored simple metaphors like wheel, tree and ship. Instead he considered analogies, and, even then, though he preferred one over the other, did not dispense even with the one he disliked, but suggested that the state remained beyond the analogies by which men had sought to make sense of it. The reason he preferred one over the other was that it drew a better analogy between the state and language.

In sum, at first Oakeshott saw the state as a closed whole, a monad, a limit on experience, whereas later on he saw it as a riddle for the understanding, which he characterised as an open dyad, indeed, an indefinite dyad. And he insisted that this was the case, the true case about the state, as a fact or experience, even though, if he were asked, he did prefer one of the analogies to the other.

The state is not a person.[101] Certainly not according to the first theory. And according to the second, the state could at most be a person by one analogy. As Oakeshott suggested, it is possible to see the state as a person by imposing the analogy of *universitas* on it. But the state is better understood as if it is the condition of a person, or the condition of persons—we can see it both ways. But if it is a condition, then that condition remains to be characterised. And what I have claimed is that the state is a blank slate: something stripped of metaphor (even if it cannot be explained, here, without metaphor), something that is *stated* or supposed to exist before we know exactly how to characterise it. It is best elucidated through analogy, through being like something which is of similar complexity and which enables to make some sense of its own complexity. Or, rather, since there should not only be one analogy (any single analogy is likely to mislead us): it is something to be elucidated through a complex of analogies, which means, in practice, at least two. So I have argued that the word state, originally meaning only "condition", "status" or "standing", was, once it became a substantive, an empty category. It was a blank slate on which philosophers could inscribe the sense they wanted to make of political experience, using words like "sovereignty", "government", "liberty", "rights", "law" and so on, even the word "person". The state could be conceptualised in terms of both law and power. Some spoke of *Rechtsstaat*. Others spoke of *raison d'état*. Few attempted to overcome the discord. Schmitt tried in several different ways: in the "concrete order" he proposed as a third alternative to norm and decision in *On the Three Types of Juristic Thought* and in the *complexio oppositorum* he associated with the Catholic Church.[102] Rather than Schmitt's cabalistic *complexio oppositorum*, Oakeshott preferred an Augustan *concordia discors*: that is to say, instead of looking for a higher person, a sovereign or pope, who could force everything into coherence, and without supposing—as Kelsen did—that the law could suffice as the sum and substance of the state, Oakeshott accepted not incoherence but ambiguity as a condition of the political. His own early unitary conception of the state made it difficult to take sides. So his contribution to the theory of the state was to theorise it as a discordant harmony of two different characters or dispositions. This theory inscribed these two dispositions on the blank slate of the slate by analogy. And the theory was meant to be a rewriting in theory of what had happened in the historical experience of modern Europe.

Since the time of Kant and Hegel the word "state" has been taken to stand for the attempt to theorise political order without presupposition. It is a good word for that purpose, as I have shown. And since Hegel at least, the state has been used as a word for an experience of politics that came to consciousness in the sixteenth century even if explicit theories of the state were mostly the achievement of the nineteenth and twentieth centuries. Oakeshott's was perhaps the greatest attempt to bring the state into the twentieth century, by seeing it not as a harmonious entity built out of one theory or even two theories but as a *concordia discors* existing as the coincidences and consequences of two rival theories.

IX

It is possible to stop there. But it is tempting to venture a bit further.

Oakeshott's mature theory of the state is his greatest achievement as a political thinker. But is there anything to be said for Oakeshott's first theory of the state?

If the "state" is *whatever is the condition of our knowledge, experience, understanding*, then such a state is fundamental. It may be a higher or absolute order (on an analogy with *civitas Dei*) or it may be a lower or relative order (on an analogy with *civitas terrena*). If it is a lower or relative order then it is only fundamental in a mundane sense, and then it is not fully a state. It is not a *status* but a *stasis*.

Recently   Christopher   Beckwith   has   analysed   Eusebius's *Preparation for the Gospel*, written in the fourth century AD, which quoted a history of philosophy by Aristocles, written in the first century AD, which quoted Timon, a follower of Pyrrho from the third century BC. It is said to be the major surviving utterance of Pyrrho. Here is Beckwith's elaborate translation of it, broken up for clarity's sake:

> As for *pragmata* "matters, questions, topics", they are all
>> *adiaphora* "undifferentiated by a logical differentia" and
>> *astathemeta* "unstable, unbalanced, not measurable"; and
>> *anepikrita* "unjudged, unfixed, undecidable".
> Therefore, neither our sense-perceptions nor our "views, theories, beliefs" (*doxai*) tell us the truth or lie [about *pragmata*]; so we certainly should not rely on them [to do it]. Rather, we should be
>> *adoxastous* "without views",
>> *aklineis* "uninclined [towards this side or that]", and
>> *akradantous* "unwavering [in our refusal to choose]",
> saying about every single one that it no more is than it is not or it both is and is not or it neither is nor is not.[103]

This is a sceptical argument. If we agree with it, Timon declared, we would feel first indifference and then calm, the famous *ataraxia* the achievement of which, for many, was the purpose of philosophy. This *ataraxia* would be our state.

Let us look at one of the words, *astathemeta*, which Beckwith translates generously as "unstable, unbalanced, not measurable". He adds: "The second term, *astathemeta*, is an adjective from the stem *sta-* 'stand' with the negative prefix *a-*, literally meaning 'not standing'."[104] Here we have a term that could be translated "without state".

For a sceptic, then, the world is unstable, unbalanced and not measurable: in other words, not a state. For a state is stable, balanced and measurable: a state has statistics, is stately. The sceptic would argue that calling something or anything a state does not stop it being true that the world is *astathemeta*, or unstable, unstatic and unstatistical.

Beckwith brilliantly relates this passage to the *Trilaksana* of the Buddha.

> The Buddha says All *dharmas* [= *pragmata*] are
> *anitya* "impermanent"…
> *duhkha* "unsatisfactory, imperfect, unstable"…
> *anatman* "without an innate self-identity".[105]

The *Trilaksana* is considered to be older than either the Four Noble Truths or the Eightfold Path. Beckwith shows that the famous word *duhkha* (usually translated as "suffering") is related to the root *sta-*. It derived from *duh-stha*, which meant standing badly, unsteady, uneasy or disquieted. Beckwith is therefore convinced that this word is an exact equivalent of the Greek term *astathemeta*. Buddhism, as it was established in the centuries after the Buddha, was therefore understood to be primarily concerned with dealing with the fact that the world was not stable, that one could not stand rightly in it, that, in short, *there was no state*.

If we follow this argument, there has never been a state in this world. And yet there *is* a state, perhaps not of this world, because without such a state there is no way for us to even begin to make sense of this world.

X

Finally, it is fitting to return to this world, and to the difficulties that come of trying to make of use of the word "state" in our politics.

I have suggested that the state is an attempt to strip metaphor out of politics. But that could never be entirely successful. Language makes it impossible. Politics makes it ridiculous. Yet there seems to be something about the word "state" which turns a concrete absolute into an abstract relative. When we shifted from "the state of *x*" to "the state", everything grand or consummate that had been intimated by concepts such as king, church, empire and *polis* was abandoned entirely, only to be taken up again, if considered necessary, to make sense of the new experience of politics. The state was limited, a *mortal* god, in Hobbes's intriguing metaphor, or a limited condition, which through its abstraction or limitation might achieve a relative perfection, even if only in theory. It could be theorised as something that could subsume or incorporate into itself elements of those older concepts, or as something that would not have to do so. It could be theorised as something absolute in itself, but also as something relative, if it were theorised in relation to other entities or ideas that it could recognise but not subsume into itself. There is something about the word "state" which suggests limited perfection. I have myself used the metaphor of a blank slate in order to make sense of the state. And here is another metaphor. For is there not something statuesque or sculpted about the state? If it were to be a person the state would neither be a living person, nor a fictional person, nor even a moral person (whatever that is): it would be more like a statue, a fixing of something living in stone, something classical, limited, polished, finished, and yet, like Greek statuary, immortal, attaining an odd impersonality and almost godlike humanity. It might be knocked off its pedestal but until that were done it would remain the symbol of a human condition.

"The state wants men to render it the same idolatry they used to render the church", wrote Nietzsche. And: "State is the name of the coldest of all cold monsters. Coldly it lies; and this lie slips from its mouth: 'I, the state, am the people'."[106] Perhaps so. Yet smash the cold idol and then what is our condition, or state, to be? Abandon the metaphor, if you can, and ask the question again. It is this question, I think, which explains why Oakeshott never abandoned the state, even when he chose to theorise it as a contradiction, as "an unresolved tension between two irreconcilable dispositions". The state has to be something in this world, even if it is a contradiction.

Notes

1. Michael Oakeshott, *On Human Conduct* (Oxford: Clarendon Press, 1975), 233.
2. Michael Oakeshott, "The Concept of a Philosophical Jurisprudence," in Michael Oakeshott, *The Concept of a Philosophical Jurisprudence: Essays and Reviews 1926–51*, ed. Luke O'Sullivan (Exeter: Imprint Academic, 2007), 154–83, at 171.
3. Quentin Skinner, "Hobbes and the Theory of the State," in Quentin Skinner, *From Humanism to Hobbes: Studies in Rhetoric and Politics* (Cambridge: Cambridge University Press, 2018), 341–83, 377.

4. Moses Finley, *Politics in the Ancient World* (Cambridge: Cambridge University Press, 1984), 8.

5. Harold Laski, *The State in Theory and Practice* (1935), quoted in ibid., 8.

6. Michael Oakeshott, "The Philosophical Approach to Politics," in Michael Oakeshott, *Early Political Writings 1925–1930* (Exeter: Imprint Academic, 2010), 168–69.

7. Skinner, "Hobbes and the Theory of the State," 379.

8. Much has been made of the analogy between a state and a person by those who study Hobbes and Pufendorf. See Skinner, especially ibid., David Runciman, "What Kind of Person Is Hobbes's State? A Reply to Skinner," *Journal of Political Philosophy* 8 (2000), 268–78, and now Benjamin Holland, *The Moral Person of the State: Pufendorf, Sovereignty and Composite Polities* (Cambridge: Cambridge University Press, 2017). It seems to me that all of this debate has fallen victim to the admittedly highly suggestive analogy of person as if it is much more than an analogy. Here, again, Oakeshott's caution seems exemplary.

9. Hans Kelsen, *Essays in Legal and Moral Philosophy* (Dordrecht: D. Reidel Publishing Co., 1973), 69.

10. Carl Schmitt, *Political Theology II*, trans. Michael Hoelzl and Graham Ward (Cambridge: Polity Press, 2008), 123.

11. *The Oxford Latin Dictionary*, ed. P.G.W. Glare (Oxford: Clarendon Press, 1994), 1816. Compare Lewis and Short, *A Latin Dictionary* (Oxford: Clarendon Press, 1987), 1755–56.

12. This is implicit in Skinner, "The State," in *Political Innovation and Conceptual Change*, eds. Terence Ball, James Farr, and Russell Hanson (Cambridge: Cambridge University Press, 1989), 90–131, at 91–92, where he says the word at first referred to "the state or standing of the rulers themselves" and later to "the state of condition of a realm of commonwealth". It is explicit in Harvey Mansfield, "On the Impersonality of the Modern State: A Comment on Machiavelli's Use of Stato," *American Political Science Review* 77 (1983), 849–57, at 851: "The word 'state' does indeed occur in political contexts in the Middle Ages, but to name the regime, not a neutral, impersonal state. In this usage the Latin *status* does not stand alone, but requires some accompanying word or person to specify whose *status*."

13. *The Oxford English Dictionary* (Oxford: Oxford University Press, 1933/1978), Vol. 10, 849–53.

14. Michael Oakeshott, *Lectures in the History of Political Thought*, eds. Terry Nardin and Luke O'Sullivan (Exeter: Imprint Academic, 2006), 361.

15. Sociologists prefer the formulation "States state". See Pierre Bourdieu, *On the State: Lectures at the Collège de France 1989–1992*, trans. David Fernbach (Cambridge: Polity Press, 2014), 11.

16. Skinner, "The State," 120.
17. Walter Ullmann, *Principles of Government and Politics in the Middle Ages* (Routledge: London, 1978), 19–26.
18. Frank R. Ankersmit, "Metaphor in Political Theory," in *Knowledge and Language*, Volume III, *Metaphor and Knowledge*, eds. F.R. Ankersmit and J.J.A. Rooij (Dordrecht: Kluwer Academic, 1993), 155–202, at 195.
19. Ian Robinson, *The Establishment of Modern English Prose in the Reformation and the Enlightenment* (Cambridge: Cambridge University Press, 1998), 160. For a similar point, see David Runciman, *Political Hypocrisy: The Mask of Power, from Hobbes to Orwell and Beyond* (Princeton: Princeton University Press, 2008), 127; Frank Ankersmit, *Aesthetic Politics: Political Philosophy Beyond Fact and Value* (Stanford: Stanford University Press), 155.
20. George Cornewall Lewis, *Remarks on the Use and Abuse of Some Political Terms* (1832), in a facsimile reproduction (Columbia: University of Missouri Press, 1970).
21. Charles Taylor, *The Language Animal: The Full Shape of the Human Linguistic Capacity* (Cambridge, MA: Belknap Press, 2016).
22. H.M. Drucker, "Just Analogies: The Place of Analogies in Political Thinking," *Political Studies* 18 (1970), 448–60, at 457–58.
23. Elliot Zashin and Phillip C. Chapman, "The Uses of Metaphor and Analogy: Toward a Renewal of Political Language," *The Journal of Politics* 36 (1974), 290–326, 311.
24. Ibid., 292.
25. Michael Oakeshott, "A Discussion of Some Matters Preliminary to the Study of Political Philosophy," in *Early Political Writings 1925–1930*, 37–138.
26. Oakeshott, "The Philosophical Approach to Politics," 139–226.
27. Michael Oakeshott, "The Authority of the State," in Michael Oakeshott, *Religion, Politics and the Moral Life*, ed. Timothy Fuller (New Haven: Yale University Press, 1993), 74–90.
28. Stephen Gerencser, *The Skeptic's Oakeshott* (London: Macmillan, 2000), 68–69.
29. Michael Oakeshott, "The Concept of a Philosophy of Politics," in *Religion, Politics and the Moral Life*, 119–37, at 126.
30. Oakeshott, "The Concept of a Philosophical Jurisprudence". The question of the transition in Oakeshott's thought is one that has been discussed more in the abstract than with close attention to his writings. Luke O'Sullivan and Efraim Podoksik find a transition in the *Social and Political Doctrines of Modern Europe* in 1939. See Luke O'Sullivan, "Michael Oakeshott on European Political

History," *History of Political Thought* 21 (2000), 132–51, at 137, citing Oakeshott, *Social and Political Doctrines*, xxii note 1, and also Efraim Podoksik, *In Defence of Modernity: Vision and Philosophy in Michael Oakeshott* (Exeter: Imprint Academic, 2003), 174. But I think Oakeshott's distinction between planning and not planning was not yet a positive conception. It was only a polemical one. Far more influential in forming his distinctive dyadic way of thinking may have been a lecture by G.C. Field which he reviewed with acclaim in 1949. I shall perhaps write about this elsewhere. But those interested in Oakeshott's development should read Field's *Principles and Ideals in Politics* (London: Geoffrey Cumberlege, 1948). For instance, on p. 13 we find: "From one point of view the whole subsequent history of political ideas can be considered in terms of the tension between these rival points of view, the Greek or purposive and the Roman or legalistic."

31. Oakeshott, "The Concept of a Philosophy of Politics," 131.
32. Michael Oakeshott, *The Politics of Faith and the Politics of Scepticism*, ed. Timothy Fuller (New Haven: Yale University Press, 1996).
33. Michael Oakeshott, *Morality and Politics in Modern Europe*, ed. Shirley Robin Letwin (New Haven: Yale University Press, 1993), here quoted at p. 19. As in the lectures from the 1960s Oakeshott begins with a triad but dismisses the first variant and so ends with a dyad.
34. See note 14.
35. Michael Oakeshott, "The Vocabulary of a Modern European State," in Michael Oakeshott, *The Vocabulary of a Modern European State*, ed. Luke O'Sullivan (Exeter: Imprint Academic, 2008), 232–66.
36. Michael Oakeshott, "The Rule of Law," in Michael Oakeshott, *On History* (Indianapolis: Liberty Fund, 1999), 129–78.
37. Oakeshott, "A Discussion of Some Matters Preliminary to the Study of Political Philosophy," 77.
38. In Oakeshott, "The Authority of the State," 83.
39. Oakeshott, *Lectures in the History of Political Thought*, 371.
40. Ibid., 364
41. Oakeshott, *On Human Conduct*, 200–01.
42. Oakeshott, "A Discussion of Some Matters Preliminary to the Study of Political Philosophy," 47 and 50.
43. Ibid., 81.
44. Ibid., 75.
45. Ibid., 85.
46. Ibid., 117.
47. Ibid., 124.
48. Ibid., 77.

49. Oakeshott, "The Authority of the State," 81.
50. Ibid., 83.
51. Ibid., 84
52. Oakeshott, "The Philosophical Approach to Politics," 169.
53. Ibid., 222–23.
54. Jens Bartelson, *The Critique of the State* (Cambridge: Cambridge University Press, 2001), 5.
55. Peter Steinberger, *The Idea of the State* (Cambridge: Cambridge University Press, 2004), 21.
56. Bernard Bosanquet, *The Philosophical Theory of the State* (London: Macmillan, 1925), 3; Gilles Deleuze and Felix Guattari, *Nomadology: The War Machine* (New York: Semiotext(e), 1986), 15; and Oakeshott, "A Discussion of Some Matters Preliminary to the Study of Political Philosophy," 75.
57. See Henri J.M. Claessen and Peter Skalnik, "The Early State: Theories and Hypotheses," in *The Early State*, eds. Claessen and Skalnik (The Hague: Mouton, 1978), 3–29; Patricia Crone, "The Tribe and the State," in *States in History*, ed. John A. Hall (Oxford: Basil Blackwell, 1986), 22–47.
58. In short, everyone who follows Quentin Skinner in "The State".
59. Oakeshott, *The Concept of a Philosophical Jurisprudence: Essays and Reviews 1926–51*, 88.
60. Oakeshott, *The Politics of Faith and the Politics of Scepticism*, 21. See also "The Idea of 'Character' in the Interpretation of Modern Politics," in *What Is History? And Other Essays*, ed. Luke O'Sullivan (Exeter: Imprint Academic, 2004), 275–76; Oakeshott, *The Vocabulary of Modern Politics*, 100, both from around 1955.
61. Oakeshott, *The Politics of Faith and the Politics of Scepticism*, 118.
62. Oakeshott, *The Concept of a Philosophical Jurisprudence: Essays and Reviews 1926–51*, 99.
63. Ibid., 173.
64. A phrase used in *The Politics of Faith and the Politics of Scepticism*, 39, 90, 118, which Oakeshott took from Ovid or Horace (perhaps also under the influence of Dr. Johnson, though he preferred *discordia concors*).
65. Many commentators misunderstand it, assuming that Oakeshott sketched two rival theories only in order to argue for one and against the other. See, for instance, the comments ("grudging", "reluctant") in Nehal Bhuta, "The Mystery of the State: State Concept and State Making in Schmitt and Oakeshott," in *Law, Liberty and State: Oakeshott, Hayek and Schmitt on the Rule of Law*, eds. David

Dyzenhaus and Thomas Poole (Cambridge: Cambridge University Press, 2015), 10–37, at 33; and Thomas Poole, "The Mystery of Lawlessness: War, Law and the Modern State," in ibid., 153–85, at 180. The fact that Oakeshott thought one of the dyads more satisfactory as a pure theory than the other, and enjoyed polemically saying so, has nothing to do with the fact that he himself insisted, again and again, that the state or politics as we have experienced them is constituted by both. See, for instance, *The Politics of Faith and the Politics of Scepticism*, 90.

66. Johann Kaspar Bluntschli, *The Theory of the State*, 3rd English ed. from 6th German ed. (Oxford: Clarendon Press, 1895), 1–2; Duncan Kelly, "Revisiting the Rights of Man: Georg Jellinek on Rights and the State," *Law and History Review* 22 (2004), 493–529, at 522.

67. Max Weber, "On Legal Theory and Sociology" (1911), in *Weimar: A Jurisprudence of Crisis*, eds. Arthur J. Jacobsen and Bernhard Schlink (Berkeley: University of California Press, 2000), 50–54, at 51.

68. Hans Kelsen, *General Theory of Law and State*, trans. Anders Wedberg (Cambridge, MA: Harvard University Press, 1945), 182.

69. Schmitt, *The Concept of the Political* (Chicago: The University of Chicago Press, 1996).

70. See the essays of Dyzenhaus and Vinx in David Dyzenhaus and Thomas Poole, *Law, Liberty and State: Oakeshott, Hayek and Schmitt on the Rule of Law* (Cambridge: Cambridge University Press, 2015); Chantal Mouffe, *The Democratic Paradox* (London: Verso, 2005).

71. Hans Sluga, *Politics and the Search for the Common Good* (Cambridge: Cambridge University Press, 2014), 139.

72. Oakeshott, *Lectures in the History of Political Thought*, 404.

73. I paraphrase: "What is a modern European state *like*?" is the actual question. Ibid., 402.

74. Ibid., 404.

75. Ibid., 404–11, esp. 410.

76. Ibid., 414.

77. Ibid., 417.

78. Ibid., 421.

79. Ibid., 421–22.

80. Ibid., 420.

81. Ibid., 423.

82. Ibid.

83. Ibid., 422.

84. Ibid. It is important to acknowledge that Oakeshott also mentioned another possible analogy in "landscape", as a blend of what is natural and artificial, "necessary and chosen, given and made". Ibid., 424. But he obviously preferred the analogy of "language", as it was the only one used in *On Human Conduct*.

85. Ibid., 425. But compare 423, where Oakeshott admitted that the third was superior. In general, and this is a point for those who study Oakeshott everywhere, there is always a tension between Oakeshott's desire to do justice to both elements of the dyad as elements of actual historical experience of the state, and his desire to explain why one element was obviously superior to the other as a theory. Crude critics of Oakeshott tend to find this a contradiction. But it was not. See note 65.

86. Oakeshott, *On Human Conduct*, 198.

87. Ibid., 199.

88. F.W. Maitland, "Translator's Introduction," in Otto Gierke, *Political Theories of the Middle Age* (Cambridge: Cambridge University Press, 1900), vii–xlv, at xxii.

89. Ibid., 199.

90. Ibid., 200.

91. Ibid., 200–01.

92. Ibid., 201.

93. Ibid., 203.

94. Ibid., 141. Since he admits, in the subsequent section, 141 ff., that *lex* is not enough by itself, since rules must be accompanied by ruling and rulers, it is evident that Oakeshott's view of language—here—resembles Hobbes. That is to say, Oakeshott does not have the view of language taken by the Oxford English Dictionary, in which "anything goes"— that language is what it is: rather, it seems that he takes a rather more stipulative view of language, the view of language taken by Swift and Johnson, in which some Academy—like the *Académie Française*— should legislate for the authorised meanings of words.

95. Ibid., 205.

96. Oakeshott, "The Vocabulary of a Modern European State," 233.

97. Ibid., 254.

98. Michael Oakeshott, "On Misunderstanding Human Conduct," in *The Vocabulary of a Modern European State*, 267–79, at 273.

99. Oakeshott, "The Rule of Law," 178.

100. Oakeshott, *Lectures in the History of Political Thought*, 378.

101. Consider again the literature referred to in note 8.

102. Carl Schmitt, *On the Three Types of Juristic Thought*, trans. Joseph W. Bendersky (Westport, CT.: Praeger Publishers, 2004); Carl Schmitt, *Roman Catholicism and Political Form*, trans. G.L. Ulmen (Westport, CT: Greenwood Press, 1996).

103. Christopher Beckwith, *Greek Buddha: Pyrrho's Encounter with Early Buddhism in Central Asia* (Princeton: Princeton University Press, 2015), 23.

104. Ibid., 27.

105. Ibid., 29.

106. Quoted conveniently in Sue Prideaux, *I Am Dynamite: A Life of Friedrich Nietzsche* (London: Faber and Faber, 2018), 390.

CHAPTER 3

The Problem of Liberal Political Legitimacy

David D. Corey

I

This essay addresses one of the most fundamental questions of liberal-democratic politics in the modern West, the question of *political legitimacy*. Stated in succinct form, the question is, "What legitimizes the exercise of 'rule' by some citizens over others in a political community where *all* citizens are recognized as free and politically equal?" In order fully to grasp this question, one must understand that by "rule" is meant the power to compel someone to do something *without his or her consent*. There may be instances—though I suspect they are extremely rare—in which all members of a political community consent to a decision or a course of action. In such instances, "rule" is neither necessary nor present. But the usual situation in liberal-democratic politics is for *some* citizens to compel others to do something they do not want to do, because they disagree over what, if anything, ought to be done. The ultimate instrument of rule is coercion or the threat of it, and no one likes to be

D. D. Corey (✉)
Honors Program, Baylor University, Waco, TX, USA
e-mail: David_D_Corey@baylor.edu

© The Author(s) 2019
E. S. Kos (ed.), *Michael Oakeshott on Authority, Governance, and the State*, Palgrave Studies in Classical Liberalism,
https://doi.org/10.1007/978-3-030-17455-2_3

coerced. Thus, again, the question that rule prompts, especially in the minds of those who experience it (i.e., the ruled), is: "Why is this legitimate?" "Who or what gives *you* the right to rule me?"

Michael Oakeshott was deeply concerned about political legitimacy. He thought that during his lifetime, liberal regimes had grown dangerously indifferent to it, and he thought this could be their undoing. Why? Because, as Oakeshott scholar Noël O'Sullivan puts it, an "indifference to legitimacy" leaves liberal democracies "unprotected against arbitrary power."[1] The question of what separates *mere* power from *legitimate* power, or what Oakeshott called "authority," could not be answered by the bare fact of "success"—however *that* is defined. Yet this is precisely what Oakeshott thought contemporary liberal regimes were supposing:

> Governments have become inclined to commend themselves to their subjects merely in terms of their *power* and their *incidental achievements,* and their subjects have become inclined to look only for this recommendation. Indeed, it is long since *this rejection of the idea of authority began to infect our thoughts about the constitutions of governments.*[2]

To ground legitimacy (or authority) on the success of power would be to reduce a fundamentally *moral* question to something thoroughly amoral. This was a solution Oakeshott refused to accept. Instead, he thought legitimacy was more solidly grounded in a certain form of non-instrumental moral relationship, which he called "civil association."[3]

In his essay on Oakeshott's approach to political legitimacy, Noël O'Sullivan criticizes Oakeshott for "confer[ing] a monopoly of the claim to moral legitimacy on civil association."[4] Because civil association is an ideal difficult to achieve in politics in general, and because certain features of contemporary politics seem to demand a more instrumental approach to government, O'Sullivan questions the adequacy of Oakeshott's theory. More specifically, he argues that Oakeshott's strong preference for civil association led him to exaggerate the crisis of political legitimacy and even "to share the experience of wholesale alienation from the modern world found in thinkers like Nietzsche and Heidegger on the right, and members of the Frankfurt School like Adorno and Horkheimer on the left."[5] O'Sullivan for his part tries to revise Oakeshott's approach in the direction of a "hybrid theory of legitimacy." Within such a hybrid theory, "Oakeshott's exclusively formal or procedural conception of the conditions for legitimacy … is incorporated into a more comprehensive one which includes political debate about the substantive purposes associated with the modern state, as well as about the constitutional issues that civil association presents."[6]

In my view, O'Sullivan's recognition of the need for ongoing "political debate" about the substantive purposes of the state is a welcome supplement to Oakeshott's theory of legitimacy, as long as we understand that this revision aims at the *practical* success of that theory. In other words, it brings the theory into closer alignment with real-world politics. Oakeshott himself, of course, tried to distance himself from understanding political theory as something to be "applied" to political goings-on in the world. Political theory was for him more like the "Owl of Minerva," which attains insight just as the phenomena it ponders are complete, or nearly complete. But be that as it may, there is nothing to stop those of us who hold a different view about the relationship between theory and practice to conjure with the possibilities of a "revised" Oakeshottean approach. I for one happen to share (what I take to be) O'Sullivan's slightly more practical orientation to the status of political theory in the world.

However, my own way of appropriating insights from Oakeshott would look different. In this essay, I endorse the view (without Oakeshott's vocabulary) that the ideal of "civil association" (and I stress that it is an ideal, not something likely to be found in pure form in the practice of liberal politics) *is* the only understanding of politics that meets the conditions of liberal political legitimacy. That is because the ideal of civil association alone refuses to treat citizens as anything other than "free" and "politically equal," and these are the bedrock commitments of liberalism itself. And yet I do not believe that political legitimacy is the only, or even the most fundamental, problem in politics. Often a more "instrumental" approach to governments is *necessary* (as opposed to legitimate). Indeed, at times the very survival of liberal democracies requires moments of strongly telic government. Thus, instead of following O'Sullivan in deeming such instrumental moments "legitimate" insofar as they emerge from political debate, I would be more inclined to deem them "illegitimate but necessary," except in cases where political debate produces something approximating consensus, which is almost never the case. Might this also have been Oakeshott's view? I do not pretend to know, given the subtlety of Oakeshott's account. But I do believe that this way of approaching the problem of legitimacy will have practical consequences that are preferable (to the extent I can foresee them) to the consequences of O'Sullivan's approach.[7]

My argument unfolds in two stages. First, I argue (rather boldly) that no effort to solve the problem of liberal political legitimacy in the real world—as opposed to the ideal world—has succeeded, either from among the early moderns or from among our contemporaries. This constitutes the bulk of the essay ahead. Next, I argue that the consequences of this failure should be a decrease in the power and scope of government at the national level. In other words, I derive a moral argument for limited government from the absence of a solid ground for political legitimacy in modern liberal politics. Throughout the essay, I have the special case of American liberalism in the back of my mind, and as I begin to draw practical conclusions near the end, I intend to limit these conclusions to American liberalism in particular, where the unique conditions of federalism, social pluralism, and extreme political polarization inform the positions I take.

II—On the Legitimacy of Rule

Among people regarded as free and politically equal, how or why is it legitimate for one person or group to exercise rule over others? The history of modern political thought is replete with attempts to answer this question. Hobbes, Locke, Rousseau, Kant, Bentham, and Mill have each tackled it in distinct ways. In contemporary political philosophy, John Rawls, Robert Nozick, Elizabeth Anscombe, and Joseph Raz have also made attempts. In fact, so many theorists have turned their attention to the problem of legitimacy that I face an expository dilemma. How can I survey all the relevant theories in a reasonable amount of space? And yet, if I do not survey them all, how can I conclude (as I shall in fact conclude) that the practice of rule under conditions of freedom and political equality appears to be illegitimate?

A way forward recommends itself in the fact that all theories of legitimacy of which I am aware—those of the authors listed above and others as well—fall into three basic categories.[8] Of course, minor and sometimes major differences exist among the theories within each category, but enough commonality exists too, namely in the basic approach that is taken, that when one evaluates the argumentative strengths and weaknesses of each category, one also identifies the strengths and weaknesses of all the theories within it. What I propose, then, is to evaluate the three basic approaches using select theorists and theories for illustrative purposes.[9] If one or more of the approaches looks promising, then perhaps

Oakeshott did indeed exaggerate the "crisis of legitimacy." But if none looks promising, then liberal democracies have a problem. Of course, this method does not permit one to conclude that no "real-world" (as opposed to ideal) theory of legitimacy will ever be successful. But it does (if all three approaches fail) suggest that there may be no ready-to-hand escape from the problem of liberal legitimacy.

All theories of legitimacy that assume freedom and political equality on the part of citizens take one or more of three possible forms. They ground legitimacy in consent, or they ground it in certain benefits citizens are said to receive (whether or not citizens consent), or they ground it in procedural fairness (whether or not citizens consent and whether or not the procedures prove beneficial to all citizens). Consent theories, benefit theories, and procedure theories are all there are. I consider consent theories first.

Consent Theory: John Locke

The classic consent theorist is John Locke, though it is worth noting that versions of consent theory go as far back as Greek antiquity. Even in the early modern period, Locke was not the first to claim that consent is the ground of legitimate rule. But Locke's version of the theory is the one that resonates most strongly with American political history and culture. For this reason, I take it as my example. The idea of consent factors into Locke's theory at several different points, and it is useful to distinguish the roles it plays. His initial (and most famous) claim is an historical one that the consent of individuals constitutes the only legitimate *beginning* of political communities. In other words, when a political community is emerging from what Locke calls the "state of nature," everyone who wants to be part of that community must signal his or her consent. Those who do not are neither part of, nor subject to the rules of, that community—with one exception: Individuals who are not part of the political community but possess or enjoy the use of property within its territory *are* subject to the rules of the community, whether they consent to be subject or not. The bare fact that they use property in the community's territory is said to signal their "tacit consent."

In addition to legitimating political communities, consent also plays a second role for Locke. In his view, the very act of consenting to be part of a newly emerging political community entails also *consent to obey the rule of the majority* of the community, at least initially, until the question of the form of government can be settled. Here, consent plays the crucial role of legitimating not a political community but an inaugural decision-making procedure. And it is worth underscoring the fact that, while universal consent is required for the establishment of a political community, only *majority* consent is required for its first major decisions.[10] This means (contrary to what one might infer from the neighbor analogy) that the rule of some citizens over others *is legitimate* according to Locke merely by virtue of individuals' consenting to join in community with each other. How and why is this so?

Locke furnishes an elaborate answer—two different argumentative strategies meant to persuade readers that consent to political community means perforce consent to majority rule (thereby legitimating "rule" on grounds of consent). The first argument employs a body metaphor and turns on a claim about the necessity of force.

1. When individuals consent to make a community, they consent to make one body with a power to act as one body (§96.3).
2. It is necessary for one body to move one way (§96.6–7).
3. It is necessary for a body to move the way the greater force carries it (§96.7–8).
4. The majority is the greater force (§96.8–9).
5. Therefore, only majority rule enables a compound body to act as one (§96.4).
6. And it follows that every person, who consents to make a community, "puts himself under an *obligation* to every one of that community to submit to the determination of the majority" (§96.11–12 and §97.2–4).

This argument may have some rhetorical appeal, but it does not supply sufficient grounds for the legitimacy of majority rule (or any form of rule, for that matter). What it claims is (a) that majority rule is *necessary* if political community is to exist at all and (b) that if it is necessary, it is legitimate.

But both claims are false. History is replete with examples of political communities formed and maintained by the will not of a majority, but of a minority with sufficient power or cunning to uphold its superior position.[11] It is simply wrong to say that majority rule is required for the existence of political communities.[12] But, supposing that majority rule was necessary, does it follow that it is therefore legitimate? The way Locke frames the issue as a contest between a "greater force" and a "lesser force," one of which *must* prevail if the body is to move at all, makes it seem so. But this distracts attention from a much more plausible ground of legitimacy than majority rule, namely unanimity. Rule is legitimate (and simultaneously ceases to be "rule" in the technical sense) when *all* citizens reach an actual agreement on what "motion" is to be made by their compound "body." Of course, Locke knows (and later says) that unanimity is virtually impossible to attain in politics. But does this fact alone tell us anything about the legitimacy of the alternatives? Locke's argument is simply that the "greater force of the majority" will *necessarily compel* the corporate body to move the way it wills. But as far as legitimacy is concerned, this amounts to nothing more or less than the claim that might make right. This is to dismiss rather than solve the problem of legitimacy as opposed to a mere exercise of power.

Perhaps a better way to interpret Locke's argument is in terms of some kind of tacit consent. At the moment individuals expressly consent to join a political community, they also tacitly consent—or must be understood as tacitly consenting—to obey majority rule in whatever is to be their next step (presumably choosing a form of government). They can be so understood, because majority rule alone is necessary—it is simply the only expedient—for moving forward at all. Here, the idea of necessity is still present, but the fact of tacit consent is what really counts. And in fact, Locke now offers a second argument (a *reductio ad absurdum*) that entails just such an assumption of tacit consent.

1. *If* the consent of the majority is not accepted as dispositive, then nothing but the consent of every individual will do.
2. But this is nearly impossible given various obstacles citizens face in attending political meetings, as well as the fact that citizens hold contrary opinions and interests.
3. The result of insisting upon unanimity is that political community would immediately dissolve.
4. But we cannot suppose that individuals who consent to form political communities' desire also that they immediately dissolve.
5. Therefore, individuals who consent to form political communities also consent (albeit tacitly) to be bound by majority rule—*provided* the majority moves toward the *ends* for which individuals united into political community in the first place.

Locke's thought is that citizens who consent to form a community also consent to allow the majority of the community to decide what form of government shall be established (monarchy, oligarchy, or democracy) and then to abide by that decision—to be "ruled" by it. Why? Because when someone consents to certain ends, he consents also to the necessary means, and majority rule is deemed necessary.

But is this true? First, it seems false that consent to specific ends implies always and everywhere consent to every necessary means. This depends on what those means are. Some initial consenters may decide to abandon some ends rather than to tolerate means they find unacceptable. But secondly, and more problematically, Locke gives readers no credible reason to suppose that citizens ever have or ever will regard the ends of political community as beyond dispute. Of course, Locke employs his "state of nature" image in order to make a clear case for the priority of certain ends. Imagining that people's lives, liberties, and estates are in constant danger in the state of nature, he asserts that the "great and chief end" of political community is the preservation of private property (our lives, liberties, and estates) through the establishment of a common law, an impartial judge, and an executive with sufficient strength to punish those who would break the law.[13]

But must everyone share Locke's view of the ends of government? If not, how can citizens determine (legitimately) which ends are most important? Or how will they decide how best to balance or otherwise adjudicate among competing claims about government's ends? Such questions prove consequential, because the ends (see the proviso in step 5 above) turn out to be *the standard* by which citizens judge the legitimacy of any and every political act, including the constitutional act of establishing a form of government. But if different citizens have different understandings of the ends of government (as citizens in fact do), then Locke's argument for legitimacy (both the legitimacy of majority rule and the legitimacy of all subsequent rule) amounts to little more than saying, "all rule is legitimate to the extent that one agrees with its ends and means." But this is tantamount to saying that all rule is legitimate as long as it isn't "rule," i.e., as long as it isn't something to which one happens to object.

These problems seem fatal for Locke's consent theory of legitimacy, and similar problems arise with other well-known consent theories. Again, space does not permit a full survey. However, a well-established criticism of all consent theories of legitimacy is that they involve an obvious fiction. In reality, no existing state (not even the USA) actually seeks—much less garners—the consent of all its citizens. Certainly, the adoption of our constitution did not secure this consent, not only because it was ratified by the states rather than by individuals, but also because the generation that ratified it has long since departed, and the "consent of the fathers" does not "bind the children," as David Hume once famously pointed out.[14] Neither does the fact of citizens' remaining in a country rather than emigrating constitute some kind of tacit consent. Morally valid consent must be informed and voluntary. But the USA does not inform citizens that the mere act of continued residence constitutes tacit consent to be ruled. Nor do many citizens have any practical options besides continued residence. Emigration presupposes financial resources, a place to go, and prospects for employment, and often there are language barriers and legal hurdles that prove insurmountable to all but an exceptional few. The idea, then, that consent (express or tacit) supplies grounds for legitimate rule is simply wishful thinking.[15]

Hypothetical Consent Theory: John Rawls

Before turning to benefit theories of legitimacy, I pause to consider a substantially revised version of consent theory that tries to overcome the problems just described. According to John Rawls (who follows Immanuel Kant in this),[16] the kind of consent required to render the state's use of coercion legitimate is neither actual consent nor tacit consent, but rather something we might call "hypothetical consent."

For Rawls, the whole problem of political legitimacy in contemporary liberal-democratic regimes boils down to two awkwardly related facts: the fact of "reasonable pluralism" that a plurality of reasonable comprehensive doctrines exists today and is not going away anytime soon and the fact that citizens view themselves as fundamentally free and equal, at least doctrinally if not in fact. Rawls rightly perceives that these two basic facts pose a problem for legitimacy: "If the fact of reasonable pluralism always characterizes democratic societies and if political power is indeed the power of free and equal citizens, [then] in light of what reasons and values—of what kind of a conception of justice—can citizens *legitimately* exercise that coercive power over one another?"[17]

Rawls's answer is as follows: "political power is legitimate only when it is exercised in accordance with a constitution (written or unwritten) the essentials of which all citizens, as reasonable and rational, can endorse in light of their common human reason."[18] Rawls does not require actual endorsement of any constitutional essentials. He requires only that citizens "can endorse" or "might endorse"[19] the essentials by reference to "common human reason" (as opposed to their particular and oftentimes incompatible comprehensive worldviews). Thus, he grounds legitimacy in a kind of consent that is not actual, but merely hypothetical.

Interestingly, Rawls does not believe that *every act* of government requires grounding in consent (hypothetical or otherwise). Rather, he believes that the most basic understanding of justice requires such grounding, along with the essential articles of the constitution. Once some principles of justice are agreed to, Rawls explains, and then a constitution can be created by reference to those principles. After that, laws can be enacted according to the constitution, and administrators and judges can deal with specific cases. The whole framework is legitimate, Rawls thinks, because of a hypothetical agreement to the principles of justice ensconced in the constitution.[20]

But three problems arise when political legitimacy is approached in this manner. The first problem is that no such agreement about the basic principles of justice, let alone the "constitutional essentials," may be forthcoming. Rawls is aware of this. He writes, "there is plainly no guarantee that justice as fairness, or any reasonable conception for a democratic regime, can gain the support of an overlapping consensus and in that way underwrite the stability of its political constitution."[21] But if no agreement is forthcoming—and this is unfortunately our present state of affairs in the USA and in every contemporary liberal regime of which I am aware—then the problem of legitimacy remains unsolved. In fact, we continue to face the exact problem with which we began: Without any agreed solution to the problem of legitimacy, the state nevertheless employs coercive power, because it must do so if the regime is to be maintained. Coercion is apparently necessary, but illegitimate.

A second problem is that Rawls' argument for legitimacy is too procedural. He thinks that once a just constitution is set up, and assuming that just economic and social institutions are in place, then the results, *whatever* they happen to be, will be legitimate. He writes,

> [T]here is no independent criterion for the right result [of laws and policies]: instead there is a correct or fair procedure such that the outcome is likewise correct or fair, *whatever it is*, provided that the procedure has been properly followed.[22]

Rawls terms this approach to political legitimacy "pure procedural justice." And he holds firmly to it throughout his long career. This means that Rawls's basic approach is not merely one of (hypothetical) consent, but also one of proceduralism, the third family of theories discussed below. But this also means that Rawls's theory should display—and in fact does display—the typical weakness of pure procedural theories, which is that they cannot respond to bad outcomes.[23] Indeed, by refusing to offer *any* criteria by which to evaluate the outcomes of political decision-making, Rawls simply has nothing to say when political outcomes turn out to be unjust or politically deleterious. And he has no response for the citizen who might understandably view the legitimacy of the regime as relating in some way to the moral quality of its actual policies.[24] In short, Rawls fails to go far enough in ensuring that the state's use of coercion is morally legitimate all the way down.

Finally (and this criticism goes for all hypothetical consent theories), Rawls believes he knows better than individuals themselves what they *ought* to consent to. There is more than a whiff of paternalism here. For Rawls, individuals ought to consent to whatever is "reasonable," and he takes the liberty of defining for his readers what this means.

> As applied to the simplest case, namely to persons engaged in cooperation and situated as equals in relevant respects ... reasonable persons are ready to propose, or to acknowledge when proposed by others, the principles needed to specify what can be seen by all as fair terms of cooperation. Reasonable persons also understand that they are to honor these principles, even at the expense of their own interests as circumstances require, provided others likewise may be expected to honor them. It is unreasonable not to be ready to propose such principles, or not to honor fair terms. ... It is worse than unreasonable if one merely seems, or pretends, to propose to honor them but is ready to violate them to one's advantage as the occasion permits.[25]

That the "reasonable" is defined in terms of "cooperation" and "honoring fair terms of cooperation" is not a trivial fact. Rather it constitutes an undefended plank in Rawls's argument for legitimacy. For, a barebones way of presenting his argument is as follows: (a) *If* American society is understood as a "fair system of cooperation," and (b) *if* "reason" requires that people who are engaged in cooperation as equals should "honor fair terms of cooperation" when offered, *then* (c) reason requires that citizens honor Rawls's two principles of justice (or better ones, if they can find them). Rawls thus supposes his theory will gain the hypothetical consent of all citizens—not their actual consent—insofar as people ought to consent to what is "reasonable," a concept Rawls defines on our behalf.

But the problem with this paternalist attempt to tell citizens what is reasonable is that citizens actually have *their own ideas* about reasonableness.[26] And one idea that many citizens no doubt hold (rightly in my view) is that there are times in political life when what is reasonable is precisely *not* to honor fair terms of cooperation, for instance, when legitimate procedures produce very bad results.[27] I need not review specific instances of this phenomenon, which has been all too common in American democratic life and in other democracies, such as the Weimar Republic. Sometimes, even though fair procedures were followed, the political results prove unacceptable. And this casts a shadow of illegitimacy over particular laws and *in extremis* over the regime itself. Unfortunately, Rawls's notion of the "reasonable," which underlies his paternalist theory of legitimacy, cannot account for this reality.

This concludes my consideration of the consent approach to legitimacy. The attempt to ground legitimacy on actual or hypothetical consent does not succeed, because no regimes actually secure (or could secure) the full consent of the governed. In order to overcome this problem, Rawls proposes a form of hypothetical consent. But this fails to be practicable for the reasons just enumerated. Thus, if the practice of rule is to be deemed legitimate, it will have to be through some other avenue than consent theory. Let us try another approach.

Benefit Theory I: Joseph Raz

The second major approach to the problem of legitimacy maintains that a state's right to coerce citizens who are otherwise regarded as free and equal stems from certain benefits the state bestows. Versions of this approach have been advanced by utilitarian writers such as Bentham, Mill, and Sidgwick, but I do not select their versions as my exemplars, because they have been subject to withering criticism, and I wish to test the strongest representatives of the approach. The basic claim of utilitarian theories is that the state is legitimate when it contributes to the greatest net balance of satisfaction summed over all the citizens—to which the standard criticism is that such theories pay insufficient regard to individual rights. The "net balance of satisfaction" can be increased without every citizen experiencing the increase. Indeed, utilitarian theories do not prevent the deliberate sacrifice of some citizens' satisfactions to the greater "net balance" for all.[28]

The benefit theories I select are therefore ones designed to meet this objection, beginning with Joseph Raz's "service conception" of legitimacy. The "service conception" grounds legitimacy in benefits, as the utilitarians tried to do, but the benefits extend to all citizens and relate not to their pleasure satisfactions but to their exercise of practical reason.

Consider what happens in the mind of a practical reasoner when a legitimate authority issues a command. Suppose a person is weighing reasons for and against performing a certain act (say, making a left turn onto MacArthur Drive), when, suddenly, a traffic guard on the corner of MacArthur raises a stop sign and shouts, "Stop!" What happens in the mind of the practical reasoner, according to Raz, is that a new reason appears in addition to whatever other reasons may have been present for *not* turning left onto MacArthur. But this new reason is different from the others, because it is not meant to be weighed equally with them but to override and exclude any competing reasons. Raz refers to this as his "preemption thesis."

> The fact that an authority requires performance of an action is a reason for its performance which is not to be added to all other relevant reasons when assessing what to do, but should exclude and take the place of some of them.[29]

The preemption thesis helps clarify the difference between legitimate authority and mere de facto authority for Raz. A de facto authority might successfully command people to do or refrain from doing certain acts, and people might do what they are told out of fear or some other concern. But only a legitimate authority successfully *changes the reasons* people have for acting or refraining from acting.[30] Another way Raz puts this is to say that people sometimes "conform" to the reasons given by de facto authorities (they perform the act required of them), but they "comply" with reasons given by legitimate authorities (they act *for the reason that* the authority is legitimate).[31]

But what makes an authority legitimate? Under what conditions would citizens rightly allow someone else's command to become a reason for their action? Before presenting Raz's answer, I prepare the way by pointing out that we often do this very thing outside the domain of politics. We allow, for instance, a doctor's order to determine what medicine we shall take when we are ill. And no wonder: While we have our own reasons to act— our illness and desire to recover constitute reasons to get the best medicine possible—we do not have enough expertise to act wisely. So when a doctor orders us to take such and such medicine we obey, because following his orders makes us more likely to comply with the reasons that antecedently apply to us than if we were to make a decision on our own.[32] In this case, a doctor is a legitimate authority for us with respect to medicine.

Here, now is Raz describing what he calls the normal way (but not the only way) that authority becomes legitimate:

> The normal way to establish that a person has [legitimate] authority over another person involves showing that the alleged subject is likely better to comply with the reasons which apply to him (other than the alleged authoritative directive) if he accepts the directives of the alleged authority as authoritatively binding and tries to follow them, rather than by trying to follow the reasons which apply to him directly.[33]

Raz refers to this as the "normal justification thesis," and he views it as an essential part of his "service conception" of legitimacy. The service conception is so named, because when authority is truly legitimate, it works in the service of (i.e., it benefits) those who obey it.

In addition to the "preemption thesis" and the "normal justification thesis," Raz offers another idea that supports the preemption thesis and rounds out his service conception of legitimacy. He calls this the "dependence thesis."

> All authoritative directives should be based on reasons which already independently apply to the subjects of the directives and are relevant to their action in the circumstances covered by the directive.[34]

This is a crucial feature of legitimate authority for Raz, as it constitutes a real limit to an authority's rightful power. The limit (think of the doctor/ patient example again) is that legitimate authorities can only rely on certain kinds of reasons when making decisions and issuing directives. Their reasons must "depend" on reasons that already independently apply to the subjects (such as the patient's chief reason for seeking the best medicine possible: his desire to recover from illness). In practice, of course, authorities often issue directives that do not meet this criterion of legitimacy.

They issue commands for reasons entirely their own or for reasons applicable to some people but not others. But Raz is quite clear that he is addressing the way legitimate authorities are *supposed* to function and how they *claim* to function, not how they fail to live up to their function.[35]

Before turning to evaluate Raz's theory, one clarification will help illuminate its expansive reach. As it has come to light so far, the service conception appears to be merely an argument from expertise. Authorities are legitimate insofar as they possess (like a doctor) a superior expertise to help subjects achieve what they themselves want to achieve. But in fact, expertise is not the only path to legitimate authority for Raz. Another path (and there are others besides) is for authorities to establish a beneficial "convention" that solves citizens' coordination problems. For example, during the 1970s when gasoline shortages caused long lines at gas stations, the government introduced a convention of "odd-even rationing." Drivers whose license plates ended in an odd number could pump gas only on odd-numbered days; drivers with even-numbered plates could pump only on even days. Raz would view this as an example of legitimate authority, not because the government possessed superior expertise, but rather because it exercised its ability to solve a problem that those subject to the rule had a good reason to want to be solved. Again, drivers had an independent reason to do what the directive helped them do. The directive altered their practical reasoning by introducing a new, preemptive consideration.

Raz's theory of legitimacy is sophisticated and illuminating. Certainly, it sheds light on some aspects of ruling and being ruled that relate to legitimacy. But in the end, it suffers from two fatal flaws, one of which is unique to Raz's specific version of benefit theory, while the other applies to benefit theory as a whole.

The first problem is that Raz's criteria for legitimacy are entirely substantive and not at all procedural.[36] He writes,

> Governments decide what is best for their subjects and present them with the results as binding conclusions that they are bound to follow. ... [Government] says: 'We are better able to decide how you should act. Our decision is in these laws. You are bound by them and should follow them whether or not you agree with them.'[37]

But as Scott Hershovitz has shown, democratic polities such as ours do not have the luxury of ignoring the *processes* by which decisions are reached.[38] That is because democracies view certain procedures as a necessary means to key democratic ends. For example, fair and inclusive deliberative processes are thought to (a) improve the substance of our decisions, (b) show respect for the dignity of our fellow citizens, and (c) help prevent alienation and resignation. Moreover, deliberative processes have the potential to (d) help citizens *shift* their initial (pre-deliberative) preferences in light of sound arguments made in the public political process.[39] In this way, sound democratic procedures help to keep a check (however minimal) on problematic phenomena such as pluralism and polarization. If this is right, then it is possible for an authoritative decision to be substantively good but procedurally illegitimate. Considerations such as these suggest that Raz's normal justification thesis falls significantly short of constituting a workable ground for the legitimacy of rule.

Secondly, it seems simply wrong to suppose that coercion can be made legitimate by the mere fact that benefits have been bestowed. This is where the doctor/patient analogy badly misleads. When patients visit doctors, they do so voluntarily; they also know in advance that doctors' services require payment in return. Moreover, when patients allow doctors to prescribe medicine, they do so knowing they are free to follow their doctors' (authoritative) advice *or not*. But in politics, everything looks different. Involvement in political life is compulsory, not voluntary. Citizens do not always (or usually) actively seek the "benefits" that government supplies. Nor do citizens typically have the opportunity to decline them. So why should we suppose that the mere fact of receiving benefits (neither asked for nor voluntarily accepted) obligates citizens to regard the state's coercive power over them as legitimate? This is not to deny, of course, that individuals who receive benefits ought to be grateful. Perhaps they should even desire to give something back in return. But the idea that people should be required to give up an unspecified portion of their *liberty* for benefits that were themselves forced upon them does not seem to constitute a plausible ground for political legitimacy.[40]

Benefit Theory II: Christopher Wellman

This fundamental weakness of benefit theories may seem fatal for the approach as a whole. But there is, in fact, another way of construing benefits that might hold out some promise. Christopher Wellman has argued that the legitimacy of rule rests not (or not merely) on the benefits it bestows upon me as an individual, but rather on the benefits it bestows upon *others*, my fellow citizens. Were it not for the coercive power of the state, Wellman explains, political life would devolve into an anarchic state of nature, and individuals would suffer at the hands of the violent. The state saves individuals from this disaster by establishing rules backed by force. But it can only do this successfully if everyone within the boundaries of the state actually participates in its order. If people are free to opt out and yet still reside in state boundaries, the state cannot perform its functions. Therefore, Wellman concludes, people have a moral duty not to opt out; every individual is duty bound to obey the coercive power of the state in order to save everyone else from harm. This is a principle he refers to as "samaritanism."[41] Just as we have a duty to help a stranger who is imperiled, provided we can do so at no unreasonable cost to ourselves, so we have a duty to help our compatriots avoid the perils of a state of nature, provided (again) that we can do so at no unreasonable cost to ourselves.

Wellman thus grounds the legitimacy of the coercive state on samaritan duties people owe to each other.[42] Is he right to do so? At first blush, he seems to have successfully dodged the main problem with all benefit theories that states cannot force benefits on people and then use this as a ground for their own legitimacy. But let us look more closely at how Wellman gets around this problem, if he in fact does.

One thing to notice about Wellman's approach is that the samaritan component of his argument, which he believes to be the key to legitimacy, is in fact not a theory of legitimacy at all, but rather a theory of political obligation. It supplies an account of why individuals are obligated to participate in the state, not an account of why or whether any given state is legitimate. Readers who are not familiar with this distinction may fail to appreciate its significance. But as many political philosophers have noticed, a state can be illegitimate but nevertheless secure my obedience for prudential reasons. Likewise, a state may be perfectly legitimate and yet have no claim to my obedience—if, for example, I choose to submit myself to a different state or no state at all. Obligation and legitimacy are thus closely related, but distinct enough that arguments for the one often prove insufficient to establish the other.

This is the case with Wellman's approach. He offers an account of political obligation grounded in the idea of samaritanism, but he says nothing about what makes the coercive state *legitimate*. If we, for our part, try to press this question, we unfortunately have nothing to fall back on except the very kind of benefit theory that Wellman himself rejects. We fall back on the fact that Wellman's state bestows the enormous benefit of saving people from a violent state of nature. Yet Wellman himself admits that benefits which are neither asked for nor voluntarily accepted cannot establish legitimacy:

> Liberals understand each person to occupy a position of dominion over her own affairs. Given this personal sovereignty, every individual has the right to choose whether and how to benefit herself, and no one may constrain someone against her will, even in the interest of benefiting her. In light of this individual autonomy it remains unclear how the benefits of a state can justify its coercion.[43]

Nothing in Wellman's theory of samaritanism removes this difficulty. If one begins by assuming that liberal citizens are "free" and "politically equal" (in my language) or "sovereign" and "autonomous" (in Wellman's), then the effort of states to establish their legitimacy by coercively bestowing benefits seems illegitimate.

A second thing to notice about Wellman's approach is that, even as a theory of political obligation (as opposed to legitimacy), its reach is quite limited. That is because the samaritan duty on which he grounds obligation only arises under two narrowly circumscribed conditions. First, people must be in "extreme peril," as Wellman imagines they would be in a "state of nature." And, second, the samaritan must be able to assist them at "no unreasonable cost" to himself.[44] Wellman is explicit that "both conditions are necessary for a samaritan duty to obtain, so that if the scenario were altered on either count, no duty would exist."[45] But it is hard to see what this accomplishes. Setting aside any number of questions one might raise about Wellman's understanding of the state of nature, or his belief that only a sizable state with monopolistic authority can rescue individuals from it, we must nevertheless ask: which functions of the modern liberal state actually meet the conditions of saving people from "extreme peril" and doing so at "no unreasonable cost?" Perhaps the military and police functions of the state meet the first criterion. But it is hard to imagine much beyond this. Wellman's "extreme peril" condition thus limits political obligation to something like a "night watchman" state. But the "no extreme cost" condition limits it even further. As George Klosko has noted, this condition would rule out obligations to "pay burdensome taxes or to obey other costly laws, let alone to undertake military service—to fight, possibly to die—for one's country."[46] Thus, even the military and police functions of the state seem undermined by the twin conditions of samaritanism.

This means that despite initial appearances, Wellman's samaritan approach to benefit theory proves unworkable as a ground for the legitimacy of rule.

Procedure Theory

A final family of theories attempts to ground the legitimacy of rule in the procedures that lead up to any given law or policy, arguing that if the procedures themselves are fair (or in some other way commendable), then the results must be legitimate, whatever they happen to be. This is another effort, as with benefit theory, to sidestep the whole problem of consent, since unanimous consent *even to procedures*, let alone political outcomes, seems impossible to secure. The idea here is that if the procedures can fulfill certain legitimizing conditions, then citizens have no right to withhold consent. Non-consent will simply be regarded as null, and rule will be deemed legitimate.

Most procedure theories suffer from a common weakness (one of the problems mentioned in connection with Rawls's approach above), which is that they lack procedure-independent resources to declare some outcomes simply bad. Since this weakness has been widely acknowledged, I here disregard the theories that suffer from it[47] and instead focus on a well-known attempt to overcome it. In his book *Democratic Authority*, David M. Estlund defends a theory of legitimacy he calls "epistemic proceduralism."[48] His goal is to avoid pure proceduralism on the one side by introducing some epistemic (substantive) criteria for legitimacy, while avoiding what he calls "correctness theory" on the other side, any account of legitimacy that rests on expert knowledge of what is true, or best, or just, in politics. Correctness theory, Estlund explains, is no longer available in our current state of radical pluralism.[49] "Qualified citizens will disagree about who counts as an expert."[50] Thus, we cannot fall back on correctness theory without violating our basic commitments to the freedom and political equality of citizens who disagree.

The question then becomes: How can one introduce epistemic standards without privileging expertise? Estlund's ingenious move is to claim that when democratic procedures are approached in the right way, they produce enough epistemic value to secure legitimacy without ever relying on putative experts. How so? Estlund commits himself to two claims. First, democracy tends on average to get things right.[51] Certainly, it is more epistemically valuable than, say, a coin toss—which is Estlund's famous example of a perfectly fair procedure with no epistemic value at all.[52] Thus, if the test of legitimacy is a tendency to get things right, then Estlund believes democracy passes that test. But second, beyond being "better than random," democratic processes are also, according to Estlund, better than all rival procedures that are morally available. By "morally available," he means procedures which, unlike those associated with "correctness theories," should be acceptable from "all qualified points of view," or what Rawls would call "reasonable" points of view.[53]

One of the strongest aspects of Estlund's argument is the way he bolsters his case for epistemic proceduralism by likening it to the jury system.[54] In the case of juries, we find panels of citizens with no special claims to expertise. We are aware of the fact that juries can err, and yet we know they tend on average to get things right. And we regard their decisions as legitimate not only because they are epistemically better than random, but also because they constitute the best system available for deciding cases without relying on putative experts.

Estlund's argument is that if we find the authority of juries legitimate (even though they sometimes make mistakes), then we should find democratic rule legitimate as well.

> The essential elements of the argument for the authority of the jury system are all present in a democratic system of government. First, there is a very great value, one that no qualified point of view could deny, to having laws and policies that are substantively just. Second, a proper democratic procedure, like a jury, is (or can be) demographically neutral. ... Third, a democratic procedure involves many citizens thinking together, potentially reaping the epistemic benefits this can bring. ... So, fourth, I conjecture there is no nondemocratic arrangement that all qualified points of view could agree would serve substantive justice better. In light of all this, citizens would be morally required to consent to the new authority of such a democratic arrangement if they were offered that choice. Non-consent would be null, and so the fact that no such consent is normally asked or given makes no difference, and so any existing democratic arrangement that meets these conditions has authority over each citizen just as if they had established its authority by actual consent.[55]

Estlund's intention is not to rest his case for epistemic proceduralism on the jury analogy, but simply to use it for support. Again, if the authority of juries is regarded as legitimate, then, *mutatis mutandis*, the authority of democratic procedures should be too.

Estlund's theory has attracted a great deal of scholarly attention, and it has been criticized from a number of different angles. Here, I will only mention one weakness, which unfortunately prevents it from performing the task we have set for it, that of grounding the legitimacy of rule for citizens who regard themselves as free and politically equal. Estlund's argument requires not only that democratic procedures be fair, but also that they result in outcomes that are (1) better than random and (2) better than all rival political procedures that are acceptable from a qualified point of view. Granting that democratic processes can be construed in ways that make them arguably fair, the problem remains of demonstrating that democracy meets conditions (1) and (2).[56] Unfortunately, Estlund's account leaves much to be desired on these points.

With respect to (1), demonstrating that democracy is better than random, Estlund offers an "imaginary model [of] epistemic deliberation" that resembles the kinds of considerations found in the deliberative democracy literature. He requires, for instance, that "everyone has full and equal access to the forum," that "everyone has the same chance to speak as everyone else," and that "people only says things that they believe will help others to appreciate the reasons to hold one view or another among those that are in question," et cetera.[57] But, as Estlund must admit, this exercise does not in fact demonstrate that democracy produces outcomes better than random. It merely lists some conditions that "*make it plausible*" that outcomes will be "better than if they had been made randomly."[58] In other words, Estlund's way of demonstrating democracy's epistemological superiority ignores empirical reality—after all, actual democracies have arrived at some notoriously bad policy decisions in the past. Aware of this potential objection, Estlund responds: "That would be a fair point if the disappointing empirical results were observed in contexts where the preceding conditions are met, but they obviously do not, since no empirical context *could* meet the conditions."[59] Thus, what Estlund in fact demonstrates, if anything, is that in an imaginary democracy the likes of which is impossible fully to realize on earth, political outcomes would likely be better than random. This is hardly a convincing case for the legitimacy of actual democratic rule.

With respect to (2), democracy's superiority over other systems that are acceptable from a qualified point of view, it is never clear in Estlund's account which systems (including democracy itself) would actually belong to this set, much less how one would evaluate the contenders vis-à-vis a form of democracy that is only imaginary.[60]

In a regrettable but not unexpected way, then, Estlund's argument for epistemic proceduralism fails to live up to its aspirations. Its goal is to strengthen the procedural approach in general by demonstrating that democracy is not only procedurally fair, but also epistemically commendable, indeed that democracy's epistemic value is superior to all other procedural rivals that are acceptable from a qualified point of view. But in failing to demonstrate that democracy outperforms even random decision-making, Estlund leaves us only with its fairness as a ground for legitimacy. This means that Estlund's approach suffers in the end from the same weakness that other procedural theories suffer from: It has nothing substantive to say when fair procedures produce bad outcomes. It has no procedure-independent mechanism for declaring some democratic decisions unacceptable.[61]

III—Practical Implications

If the argument above seems sound and we really do lack convincing arguments from within the liberal tradition for the legitimacy of rule, does this have any significant implications for how we ought to practice politics today? I believe it does.

American politics has for many years—probably since its origins—relied more or less on de facto legitimacy. What I mean is that we have never been able (and rarely have we tried) to offer an airtight philosophical case for the legitimacy of the coercive powers of government. Instead, we have proceeded on the happy assumption that if government does its job tolerably well, if it protects citizens from harm and enacts laws that contribute to our general well-being, then most people most of the time will be satisfied enough not to rock the boat. This was precisely what worried Michael Oakeshott: We have developed an insensitivity to the problem of legitimacy, one which may eventually leave us defenseless against the exercise of arbitrary power and benevolent despotism. Of course, there have been significant periods in our history when the coercive powers of government led some segments of society to perceive a lack legitimacy—the Civil War and its aftermath, the New Deal, the "separate but equal" policies prior to the Civil Rights Movement, and the prosecution of the Vietnam War—but Americans have always managed to overcome these crises in one way or another. Thus, de facto legitimacy has served us well enough.

However, there are strong reasons to believe that the de facto legitimacy of American government will not survive the future. I cannot expand on the reasons here, but I can at least list them. Americans are currently more deeply pluralistic and ideologically polarized than ever before in our history. (This has been measured by the Pew Foundation.) At the same time, the power and scope of government have been constantly increasing to the point at which, today, there is scarcely a single area of private life untouched by regulations backed by coercion. Yet, these two basic facts—(1) pluralism and polarization, with (2) virtually unlimited government power—when taken together, are simply incompatible with de facto legitimacy. The reason is that an increasingly active and powerful government will necessarily alienate larger and larger sections of political society as it creates policies designed to please some constituents but not others. And with the political atmosphere as charged as it is today (thanks to government encroachment combined with extreme political polarization), citizens who stand to lose will vociferously object that the powers arrayed against them are simply illegitimate. This perhaps goes some way to explaining the slogan "Not my president!" that is currently on the lips of so many Americans on the right and left as I compose this essay. This is a protest against President Donald Trump's *legitimacy*, not because he lost the election (he won it), but because the policies he wants to enact are objectionable to large sectors of an intensely polarized society, and he seems bent on enacting them anyway.

The question, then, is what can be done when a regime's *de facto* legitimacy shrinks to such crisis levels that violence begins to break out in the streets, as it has today in many liberal democracies. The answer cannot be, of course, to fall back on some philosophically sound argument for legitimacy. No such arguments exist—or at least I cannot find them. And yet some degree of political coercion remains *necessary* if order is to be maintained and liberty defended.

My answer is as follows: Just to the extent that rule is necessary but apparently illegitimate, it becomes prudent to limit the occasions of rule as much as possible and to ensure that its quality is such that it feels as little like rule as possible. To limit the occasions of rule means abandoning the old political question, "What policies would we (the party in power) like to enact?" and asking instead, "What policies do we (the American people in general) need minimally in order to maintain ourselves as a polity?"

In other words, limiting the occasions of rule means limiting government scope and power to levels proportionate to our actual levels of political agreement. General rule: The more pluralistic and polarized a society becomes, the less its government should do. And the philosophical ground for this claim is that our bedrock commitments to freedom and political equality do not permit otherwise.

To ensure that the *quality* of rule feels as little like rule as possible it is necessary to garner as much consent as possible. One way of doing this is by returning to a more federal approach. Because our national character is so badly fractured, consent will remain elusive. However, by returning power to local areas, where people have more in common, rule will feel less like coercion, more like what "we" want to do as a whole. A second way of affecting the quality of rule is through a more concerted effort at statesmanship. Rather than approaching politics as if it were a war between one side and another, we must approach it (credibly) as an effort to garner support for the best solutions for all. To the extent that this effort succeeds, de facto legitimacy will remain intact. To the extent that it fails, government will seem illegitimate and increasingly irksome to American citizens who take their commitments to freedom and political equality seriously.

One more change is, I believe, necessary to fend off the crisis of legitimacy and avoid political dissolution. The republican theory laid out in Madison's Federalist #10—the idea that factions will counter factions and that, therefore, whatever survives the process of factional contestation will approximate the common good—has not worked. American liberalism is today dominated by factions. The notion that factions would neutralize each other in an almost mathematical way was a product of Enlightenment rationalism. It was too clever by half. But, worse than not working, it has actually had a corrosive effect on our political culture. It has encouraged individuals and groups to fight as hard as they can for political victory, all the while assuaging their consciences that this constant antagonism is fundamental to the success of our system.

In my view, the theory of Federalist #10 went too far in supposing that wise political institutions and practices could function even without virtuous citizens. If so, we need to develop publicly recognized principles of civility and political restraint that can serve as criteria by which to shame political actors who use our shared government to pursue highly controversial ends. This is not a return to the more ancient view that civic virtue alone can promote a healthy politics. But it is a move toward a more moderate view on this score. A combination of sound institutions with much more serious attention to the cultivation of political virtue (especially the virtue of restraint) is necessary for long-term civic health. If we are to remain a polity animated by love of freedom and respect for the political equality of our fellow citizens, then we need to teach that violation of these goods poses a fundamental threat to our regime.

IV—CONCLUSION

The problem of liberal legitimacy involves the question, "What legitimizes the exercise of 'rule' by some citizens over others in a political community where *all* citizens are recognized as free and politically equal?" Michael Oakeshott's primary way of responding to this question was to point to his ideal of "civil association," a form of moral relationship in which the state regards citizens on the one hand as "free" to pursue their own ends, as long as these do not conflict with a like freedom for all, and on the other hand "equal" in the sense that no citizen has a right to arbitrarily impose his preferences on others in the private sphere or especially in the public sphere by using the state to enforce some collective purpose. Oakeshott's theory of civil association was admittedly "ideal," and he did not think modern liberal politics could ever be characterized by civil association alone. Rather he thought modern politics would involve an ongoing tension between civil association and the form of instrumental association toward collective ends, which he called "enterprise association."

This essay has explored the implications of Oakeshott's view for contemporary liberal politics, especially his view (if it was his view) that civil association alone meets the criteria of liberal legitimacy. If Oakeshott was right, then it would stand to reason that other philosophical attempts to solve the problem of legitimacy, no matter how prominent they are or deep-seated in the liberal tradition, must be flawed to the extent to which they deviate from the ideal of civil association. In order to show that this is in fact the case, I have analyzed the philosophical strengths and weaknesses of all three well-known approaches to political legitimacy and found them wanting.

The practical implications of this finding are significant. Over the past century or more, liberal governments have increased exponentially in scope and power, yet the lack of legitimacy that this essay underscores suggests that they should be *decreasing* in scope and power.

Furthermore, over the past century the locus of government has shifted radically from cities and states to the national level, yet the problem of political legitimacy at the national level is significantly worse than at the local. This study in the problem of political legitimacy has therefore yielded results that may be applicable in the real world as liberal democracies such as the USA attempt to navigate the "crisis" of legitimacy that unfolds before us.

Notes

1. Noël O'Sullivan, "Oakeshott on Modernity and the Crisis of Political Legitimacy in Contemporary Western Liberal Democracy," *Cosmos and Taxis* 1, no. 3 (2014), 21.
2. Michael Oakeshott, *On Human Conduct* (Oxford: Oxford University Press, 1975), 192. Quoted in O'Sullivan, who also adds the italics.
3. Terry Nardin describes civil association as follows: "Civil association implies a state whose laws leave citizens free to pursue their own self-chosen goals within limits that secure that freedom for all: a state that is premised on the independence of those associated and is therefore hostile to the domination that occurs when one person seeks to arbitrarily impose his preferences on others or when the state itself is organized to impose a collective purpose on everyone." Terry Nardin, "Michael Oakeshott," *The Stanford Encyclopedia of Philosophy* (Winter 2016 Edition), ed., Edward N. Zalta. https://plato.stanford.edu/archives/win2016/entries/oakeshott/.
4. O'Sullivan, "Oakeshott on Modernity," 25. In support of this claim, O'Sullivan cites Efraim Podoksik, *In Defense of Modernity: Vision and Philosophy in Michael Oakeshott* (Exeter: Imprint Academic, 2003).
5. Ibid., 21. Cf. page 25, the first paragraph of the conclusion.
6. Ibid., 25.
7. I say nothing more about the likely consequences of O'Sullivan's approach in the body of this essay, but my worry is that his desire to protect liberal democracies from arbitrary power and to school them in the crucial distinction between power and authority will not be well served by resting political legitimacy on the mere fact of political debate. Such an approach exposes liberal democracies to the "tyranny of the majority" and even to the tyranny of a cunning *minority*.
8. When I say "all theories of legitimacy," I mean those that assume freedom and political equality on the part of citizens. Many theories of legitimacy, particularly ancient and medieval ones, depart from these assumptions. Most

still fit into the three basic categories. But since they are not relevant to current American political conditions, I do not consider them further here.

9. My method is similar to that of A. John Simmons in *Political Philosophy* (Oxford: Oxford University Press, 2008), 39–66, except that Simmons is concerned with the problem of obligation rather than the related but distinct problem of legitimacy.

10. Even at the inauguration of political community, some will likely dissent. Locke's thought is that they are perfectly free to dissent and maintain their current status in the state of nature. Thus, the creation of a new political community harms them in no way. But Locke here assumes ample land and resources for these dissenters, an assumption that is obviously not solid in contemporary life.

11. The surprising frequency of cases where a majority grants obedience to a ruthless minority was the subject (more than a century before Locke's *Two Treatises*) of Étienne de La Boétie, *The Politics of Obedience: The Discourse of Voluntary Servitude* (1576).

12. Perhaps what gives Locke's argument the semblance of plausibility is its seductive, Newtonian language. "Body," "force," and "motion" are the key terms used in Newton's *Principia Mathematica*, published in 1687. I would not argue that Locke's *Second Treatise* (composed between 1679 and 1681) was directly influenced by Newton's *Principia*, which came later. But both thinkers had a deep interested in natural science, and they became close friends after (if not before) Locke wrote a favorable review of the *Principia*. My argument is only that Newton's *Principia* would have lent rhetorical support to Locke's language here. On the friendship between Newton and Locke, see further, Peter R. Anstey, "Newton and Locke," in *The Oxford Handbook of Newton*, ed. Eric Schliesser and Chris Smeenk (*Oxford Handbooks Online*, February 2017). http://www.oxfordhandbooks.com/view/10.1093/oxfordhb/9780199930418.001.0001/oxfordhb-9780199930418.

13. See Locke, Ibid., §§123–131.

14. David Hume, "Of the Original Contract," in David Hume, *Political Essays*, ed. Knud Haakonssen (Cambridge: Cambridge University Press, 1994 [1748]), 189. See also, David Copp, "The Idea of a Legitimate State," *Philosophy and Public Affairs* 28, no. 1 (1999), 31–32, who calls this the "pedigree view" of legitimacy, and rejects it.

15. Some people believe that acts of political participation such as voting amount to tacit consent. Others believe the opposite that non-participation amounts to tacit consent and that those who do *not* consent need to protest actively in order to signal their opposition. Both beliefs are persuasively controverted by Simmons, *Political Philosophy*, 114–15.

16. See Immanuel Kant, "On the Common Saying 'This May Be True in Theory But It Does Not Apply in Practice'," in *Kant: Political Writings*, ed. Hans Reiss (Cambridge: Cambridge University Press, 1991), 79.

17. John Rawls, *Justice as Fairness: A Restatement*, ed. Erin Kelly (Cambridge, MA: Belknap Press of Harvard University, 2001), 40–41, my italics.

18. Ibid., 41.

19. Ibid., 84.

20. Rawls, *Justice as Fairness*, 48–49.

21. Ibid., 37.

22. John Rawls, *A Theory of Justice*, rev. ed. (Cambridge, MA: Belknap Press of Harvard University, 1999), 75, my italics. Cf. Rawls, *Justice as Fairness*, 51.

23. Rawls prescinds from offering criteria of evaluation because he assumes deep disagreement about such criteria. On this problem, see further, Gerald F. Gaus, "Reason, Justification, and Consensus: Why Democracy Can't Have It All," in *Deliberative Democracy*, ed. James Bohman and William Rehg (Cambridge, MA: MIT Press, 1997), 205–42.

24. See further, David M. Estlund, *Democratic Authority: A Philosophical Framework* (Princeton: Princeton University Press, 2008), esp. Chapter 5, "The Flight from Substance."

25. Rawls, *Justice as Fairness*, 6–7; cf. p. 81, where Rawls's strong connection to Kant is made clear. Despite his protests that his conceptions of justice are strictly "political" and do not depend on any comprehensive doctrine, Rawls' dependence on Kant's account of what is "reasonable" is unmistakable here.

26. Jeremy Waldron, "Theoretical Foundations of Liberalism," *Philosophical Quarterly* 37, no. 147 (1987), 144, puts this point forcefully: "When we move from asking what people actually accept to asking what they *would* accept under certain conditions, we shift our emphasis away from will and focus on the *reasons* that people might have for exercising their will in one way rather than another. Doing so involves certain dangers for the liberal. Real people do not always act on the reasons we think they might have for acting: the reasonableness of the actors in our hypothesis may not match the reality of men and women in actual life."

27. I want to be clear that I do not object to the ideas of cooperation and fairness that animate Rawls's work. But I do not think Rawls supplies real arguments to defend these ideas. He defends them on the one hand by claiming to "work them up" from our political culture (Rawls, *Justice as Fairness*, 5) and on the other hand by merely asserting that they are the very essence of reasonable. My own defense of values such as cooperation and fairness is that they produce results that are more sustainable than the known alternatives.

28. See Rawls, *Theory of Justice*, 20–21, 160–68, for this criticism.
29. Joseph Raz, *The Morality of Freedom* (Oxford: Clarendon Press, 1988), 46.
30. Joseph Raz, *The Authority of Law: Essays on Law and Morality*, 2nd ed. (Oxford: Oxford University Press, 2009), Ch. 1, "Legitimate Authority," 19.
31. See Joseph Raz, *Practical Reasons and Norms* (Oxford: Oxford University Press, 1999), 178 and Scott Hershovitz's helpful discussion in his "Legitimacy, Democracy, and Razian Authority," *Legal Theory* 9 (2003), 202.
32. I have adapted this example from Hershovitz, "Legitimacy, Democracy, and Razian Authority," 207.
33. Raz, *The Morality of Freedom*, 53.
34. Ibid., 47.
35. Ibid.
36. This is the opposite of the problem I noted with Rawls. Rawls emphasized just procedures to the complete exclusion of substantive evaluation. Raz emphasizes substantive value to the complete exclusion of procedure. Neither approach will do for reasons I articulate above.
37. Joseph Raz, "Government by Consent," in *Ethics in the Public Domain: Essays in the Morality of Law and Politics*, rev. ed. (Oxford: Clarendon Press, 1994), 359.
38. Hershovitz, "Legitimacy, Democracy, and Razian Authority," 213–16.
39. I add this point to the previous ones made by Hershovitz. On the process of shifting preferences, see further the classic essay, Jon Elster, "The Marketplace and the Forum: Three Varieties of Political Theory," in *Foundations of Social Choice Theory*, ed. Jon Elster and Aanund Hylland (Cambridge: Cambridge University Press, 1986), 103–32.
40. See further A. John Simmons, *Justification and Legitimacy: Essays on Rights and Obligations* (Cambridge: Cambridge University Press, 2001), 56–57; cf. Simmons, *Political Philosophy*, 56, 58.
41. Christopher Wellman, "Liberalism, Samaritanism, and Political Legitimacy," *Philosophy & Public Affairs* 25, no. 3 (1996), 211–37.
42. Ibid., 216.
43. Ibid., 213.
44. Ibid., 215.
45. Ibid.
46. George Klosko, "Samaritanism and Political Obligation: A Response to Christopher Wellman's 'Liberal Theory of Political Obligation'," *Ethics* 113, no. 4 (2003), 838.
47. Besides Rawls' "pure proceduralism," I have in mind most theories of deliberative democracy such as those associated with Jürgen Habermas and Joshua Cohen.
48. Estlund, *Democratic Authority: A Philosophic Framework*, Ch. 6.

49. Estlund's rejection of "correctness" in politics is too sweeping, but I shall not dwell on that as a criticism. He needs, but does not supply, a more refined map of the epistemological terrain of politics. Not every decision turns on what is "true"; not every decision turns on what is "just." Estlund shows no signs of recognizing that some decisions demand genuine expertise and that citizens do not always find this objectionable.
50. Ibid., 102.
51. Ibid., 8.
52. Ibid., 66.
53. Ibid., 44.
54. Ibid., 10–12, 156–58.
55. Ibid., 157.
56. This is noticed by Gerald Gaus, "On Seeking the Truth (Whatever That Is) Through Democracy: Estlund's Case for the Qualified Epistemic Claim," *Ethics* 121, no. 2 (2011), 270–300.
57. Estlund, *Democratic Authority*, 175. He offers nine provisions in total.
58. Ibid., 176.
59. Ibid., 176. My italics.
60. See further, Gaus, "On Seeking the Truth," 277ff.
61. I am aware that Estlund has a list of "primary bads" which he thinks democracy will do a good job of avoiding: "war, famine, economic collapse, political collapse, epidemic, and genocide" (p. 163). The problem is these "bads" are themselves controversial. They seem to come out of nowhere. And reasonable citizens will disagree about their relative badness under varying circumstances. See further, Gaus, "On Seeking the Truth," 293–96.

CHAPTER 4

Oakeshott on the State:
Between History and Philosophy

Gary Browning

I

Oakeshott was a philosopher as well as an historian. He engaged in philosophy by reflecting upon the character of experience and was an historian of political thought in examining the historical conditions in which distinct forms of political thinking arise. For Oakeshott, these two activities are separate. Philosophy understands experience in an unconditional and general way. It understands the postulates of activities, such as art, history, and practical life. It conceptualizes the experiential orientation of thinking historically, practicing science, contemplating artistic images, and negotiating the twists and turns of practical life. Insofar as it is philosophical, thought does not engage with practical tasks, recognize how the past has changed into the present, contemplate scenes artistically, or generate hypothetical scientific laws. Rather

G. Browning (✉)
Oxford Brookes University, Oxford, UK
e-mail: gkbrowning@brookes.ac.uk

E. S. Kos (ed.), *Michael Oakeshott on Authority, Governance, and the State*, Palgrave Studies in Classical Liberalism,
https://doi.org/10.1007/978-3-030-17455-2_4

it conceptualizes what we are up to in undertaking practical action or in tracing antecedent events, which relate to a political action such as the referendum decision of the UK to leave the European Union. An historian's understanding an event such as Brexit, the prospective withdrawal of the UK from the European Union, relates the referendum decision to leave the EU to past events that preceded it and rendered it possible. So a series of events and developing attitudes within the Conservative Party might be invoked to explain why Cameron considered it useful to stage a referendum on this issue of EU membership. At the same time, historical events and developing attitudes in the UK to issues relating to UK membership of the EU might be referenced to explain the vote for Brexit. The historian by his study of events preceding the referendum decision to withdraw from the EU would not be committed to either supporting or denouncing Brexit. The moral and instrumental preferences of practical life are irrelevant to historical understanding. Likewise, the historian does not have to frame a philosophical understanding of the postulates of history to justify her narrative. The past may be real or imagined, and the status of beliefs and practices unquestioned, but the historian can still provide a convincing account of an historical topic. Hence for Oakeshott, philosophy, history, and practice are separate from one another and according to some of the idioms that he uses to describe their relations, they are insulated from one another. Yet, in fact, are philosophy and history distinct from one another? Are philosophical and historical forms of inquiry to be considered altogether distinct from one another? In this essay, I will argue that they are intertwined in Oakeshott's own account of the state, notwithstanding his own reading of their distinctness.[1] Of course, to criticize Oakeshott on this score is susceptible to the caveat entertained by Minogue in his essay, "The Fate of Rationalism in Oakeshott's Thought," "As ever with Oakeshott, the detail of the argument is marvelously suggestive, and its development so subtle that it can be criticized only by the most brutish grasp of what he might be up to."[2] If critiquing Oakeshott is hazardous, to accept his self-understanding of his enterprise is misplaced if it means maintaining a sense of the independence of modes of thought from one another that cannot be sustained in practice. In what follows, I will run through Oakeshott's practice as an historian of political thought and then invoke his philosophical account of the state and in so doing show how they are not discrete activities but are inter-related.

II—Oakeshott: Historian of Political Thought

In the lecture series on the history of political thought Oakeshott delivered at the London School of Economics and Political Science in the 1960s, he provided a history of the development of political thought. These lectures, now published posthumously as *Lectures in the History of Political Thought*, differ from preceding lecture series that concentrated upon specific texts and theorists in that they set out the contexts in which historic texts of political theory are situated. They are historical in character and set out a basis for explaining political thought historically. They show Oakeshott's understanding of the contextual setting for political thought. He relates historic theories of politics to the traditions and forms of political experience associated with differing political regimes. Oakeshott outlines the political experience of the Ancient Greeks and Romans, the character of medieval government, and the nature of a modern European state. These then serve as contextual settings for the political thought of Ancient, medieval, and modern theorists. The lectures reflect Oakeshott's understanding of how political thought depends upon the historical conditions of political practice, and his method in the history of political thought is to relate theory to actual forms of political experience.[3] At the outset of the lectures, Oakeshott declares, "History I take to be a mode of thought in which events, human actions, beliefs, manners of thinking are considered in relation to the conditions, or the circumstantial contexts in which they appeared."[4] He distinguishes such an approach from a scientific one, which would provide general laws to establish a causal understanding of past phenomena. Oakeshott's historical approach renders past events, beliefs, and actions more intelligible by relating them to affiliated kinds of things, such as beliefs and actions rather than to record the regularities with which they occur. The thought is that contextualizing ideas in the broader context of a political culture enhances understanding without either establishing their necessity or justifying them in a general normative sense.[5]

In his *Lectures in the History of Political Thought*, Oakeshott is at pains to highlight how his enterprise disavows a teleological conception of the progress or regress of political thought over time, which would imply a philosophical reading of history. He emphasizes the distinctness of particular forms of past thinking to the extent that he denies the prospect of a continuous history of political thought. He observes, "I want to avoid the appearance of putting before you anything like a continuous history of European political thought."[6] Oakeshott's *Lectures in the History of Political Thought*, then, do not provide an overall account of the historical development of political thought but instead concentrate upon specific historical periods. Thompson in "Michael Oakeshott on the History of Political Thought" questions their status as exemplifying Oakeshott's notion of a history of political thought. For Thompson, "they are sophisticated lectures, but their purpose is introductory."[7] Notwithstanding their introductory character, however, they reveal key aspects of Oakeshott's notion of the history of political thought. As Thompson himself suggests, "But although the lectures are not the best source for Oakeshott's conception of the history of political thought, they do contain some important observations central to that conception."[8] In relating past political thought to the public culture of past political contexts, Oakeshott follows Hegel, whom he admires, but he is against the supervening teleology of Hegel and his philosophical history, which perceives a developmental continuity in the history of political thought. Oakeshott opposes the idea of a continuous history of political thought because he concentrates on distinct past forms of political thinking, which derive from past circumstances that are held to be necessarily distinct from the present. Oakeshott is against retrojecting onto the political past ideas without reference to their local contexts. Oakeshott may be said to be implacably opposed to grand narratives which either reduce history to philosophy or history to philosophy.[9] Rather he relates political ideas to the political cultures within which past political thinkers operated.[10]

To understand Greek political thought, Oakeshott invokes the political experience of the Greeks, analyzing the conditions of their political culture and more specifically their political vocabulary and distinctive images of the world. He then focuses upon the political thought of Plato and Aristotle taking them as sifting and criticizing the current general beliefs about politics so as formulate coherent ideas.[11] Again, Oakeshott imagines modern thinkers to be operating within a specific historical context, namely that of the emergence of the modern state. He identifies characteristics of the modern European state such as its composition of legally free human beings, its centralized and sovereign authority, and its inter-relations with other similar states as informing the theories of modern political thinkers. In considering forms of modern political thinking, he identifies an interpretation of the state, which, in relying upon organic and nationalistic formulas, suffers from its failure to register the constructed and free nature of the association of individuals in a modern state. In contrast, he recognizes how Calvin, Hobbes, Locke, Rousseau, and Mill, among others, theorize the state as an association of individuals, who associate together freely to achieve a variety of freely chosen purposes.

III—History and Other Disciplines

Oakeshott's *Lectures in the History of Political Thought* assumes history to be a constructive activity, in which the past is different from the present, and it is also separate from philosophy, science, or the practical needs of the present. In *Experience and Its Modes* (1933), Oakeshott argues for the radical insulation of modes of experience from one another. Modes of experience, save for philosophy, namely history, science, and practice, arrest experience in organizing it from a particular perspective, while philosophy reviews the conditions of experience completely, observing the limits of the other modes. Hence, history is neither linked to philosophizing nor to current practical issues. In "The Voice of Poetry in the Conversation of Mankind," an essay in *Rationalism in Politics*, Oakeshott reformulates how he sees relations between modes of experience, imagining that they relate to one another conversationally rather than operating completely independent of one another or being dependent upon one another.[12] The character of the imagined conversation of mankind is indeterminate, though it is taken to be a conversation in which no one voice is dominant.[13] The assumption is that interlocutors respect one another and that there is no supervening goal of the conversation. In "The Activity of Being and Historian," another essay in *Rationalism in Politics*, Oakeshott observes a sharp divide between the historian's study of the past and other ways of imagining it. Oakeshott insists that the past of the historian is different from the practical, scientific, and aesthetic attitudes to the past. A practical attitude to the past looks to the past in light of the present and hence assimilates the past to present concerns. For instance, a lawyer is interested in the past insofar as it relates to the concerns of his client in the present. If evidence from the past can prove the innocence of a defendant whom a barrister is defending in a criminal case, then it will be used. The barrister is not interested in the past for its own sake. The historian in contrast studies the past for its own sake and respects its distinctness from present concerns. An historian in the present who wishes to defend the Normans will not do justice to what happened at the Battle of Hastings.[14] Oakeshott's sympathy for Butterfield's studies of the past reflects his distrust of Whig interpretations of history that reduce the past to the political ideology of the present.[15] Oakeshott is categorical in his recognition of the historian's appreciation of the separation of past from present interests. Hence, Oakeshott insists that philosophy should not determine the direction of historical inquiry. Philosophy can review the postulates of historical understanding, but its review is not judged to impose a pattern upon narratives of the past. Hegel's philosophy of history supersedes the narrative of empirical pragmatic historians, but, for Oakeshott, Hegel in his philosophical history is undertaking philosophy not history. Likewise, the demands of practical political life are not to dictate to the historian an account of the past, which is not justified evidentially.

Yet Oakeshott, in fact, allows for significant connections between philosophy, political practice, and history, even if the three worlds are specified in distinctive ways. In his celebrated "Introduction to *Leviathan*" (1946), Oakeshott presents a general characterization of the history of political philosophy by identifying it in terms of three traditions. The three traditions are the rational natural tradition, the tradition of will and artifice, and that of rational will.[16] What Oakeshott has to say on this score is elliptical and yet suggestive for he implies that there are connections between philosophy, politics, and history. His identification of traditions in the history of political philosophy presumes that philosophical expertise is required. Political philosophy is a style of thought that is conceived as a distinct and highly abstract form of reflection on politics. Its style is not to be recognized by the relating of past events, the character of the style has to be appreciated and that demands firsthand expertise of the subject matter. Its identification depends upon philosophical rather than historical expertise.[17] This philosophical recognition of the character of philosophical argument is of a piece with what he has to say in his *Lectures in the History of Political Thought*. In this latter study, he maintains that a presupposition of the inquiry is a prior identification of styles of political thought so that, for instance, explanatory and practical forms of thinking are distinguished from one another.[18] In the "Introduction to *Leviathan*," Oakeshott discusses the nature of the three specified traditions of political philosophy by highlighting their textual masterpieces. Plato's *Republic* is held to be the masterpiece of the rational natural tradition. Hobbes's *Leviathan* is supreme in the tradition of will and artifice, and Hegel's *Philosophy of Right* is exemplary in the tradition of rational will. Oakeshott's identification of traditions in political philosophy unites political philosophies historically by noting their adherence to common if developing conceptual standpoints. Identification of and assessment of a tradition depends upon a mix of philosophical and historical forms of understanding. Hence, Oakeshott sees history as bearing upon philosophy and shows how the disciplines of history and philosophy are connected with one another. Again, he imagines that each of the traditions of political philosophy is aligned to practice in that each develops in relation to practical historical circumstances. The focus on will in the will and artifice and rational will traditions reflects modern developments in various spheres of conduct, which is distinct from Plato's assumptions about a natural order of things. This alignment of philosophy with historical conditions of practice is not to imply that Oakeshott either imagines that philosophy is prescriptive for practical life, or that philosophical ideas are to be reduced to practical interests or to historical moments. Its alignment with practice enables its understanding of practice but does not supply a recipe for political action. Oakeshott's understanding of the ways in which modes of experience are related is finely balanced. On the one hand, he insists upon their independence throughout his career and yet the metaphor of a conversation between experiential activities allows for engagement between them, but it is a form of engagement that is not taken to obtrude upon their character. In fact, the relations between modes of experience bear significantly upon their individual character. A history of political philosophy presumes a philosophical understanding of its nature. The development of political philosophy depends upon an historical understanding of its commerce with practice.

In "Practical Life and the Critique of Rationalism," Smith rightly observes Oakeshott's determination to isolate philosophy from practical considerations. He remarks, "The central thrust of *Experience and Its Modes* is to protect philosophy and the other modes of experience from the blandishments of praxis. 'A philosophy of life,' Oakeshott avers, 'is a meaningless contradiction.' Life—practical experience—and philosophy—the quest for intellectual coherence—remain fundamentally inimical to one another."[19] It is true that, for Oakeshott, political philosophy is not an ideology aiming to impact upon practice. In a posthumously published essay, "Political Philosophy" Oakeshott observes, "[W]e must expect from political philosophy no practical conclusions

whatsoever."[20] Yet Oakeshott aligns the identities of political philosophies to particular historical contexts and understands political philosophy as arising out of practical experience and as developing historically.
His own substantive political philosophy, which is elaborated in *On
Human Conduct*, is self-consciously related to the development of the
modern state and to a particular tradition of political philosophy. As
McIntyre notes, Oakeshott in fact takes philosophical understanding to
develop out of a practice of philosophy that resists specification in express
terms. The tradition of philosophy suggests its implication in practice
rather than abstract theory.[21]

In *On Human Conduct*, a classic work of substantive political
thought, Oakeshott employs a new and original vocabulary to specify the conditionality of political association, which is derived from
reflection upon the development of the modern European state.[22] The
work consists of three inter-related sections: (i) On the Theoretical
Understanding of Human Conduct; (ii) On the Civil Condition; and (iii)
On the Character of the Modern European State. The opening section
is a theoretical exploration of the character of human conduct by theorizing its component conditions of agency and social practice. Oakeshott
distinguishes the character of a practice from that of a process. A practice is constituted by the contingent beliefs of their human participat-
ing agents, while processes are composed of natural phenomena, which
are determined by scientific hypotheses explaining the generic recur-
rence of patterns amidst change. Insofar as the three essays are mutually complementary, the relationship between social practices and their
constituent reflective agents is held to demonstrate how individuals are
enabled to participate in a scheme of social and political cooperation,
which Oakeshott designates as civil association. Civil association, for
Oakeshott, represents an ideal mode of political association, in which
individuals consent to procedural rules of conduct, which regulate but
do not determine the behavior of individuals. These rules do not prescribe particular forms of conduct because they depend upon individual
interpretation of their application to particular circumstances. The rules
shape but do not direct their actions and hence allow for individuality
and freedom in their performance. Oakeshott's analysis of the postulates
of the human condition and his related construction of an ideal form of
civil association is followed by the third essay that reviews the historical
formation of the modern European state, which intimates the form of
civil conduct that is theorized in the preceding section, under the title,

"On Civil Association." Hence, Oakeshott's own political thought is shown to develop out of his historical understanding of the development of European politics.

In delineating the history of the modern European state, Oakeshott distinguishes between two historic forms of political association, a *societas* and a *universitas*. A *societas* is a form of political association, which constitutes what Oakeshott terms the civil condition. In a *societas*, individuals recognize the authority of a set of general laws, which provide a framework of order that permits them to follow their own independently formulated activities. It is a free association of individuals, who are united by their common commitment to establish a cooperative social framework that enables individuals to undertake their several self-chosen purposes and activities. A *universitas*, on the other hand, focuses upon achieving a common collective goal. Its members are unified by their determination to achieve a common purpose. Oakeshott takes the outlines of both forms of society to be discernible in modern European history. For Oakeshott, prospects for civil freedom are compromised by the contemporary strength of collectivism. In his account of the modern European state, Oakeshott refers to several political theorists, who have framed historic theories of a political association, which follow one or the other of his paradigmatic models of political association. His commentaries are economical but incisive. For instance, he identifies Machiavelli tellingly as a theorist of a *societas*. Likewise, Hobbes is perceived to be an outstanding theorist of a *societas*, while Bentham receives a masterly footnote that identifies him to be an energetic advocate of a *universitas*.[23] His brief but compelling analysis of Hegel as a theorist of a *societas* interprets Hegel to be a political theorist, who, in framing an authoritative political philosophy, attends carefully to the experience of agents, social practices, and states in the modern world.[24]

Oakeshott's *On Human Conduct* is an intricate analysis of the nature of human conduct, the character of an ideal civil association, and the development of the modern European state. These elements of analysis go together in that human beings are shown to be reflective and free agents, whose possibilities for undertaking freely self-chosen individual actions are enhanced by their subscription to a civil association, which in turn is shown to be intimated in historical development. While Oakeshott imagines historical understanding to be autonomous, his philosophical exploration of the conditions of political association depends upon an historical reading of modern European history. Oakeshott's carefully contrived philosophical account of a state that allows for individuality, and freedom and his antipathy toward collectivism are shaped by and in turn reflect upon his reading of European political history. His substantive political thought is constructed in light of preceding historical developments of the political experience of modern Europe and the political theorizing of philosophical predecessors, notably that of Hobbes and Hegel, and his own substantive political thought in turn shapes his interest in the development of the modern state. *On Human Conduct* is a notable contribution to modern political thought. Its value derives from its drawing upon historical and philosophical forms of understanding. The ideal of civil association is related to the conditions of reflective practice that allow for individual agency in social contexts. The ideal of individuality and the value of civil association are related to conditions of agency, but they also are intimated in the political experience of the modern world. This experience shows the feasibility of the ideals and their possibilities in concrete shape. Oakeshott blends historical and philosophical expertise in his account of the modern state which is at once philosophical and historical.

IV—CONCLUSION

Oakeshott is an idealist thinker, who was influenced by Hegel, both as a philosopher and more particularly as a political theorist. Hegel recognized the relative autonomy of a variety of modes theory and practice. He was a profoundly historical thinker, who imagined that all subjects including philosophy were historical in character. A significant difference between his philosophy and Plato's, for instance, involves his sense of the historical determination of human thought and practice.[25] Yet Hegel imagines that philosophical history superseded other forms of history in supplying an absolute understanding of things. Hence, he considered the *Philosophy of Right* to go beyond a merely historical justification of the conditions of a rational and just political association. Ultimately, it may be said that Hegel reduces history to philosophy in allowing philosophy the final reconciliatory word on mankind's engagement with experience.[26] Perhaps Oakeshott's sensitivity to the perils of advancing the claims of a single discipline over that of others informed his reading of the strict independence to be assigned to modes of experience or forms of understanding. Likewise, he was critical of what he took to be Collingwood's late dissolution of philosophy into history.[27] It is beside the point that Collingwood's later thought is best interpreted as maintaining an independence between philosophy and history, because it is clear that Oakeshott imagined that Collingwood had slipped into an error in reducing philosophy to history.[28]

Oakeshott aimed to guard against a reductive understanding of the relations between philosophy and history, just as practical undertakings are different from artistic contemplation, scientific understanding, philosophical speculation, and historical understanding. Even where he allows for relations between them, his designation of them as conversational sees each as constituted separately and engaging in talk that does not affect their identities. However, in his actual practice of history, forms of political organisation and political thought are identified in philosophical terms just as historical links between thinkers and contexts influence how their philosophies are to be interpreted. The upshot is that Oakeshott's thinking about the state operates between history and philosophy. The irony is that it is precisely this overlapping of modes of thinking that endows a value to his writings which is lacking in other perspectives. Hegel's political philosophy is a testament to considered historical and philosophical thinking, but its philosophical absolutism constitutes a grand narrative that devalues the openness and contingency of the historical process.[29]

Oakeshott's practice of the history of political thought allows him to make a variety of connections in the history of political thought. Thompson, in a careful essay on Oakeshott as an historian of political thought, observes how Oakeshott distinguishes his approach from that of Skinner by allowing for a variety of forms of political thinking, which are not to be reduced to "ideology."[30] Skinner and the Cambridge School of the history of political thought have tended to interpret forms of political thought as being designed to justify or disrupt political authority, and this "ideological" reading of political thought has been applied to Hobbes and Machiavelli among others. Skinner has been concerned to disparage "influence" as a category in the history of political thought as he is skeptical of causal claims of one thinker influencing another when they are subject to differing ideological and political contexts.[31] To deny the influence of one philosopher upon another across time implies that philosophy is not to operate as a distinct form of thinking, which appears implausible given, say Hegel's own account of the impact of Plato and Aristotle on his thought. Oakeshott's recognition that philosophy is a distinct form of thought allows for a way of reading its development that can take account of the impact of a preceding political philosopher upon a succeeding one.[32] Oakeshott's plausible criticism of Skinner turns upon his own recognition of the differing nature of particular forms of political thinking. Political philosophy is not to be reduced to history and ideology.

The value of Oakeshott's political thought and his theorizing about the state resides in its capacity to relate together differing forms of thought rather than upon its self-proclaimed sharp separation of them from one another. In *On Human Conduct*, his reading of an ideal mode of political association is linked to his reading of the historical development of forms of the state in modern Europe. Philosophy is not thereby reduced to history, just as history is not to be seen as a mere instrument to the framing of a political philosophy. But if Oakeshott avoids the reduction of one form of thinking to another, he is not to be interpreted as establishing their independence from one another. The skills of Oakeshott as an historian of political thought and a theorist of the state are that he links differing forms of thinking so as to see the messy world of practice as registering historical development that can be reflected upon philosophically. Philosophy is not set apart from history and practice but neither is to be read as a form of ideology or as superseding history by showing the historical necessity of an ideal state.

NOTES

1. In my book on the nature of the history of political thought, I argue this case at greater length. See Gary Browning, *A History of Modern Political Thought: The Question of Interpretation* (Oxford: Oxford University Press, 2016). In this monograph, my reading of Oakeshott is part of a wider argument that history and philosophy are necessarily intertwined in the practice of the history of political thought.
2. Kenneth Minogue, "The Fate of Rationalism in Oakeshott's Thought," in *A Companion to Michael Oakeshott*, eds. Paul Franco and Leslie Marsh (Pennsylvania: The Pennsylvania State University Press, 2012), 247.
3. M. Oakeshott, *Lectures in the History of Political Thought*, eds. Terry Nardin and Luke O'Sullivan (Exeter: Imprint Academic, 2006).
4. Ibid., 31.
5. Ibid., 32.
6. Ibid., 42.
7. Martyn Thompson, "Michael Oakeshott on the History of Political Thought," in *A Companion to Michael Oakeshott*, 198.
8. Ibid., 199.

9. For an account of what is meant by grand narratives in the work of Lyotard, and for a critique of his critique of them, see my earlier work on Lyotard and grand narratives. Gary Browning, *Lyotard and the End of Grand Narratives* (Cardiff: University of Wales Press, 2000). For a sympathetic if critical account of Hegel's philosophy of history, see Gary Browning, *Hegel and the History of Political Philosophy* (Basingstoke and New York: Macmillan, 1999).

10. Ibid., 73.

11. Ibid., 30.

12. See M. Oakeshott, "The Voice of Poetry in the Conversation of Mankind," in Michael Oakeshott, *Rationalism in Politics and Other Essays* (London and New York: Methuen & Co, 1962). In his posthumously published *Notebooks*, Oakeshott sketches plans for producing a text that rehearses a conversation between a number of interlocutors representing differing styles and activities in life. See Michael Oakeshott, *Notebooks: 1922–86*, ed. Luke O'Sullivan (Exeter: Imprint Academic, 2014), 307–70.

13. Ibid., 418–19.

14. Michael Oakeshott, "The Activity of Being an Historian," in *Rationalism in Politics and Other Essays*, 168–75.

15. On Oakeshott's sympathy for Butterfield, see Geoffrey Thomas, "Michael Oakeshott's Philosophy of History," in *A Companion to Michael Oakeshott*, 95–120. See also Herbert Butterfield, *The Whig Interpretation of History* (London: W. W. Norton, 1965).

16. Michael Oakeshott, "Introduction to *Leviathan*," in Michael Oakeshott, *Hobbes on Civil Association* (Oxford, Basil Blackwell, 1975), 3.

17. Ibid., 3.

18. Oakeshott, *Lectures in the History of Political Thought*, 4–3.

19. S. Smith, "Practical Life and the Critique of Rationalism," in *The Cambridge Companion to Oakeshott*, ed. Efraim Podoksik (Cambridge: Cambridge University Press, 2012), 131–52.

20. Michael Oakeshott, "Political Philosophy," in Michael Oakeshott, *Religion, Politics and the Moral Life*, ed. Timothy Fuller (New Haven and London: Yale University Press, 1993), 153.

21. Note the comment, "…philosophy is a practice like other human practices, it involves 'knowing how' to do things philosophically." See Kenneth McIntyre, "Philosophy and Its Moods: Oakeshott on the Practice of Philosophy," in *A Companion to Michael Oakeshott*, 82.

22. Michael Oakeshott, *On Human Conduct* (Oxford: Oxford University Press, 1975), 185–326.

23. Ibid., 169.

24. Ibid., 257–63.

25. See Gary Browning, *Plato and Hegel: Two Modes of Philosophizing About Politics* (Abingdon: Routledge, 2013).

26. See Gary Browning, "The Night in Which All Cows Are Black: Ethical Absolutism in Plato and Hegel," *History of Political Thought* 12, no. 3 (1991).

27. See Michael Oakeshott, "Review of R. G. Collingwood. *The Idea of History* (1947)," in Michael Oakeshott, *Selected Writings, vol. 3, The Concept of Philosophical Jurisprudence*, ed. Luke O'Sullivan (Exeter: Imprint Academic, 2014), 199.

28. For a reading of Collingwood that takes him to recognize close but non-reductive relations between history and philosophy, see Gary Browning, *Rethinking R. G. Collingwood: Philosophy, Politics and the Unity of Theory and Practice* (Basingstoke: Palgrave Macmillan, 2004).

29. See Gary Browning, "Lyotard and Hegel: What Is Wrong with Modernity and What Is Right with the *Philosophy of Right?*" *History of European Ideas* 29, no. 2 (2003), 223–39.

30. See M. Thompson, "Michael Oakeshott on the History of Political Thought," in *A Companion to Michael Oakeshott*, 69.

31. See Quentin Skinner, "The Limits of Historical Explanation," *Philosophy* 41 (1966), 199–215.

32. For a justification of the use of the concept of influence in the history of political thought, see Gary Browning, "Agency and Influence in the History of Political Thought: The Agency of Influence and the Influence of Agency," *History of Political Thought* 31, no. 2 (2010), 345–66.

CHAPTER 5

Taking Natural Law Seriously Within the Liberal Tradition

Timothy Fuller

I—Taking Rights Seriously

No one is startled by the thought of taking rights seriously in our political tradition. Yet controversies over what it may mean to do so, or over the question of our sincerity in the effort, abound.

Ours is also a tradition honoring the rule of law. There is a connection between the rule of law and taking rights seriously. Thus, to take rights seriously ultimately leads us to jurisprudential considerations, or to the controversies of the legal philosophers. Law must be protected from falling into the hands of the calculators of utility. The latter is prone to erode procedure and formality, to circumvent the fixities of the law, in order to procure a desired substantive condition of civil society whose benefits will transform retrospectively, it is claimed, the initial appearance of expedient partiality. But can the rule of law be saved in the rule of expediency whatever may be thought of the substantive condition that actually emerges? And then what of rights? Can rights be taken seriously if acknowledging them is contingent on the compatibility

T. Fuller (✉)
Colorado College, Colorado Springs, CO, USA
e-mail: tfuller@coloradocollege.edu

© The Author(s) 2019
E. S. Kos (ed.), *Michael Oakeshott on Authority, Governance, and the State*, Palgrave Studies in Classical Liberalism,
https://doi.org/10.1007/978-3-030-17455-2_5

of claims with the substantive outcomes dictated by policy? Can utility be effectively opposed by the dominant legal positivism in contemporary jurisprudence:

> Legal positivism rejects the idea that legal rights can pre-exist any form of legislation; it rejects the idea, that is, that individuals or groups can have rights in adjudication other than the rights explicitly provided in the collection of explicit rules that compose the whole of a community's law. Economic utilitarianism rejects the idea that political rights can pre-exist legal rights; that is, that citizens can justifiably protest a legislative decision on any ground except that the decision does not in fact serve the general welfare.[1]

The preference today for views of this sort rests on the rejection of classical natural law theories in favor of "empirical metaphysics." Dworkin himself intends to remain within the general framework of the dominant utilitarian-positivist outlook defending an idea of rights which is itself "parasitic on the dominant idea of utilitarianism, which is the idea of a collective goal of the community as a whole."[2] Dworkin believes that individual claims may be overridden if collective claims should prevail, but rights should be taken seriously.

According to Dworkin, even in hard cases it is the judge's duty not to invent new rights but to discover which of the parties to a dispute has a right to win. The hard case is any in which there is no obvious rule or custom, no consensus among competent experts, and hence no demonstrable conclusion in the matter. Nevertheless, Dworkin says there may be a truth in the matter and it must be pursued.[3]

The practical objection regularly made to this idea is the general fear of permitting judges to interpret law creatively: "adjudication should be as unoriginal as possible."[4] Dworkin skirts this by arguing that the judge can discover a right in the hard case, not invent one.[5] He wishes to persuade us to separate "discovery" from "originality." He denies that the appearance of originality proves that a right has been invented but not discovered. Dworkin argues that the abstract distinction between discovery and originality is, in actual social life, always in a process of mediation through judicial agency.[6] The discovery of a right in a hard case is not, then, an intuition. One might better call it an informed interpretation, which may be evaluated for its acceptability as a successful mediation between the general character of prevailing law and the disposition of the case. It has a force of "truth" despite the fact that prior to its expression by the judge it could not be known to be true. Without the agency of the judge, the truth remains hidden. Yet one can estimate whether to evaluate the decision as effectively a discovery or whether it is ineligible to be accepted that way.

Among other things, we should consider whether a decision is generally consistent with other decisions in the same area, and whether it is non-arbitrary in not serving some parties at the expense of other similar ones. But it would seem that the aim of all this is to defend a conception of the judicial function as simultaneously serving to defend rights and allowing rights to evolve as a contribution to some putative increase in general, communal welfare. The ultimate mediation, then, would be between the maintenance of those already acknowledged rights which protect subjective freedom and the "newly discovered" rights which enhance objective freedom (to use Hegelian terms) or (to use Deweyite terms) to mediate between "formal" and "effective" liberty. Dworkin refers to mediating "policy" and "principle," or transposing "political right" into "legal right." It is not a distortion, therefore, to suggest that, in Dworkin's outlook, there could and should be a continuous effort at engineering social change through judicial activity, and that this can be carried out so as to transcend, in principle, political partisanship. If so, it would be possible to show how rights could be defended by interpreting them so as to promote certain goals. Conversely, the promotion of certain goals would be necessary to the defense of rights. The political would pass over into the trans-political. Lack of universal agreement would not disprove the adequacy of the judicial decision.

According to Dworkin, a political right is the claim to an opportunity that is justified (rational) insofar as the realization of such opportunity would enhance the possible realization of a larger pattern congenial to the individual who makes the claim.[7] Is this anything more than a defense of interest group pluralism and a relativity of group ends? Only, it would seem, if the interest served would contribute to the enhancement of the collective welfare goal of a given community. Thus relativist pluralism would at most be a procedural premise for the purposes of eliciting all those expressions of interest that would permit comprehensive articulation of communal well-being. The satisfaction of some group claims as opposed to others would cease to be arbitrary when such preferences contribute to a further development toward the communal goal. But since the features of the communal goal are multifaceted there will be trade-offs between competing component elements of the general welfare.[8]

On the other hand, there can be absolute rights, presumably they are trans-political from the start, which are virtually always eligible to stand against policies even if the policies would enhance the general welfare in some way (e.g., free speech). It would appear that Dworkin has provided in his own vocabulary a combination of ideas drawn from J. S. Mill and John Rawls: From Mill, he has taken the notion of articulation of all views toward the end of progressive improvement or perfection of social life in the most comprehensive and eventually non-controversial manner; from Rawls he has taken the priority of liberty in relation to a principle of distribution ruling out unnecessary inequalities, pointing to an order in which every participant understands and can accept his social position as the best possible. The temperamental strain common to all three, and to a certain mode of liberal thinking in general, is the desire to transform the partisan into the non-partisan, the political into the consensual, without resort to significant coercion: an historically evolving social covenant without the sword.

An ideal judge will facilitate the general social enhancement by constructing an adequate theoretical understanding of how to apply the generally accepted constituting rules of a society.[9] In so doing, the judge articulates policy designed to maintain and to fill out the intention of the law. The law is always open to contested interpretations. The law cannot be self-enacting or self-interpreting. However, "decisions about legal rights depend upon judgments of political theory that might be made differently by different judges or by the public at large" and this may be so even if the decision was in some sense a "principled" decision (sincerely arrived at in an effort to do right according to a political theory taken by the judge to be correct). In short, the judge is liable to a charge of subjective decision-making.

According to Dworkin, a judge must "rely upon the substance of his own judgment at some point, in order to make any judgment at all." Hence, the real issue is the judge's decision between opposing and submitting to some prevailing authoritative opinion as to how decisions in given areas of law should come out. The decision to submit to prevailing "wisdom" is itself a personal judgment.[10]

But it would appear that this argument gains its principal strength from a prior assumption that the law is to be understood as embedded in a process of social evolution which neutralizes the preference for unoriginality over originality or "discovery." That is, Dworkin does not presume that it is the rule of law as such which is to be protected. He assumes, rather, that the process of mediating between principle and policy, or translating political claims into legal entitlements is what is to be protected. Sometimes no doubt unoriginality is fitting, but in a general sense it is what is progressive that must be served. Dworkin would appear, therefore, to be intent upon transforming the commitment to the rule of law into a commitment to social engineering. Implicitly, Dworkin's defense of a residual element of inevitable personal choice in the judge's decision-making is intended to legitimize judicial autonomy, limited primarily by the soundness of the judge's political theory and by prudential considerations of the pace of social evolution that could be hoped for. In short, the ideal judge is self-determining with regard to the definition of his judicial duty.

The ideal judge's "theory identifies a particular conception of community morality as decisive of legal issues; that conception holds that community morality is the political morality presupposed by the laws and institutions of the community. He must, of course, rely on his own judgment as to what the principles of that morality are."[11] In controversial matters, the ideal judge will "become like any reflective member of the community willing to debate."[12]

There is, however, a difference between the ideal judge and any willing debater:

> It does not follow from the fact that the man in the street disapproves of abortion, or supports legislation making it criminal, that he has considered whether the concept of dignity presupposed by the Constitution, consistently applied, supports his political position. That is a sophisticated question requiring some dialectical skill … it is not to be taken for granted that his political preferences, expressed casually or in the ballot, have been subjected to that form of examination.[13]

The ideal judge will bring genuine moral insight to bear, effectively relating principles to policies. Ordinary judges may, of course, be fallible or decide out of unreflected prejudice. Mistakes may be made. But who could know when that will happen and what group other than judges will have "better facilities of moral argument"?[14]

Taking rights seriously means here incorporating political claims into law under the auspices of a process of judicial decision-making that aims at uniting the normative and the conceptual. The union is accomplished by relating an "adequate" description of social arrangements in a positivist sense to a "discovered" right as between contending forces in the described social arrangement. The judge is ideally only the vanguard of social change, assuring "proper" direction, a privileged participant in an endless debate over the desired end-state of social order.

II—Taking the Rule of Law Seriously

While it is not uncommon to defend the idea of the rule of law, even as an intrinsic good, it is clear that taking the rule of law seriously conflicts with the intent to take rights seriously in the manner described above. With Dworkin, taking rights seriously ultimately sets up an autonomous standard, political in nature, on the basis of which one is to judge the validity of the commitment to the rule of law. Dworkin's commitment to the rule of law is instrumental in nature. Indeed, it must be so if the principal task is to take rights seriously. The most uncompromising defense of the rule of law on non-instrumental grounds is to be found in the writings of Michael Oakeshott.

According to Oakeshott, the interaction of individuals in civil society falls into two modes: The first is an

> intermittent transactional association of reciprocity in which agents, responding to their understood situations, seek the satisfactions of their wants in the responses of one another ... It is a relationship of bargainers and from it emerge whatever substantive satisfactions are from time to time enjoyed.[15]

In this mode, agents are transactionally related in an "enterprise association" agreeing upon a purpose to pursue.

There is another primary mode of association in defense of which Oakeshott challenges those theorists who "find it impossible to imagine association except in terms of a common purpose."[16] The attempt to identify the civil association with common purpose carries the "difficulty of specifying a common purpose in terms of which to distinguish civil association from all other enterprise relationship."[17] The substantive purposes of enterprises are easy enough to identify but what is the substantive purpose of civil society?

Oakeshott approaches this question by describing a mode of relationship "in terms of the conditions of a practice."[18] The "two most important practices in terms of which agents are durably related to one another in conduct are a common tongue and a language of moral converse."[19] However,

> a moral practice is not a prudential art concerned with the success of the enterprises of agents; it is not instrumental to the achievement of any substantive purpose or to the satisfaction of any substantive want ... It is concerned with the act, not the event.[20]

A practice does not

> prescribe choices to be made or satisfactions to be sought; instead, it intimates considerations to be subscribed to in making choices, in performing actions, and in pursuing purposes ... It postulates 'free' agents and it is powerless to deprive them of their freedom.[21]

> Thus, conduct *inter homines* may properly be said to be 'social' only in virtue of the manners in which 'free' agents are actually associated; that is, in respect of their being associated in a multiplicity of practices of various dimensions and complexities, degrees of independence, and differences of status. This multiplicity of association does not itself compose a 'society', much less anything that may properly be called a 'community'; but a moral practice, as the *ars artium* of agency, is agents related to one another in terms of conditional proprieties which are expressly or tacitly recognized in the conditions of all other special prudential relationships and manners of being associated in conduct.[22]

The "civil" association cannot be the implementation of theorems or propositions. It cannot be the consequence of a program or a plan. A practice reduced to these things would find itself abstracted from the contingency pervasive in human existence. By insisting that human beings as agents *subscribe* to practices, Oakeshott points to the understanding of a human being as the interpreting mediator between the features of a practice and particular occasions wherein the exercise of the practice is called forth. It is not possible to *obey* a practice or a rule. Practices and rules are not commands but modes of proceeding that have emerged in the flow of experience:

> In short, we may suppose there to be available to an agent a store of well-attested propositions purporting to be general principles of conduct, and by no means worthless. Nevertheless, what is certain is that the understanding exercised by the agent in conduct cannot be an ad hoc mobilization of his knowledge of these theorems of moral and prudential lore enlisted to tell him what to do, because they are incapable of any such utterance. These theorems cannot themselves be performed, and acting cannot be 'implementing' or 'applying' them to contingent situations because they are unable to specify actions. What the agent needs to know … is how to *illustrate* them …[23]

The chosen actions of agents illustrate practices and rules rather than implement them because in no sense are the chosen actions of individuals "correct" displays of human conduct. One will not know how to conduct oneself by knowing this or that particular human action. One conducts oneself by finding a fitting illustration of a practice for a given, contingent situation. Each human being is the exhibition of "a sequential relationship of intelligent individual occurrences where what comes after is recognized to be conditional on what went before" without a "mediator between occurrences which is not itself an occurrence, e.g., a 'law' or a 'function.'"[24] "Progress" is an extrinsic interpretation of change.

Practices qualify what human beings do but do not determine what they do. Relationships between individuals that arise from subscription to practices without the specification of a joint enterprise suggest the proper meaning of "civil" association. Citizenship in a civil association is constituted in the "acknowledgement of the authority of *respublica*," but "recognizing the authority of *respublica* is not finding its conditions to be desirable or believing that others better informed than oneself have approved of them."[25]

Acknowledgment, in this case, is not synonymous with approval of the conditions acknowledged, nor a judgment of utility or advantage, nor is it the result of a calculation that one cannot escape acknowledgment. Critics of this argument are wont to say that there must always be some background of cultural ties to make this acknowledgment possible.

Such critics are correct insofar as all real associations of actual individuals are sustained through a mixture of learned motivations. Oakeshott presents an "ideal" of civil association. What is to be gained from doing this?

The answer depends on the significance of an "ideal character." For Oakeshott, it is the delineation of a pattern intimated within a conglomeration of actual goings-on. Here what is at stake is the theorization of a relationship among individuals that does not compromise their self-identification. It is the elaboration of an inquiry, inaugurated as much by Hobbes as by anyone, into the possibility of imagining an orderly relation between selves who inevitably measure the world according to their own measure.

> This ideal character is among the instruments which may be used in seeking to understand complex, ambiguous, historic human associations ... it is ideal not in the sense of being a wished-for perfect condition of things but in being abstracted from the contingencies and ambiguities of actual goings-on in the world.[26]

The ideal character is simply a consistent interpretation of the logical requirements of order for an association of human beings who cannot help but understand themselves as individuals. The ideal condition is a "civitas" composed of "cives" who accept "respublica" as a postulate of the civil condition.[27] If subscription to authority were necessarily predicated on the reception of benefits, it would be open to doubt whether individuals, seeking benefits sharply at odds with each other, could successfully associate. Obviously, there are such associations. That they are workable, even persistent, suggests at least implicit recognition of "respublica" as a "system of moral (not instrumental) rules, specifying its own jurisdiction, and recognized solely as rules ... binding to consideration independently of their origin or likely or actual outcome in use and of approval of what they prescribe."[28]

> the only understanding of *respublica* capable of evoking the acceptance of all *cives* without exception, and thus eligible to be recognized as the terms of civil association, is *respublica* understood in respect of its authority.[29]

To consider human beings in terms of their conduct is to see them as

> reflective intelligences whose actions and utterances are choices to do or to say *this* rather than *that* in relation to imagined and wished-for outcomes. And the relationships between them to be investigated are recognized to be themselves expressions of intelligence which may be enjoyed only by their having been learned and understood and in virtue of an acknowledgement of the authority of their conditions or of a recognition of their utility ... It is a science of intelligent procedures, not processes.[30]

To emphasize procedure rather than process, intelligent response rather than caused behavior is the basis of Oakeshott's understanding of citizenship and the association of citizens: They are associated in the recognition of a rule of law, but they are not bound by necessary interests, needs, wants, or dispositions in common. These individuals do not comprise a "society" and they are not compelled by "social forces" or "independent variables." They need not be obsessed with each other's doings, nor constantly frustrated by "relative deprivation," nor are they engaged ineluctably in a perpetual siege of their resources in order to indulge in an endless transformation of "wants" into "needs," or an incessant redistribution of their possessions according to some principle of comparability which the terms of their association cannot supply.

Such people understand that they are subscribing to, not obeying, a body of laws, which laws are the result of the deliberations of rulers or officeholders in authority. Authority here is not understood as "informal" or "tacit" power or influence, but as the specific engagement to rule, associated with an office of rule, exercised under agreed-upon terms, producing rules to which citizens may subscribe.

In this view,

> Power is not identifiable with authority and it is not even among the considerations in terms of which an office of government is recognized to have authority. The difference is categorical. The contingent features of its apparatus of power are neither formally nor substantively related to the constitutional shape of the office or rule.[31]

The elucidation of the ideal character, in short, makes explicit the implicit aim of civil association to establish and maintain authoritative rule. To put it differently, one might say that it is the already existing commitment in the thinking of individuals on the road to being *cives* in a *civitas*, and it prompts their respective imaginations toward the creation of institutional relations that are separable from mere relationships of power, interest, or hope for an imagined end-state.

The clarity of this conceptual distinction will not be equaled in actuality. The achievement is in continual need of protection and renewal. Those who have sought to do this have had to assume certain attitudes about what sort of beings they and their fellows are and, in turn, what sorts of relationships they could enjoy. The fact that such beings do not perfectly exhibit the conduct that their self-understanding logically requires has nothing to do with the elucidation of that self-understanding. We are reminded of the difference between an "ideal character" and the world of historic actuality the ideal character illuminates. To conceive "power" and "authority" as separable and, as a consequence, to exercise whatever ingenuity is available to concretize that distinction in practices among individuals is a tribute to the capacity of human beings to govern themselves by the ideas they hold of the direction they ought to take.

The achievement is undermined when authority is defined as the building of consensus, the proclamation of unifying goals, or the gaining of influence by advancing interests. Authority is appropriate precisely to an association of human beings whose view of their association has already ruled out common goals and consensus, and who share no fixed principles to determine social importance. They will subscribe to rules not because they have been cajoled or paid off, not because it is in their interest, and not because they have been blackmailed or threatened, but because the rules proceed from those holding offices constituted to make rules. Consider the credibility gap of modern, democratic politics: To make building consensus, the prerequisite to exercising authority insures that no authority will be exercised since it is the lack of consensus (and the awareness of the arbitrariness of "consensus") that makes authority indispensable.

It is true that in actual political life what seems authoritative to some will seem to others to be the mere exercise of power. Perhaps there is no relation among individuals in society that can exempt itself from this ambiguous condition. Authority is an abatement of but not a permanent release from the ambiguities surrounding this engagement.

Oakeshott challenges the instrumentalism of modern thought, posing its antithesis in order to reopen the inquiry into the nature of civic association, the relationship between authority, the rule of law, and the status of the individual:

> Laws are unavoidably indeterminate prescriptions of general adverbial obligations. They subsist in advance and in necessary ignorance of the future contingent situations to which they may be found to relate ... Therefore, the second necessary condition of association in terms of the rule of law is an office endowed with authority and charged with the duty to ascertain (according to some conditional rules of evidence) what has been said or done on a particular occasion brought to its notice because it is alleged not to have subscribed adequately to an obligation imposed by law

> ... [A] court of law is concerned with a particular contingent action or utterance in respect of its conformity with the conditions of existing obligations ... Deliberation, here, is an exercise in retrospective casuistry ... Nor may it regard itself as the custodian of a public policy or interest in favour of which...to resolve the disputed obligation ... [I]n a court of law 'justice' must exhibit itself as the conclusion of an argument designed to show as best it may that *this* is the meaning of the law in respect of this occurrence.[32]

And

> Here, then, is a mode of human relationship ... abstract: a relation not of persons but of *personae*. Association, not in terms of doing and the enjoyment of the fruits of doing, but of procedural conditions imposed upon doing: laws. Relationship, not in terms of efficacious arrangements for promoting or procuring wished-for substantive satisfactions (individual or communal), but obligations to subscribe to non-instrumental rules: a moral relationship. Rule, not in terms of the alleged worth, 'rationality' or 'justice' of the conditions these rules prescribe, but in respect of the recognition of their authenticity.[33]

III—Taking Natural Law Seriously

Dworkin and Oakeshott defend conflicting strains within the complex tradition of liberalism. Each portrays an ideal whose presuppositions exclude those of the alternative. In one, taking rights seriously is the defining end of the rule of law, appealing to a possible, substantive relationship among competing political claims. In the other, extrinsic standards for assessing the *ius* of *lex* undermine the rule of law, transforming the civil association from a "moral" association, wherein agents obligate themselves to abide by rules adherence to which specifies no particular satisfaction of individual or group wants or claims, into a struggle for power even if pursued through the judicial system.

A third voice presents itself in John Finnis' reformulation of classical natural law. He seeks to pass between the normative speculations of neo-positivist or utilitarian theorists, and the stark proceduralism of the pure rule of law. He recognizes that a legal order has a symbolic meaning for political life. What the legal order forbids, promotes or permits, among the ways human beings seek to flourish, contributes to the articulation of the self-identification of a polity. If the law inevitably intimates something above and beyond its own procedures, if law has an existential meaning, then it behooves the theorist to inquire whether he must remain caught between the uncontrolled insertion of normative preferences into law which leads to imposing the view of a part on the whole; and the converse aim radically to individualize questions of meaning, rendering them essentially private, resisting or denying the need of natural sociality to express itself in a common, but supra-ideological, form that enjoys voluntary recognition.

Finnis thus engages to show that there are universal, human goods implicitly or explicitly sought by all human beings out of natural inclination. At this level, one speaks of natural desires, not of moral choices, to do this as opposed to that in actual, contingent circumstances. If human flourishing is in seeking specific ways to fulfill the natural desires in individual human lives, law is necessary to securing conditions that support such seeking. It is necessary, therefore, to relate the natural desires to the contingent conditions in which their satisfaction is sought, and law is one medium through which this may be deliberatively, reflectively done.

In reviewing the effort of modern legal theorists to analyze and comprehend law "on the basis of non-evaluative characteristics only," Finnis finds incorrigible differences of opinion about "what is *important* and *significant* in the field of data and experience with which they are all equally and thoroughly familiar."[34] At best modern legal philosophy, despite its suspicion of the possibility of knowledge of objective good, manages to retain a sense of moral evil. But this opens the way to uncontrolled moral speculation, and the connection between law and moral good must become "uncertain and floating."[35]

Continuing scrutiny of the prevailing state of affairs is undeniably important, but if disciplined knowledge is to illuminate our self-understanding and direction it must do so as an aid to converting the prejudices of the theorist, and of the theorist's culture, "into truly reasonable judgments about what is good ..."[36]

Remarkably, Finnis accepts that this cannot be accomplished "by some inference from the facts of the human situation."[37] A judgment, synthesizing insight into the natural desires or natural goods with a wide acquaintance with the actual conditions of society, must be made. There is a dichotomy between what we value and the "facts," but if the natural basis of value is acknowledged, then there is a substructure of evaluation which persists through altering contingent conditions. Judgment is to be distinguished from non-rational expressions of preference for one cultural possibility against another. A natural law theory "undertakes a critique of practical viewpoints … to distinguish the practically unreasonable from the practically reasonable … to identify conditions and principles of practical right-mindedness, of good and proper order."[38] The scientific study of law must look beyond itself for the final meaning of the search that motivated scientific investigation in the first place.

The movement from the prelegal to the legal is not the experientially final step. As a movement in self-consciousness, it opens the way to self-critical examination to discover the foundation of good which motivated the movement at the outset.

With the articulation of order appears the question of its rightness or goodness. Yet we cannot fully visualize goodness from the conspectus of wants and satisfactions through which initial response to the felt need of goodness is made. Implicit is a quest for additional insight to illuminate the deeper need that is revealed as opposed to a mere repetition in technical terms of the incomplete understanding that the order already possesses.

Efforts to mediate between need and its illumination cannot be avoided, only disguised. We are moved by the good which moves us to seek it. Our acceptance of the seeking is a choosing, but that we choose diminishes in importance as the seeking of which we are agents finally encompasses us. Self-determination is transformed into the ordering of the self in compliance with the object of its search.

Seeking well-being will not eliminate chronic disagreement about the various paths chosen to pursue well-being. Finnis presents natural law theorizing as compatible with a disjunction between "facts" and "norms" which cannot be eliminated by elucidating principles of well-being or flourishing. Man is his own agent in establishing the connection between his sensed incompletion and flourishing, and he must will to harmonize them. As Finnis puts it, one experiences "one's nature … from the inside, in the form of one's inclinations" recognizing "that the object of the inclination which one experiences is an instance of a general form of good."[39] Thereafter, one is further prompted to be reasonable in the pursuit of goods prompted by the inclinations. But to attempt to be reasonable demands that we theorize reasonableness. Natural law becomes apparent in experience but is completed by intellectual illumination constituted in reason.

Knowing of goods and understanding the requirements of reasonableness in pursuit of them can be a unity only when we make them so in action. The basic goods must be sought in all actions that can qualify as moral but they do not themselves specify actions. We act in deciding how to pursue the goods which we have identified, and we express our understanding of what we have identified in chosen actions. Reason absorbs the implications of particular experience, organizing them according to the requirements of goodness. Reasonableness, then, includes both comprehensive awareness of conditions and a self-critical awareness of the response necessary to those conditions in order to keep goodness in sight.

Finnis finds the whole of humanity bound together in search of a fulfillment that is common to all, albeit manifested in a diversity with unspecified boundaries. Inclination to good is not antithetical to diversity; it is the source of diversity.

While such natural diversity intimates the importance of "liberty" or "authenticity" as conditions of seeking good, they do not exhaust the desirabilities to be identified as good. Exclusive devotion to liberty or authenticity limits the understanding of good and distorts it. Finnis lists seven basic goods which he takes to be self-evident: life, knowledge, play, aesthetic experience, sociability/friendship, practical reasonableness, and religion.[40] They enjoy equal, non-hierarchical status. The effort to organize our experience coherently while trying to satisfy all the basic goods, now emphasizing some, now others, according to circumstances, constitutes moral existence.

The organizing judgment we make constitutes our self-interpretation implicating both the conditions under which we live and the goods we seek in the context of those conditions. Our responses show what the circumstances mean to us in light of our understanding of the goods. Such judgments are more or less adroit, but the standard will always be the responsiveness to the goods given the conditions.

Finnis thus explicitly rejects a "thin theory" of human goods which identifies "as the basic human goods those goods which *any* human being would need *whatever his objectives* … the goods identified by a thin theory will be what it is rational for any human being to want whatever else his or her preferences."[41] The defense of thin theories is based on a practical judgment of "fear that anything other than a thin theory of the good will entail an authoritarian politics."[42] This fear leads many to an arbitrary insistence on the insuperable subjectivity of all stipulations of good.

To Finnis, however, mere choosing among goods does not define human flourishing. The choice of goods to pursue, even though issuing from a subject, is open to assessment both by the subject who has chosen, and by others, independently of the fact that the manifestation of choice is associated with any particular individual. What is chosen must dignify the choosing. That is, what is chosen completes the meaning of the choosing, and any defense of the essential contribution of choosing to human flourishing will fail if the choices themselves are exempted from, or fail to be eligible for, defense. Man does not live to choose but chooses in the hope of living well (in a manner that can enjoy confirmation both by himself and others). Liberty and authenticity must

> find their proper place in any accurate (i.e. 'full', non-emaciated ...) theory of the human good. Indeed, only such a theory can make secure for them the dignity of being recognized as objective goods, truly worthwhile (rather than merely the matrix for the pursuit of 'subjective' desires and satisfactions).[43]

We are moved toward fulfillment in the full, not the thin, sense "prior to any intelligent consideration of what is worth pursuing" but what we need to know is "discernible only to one who ... intelligently directs, focuses, and controls his urges, inclinations, and impulses."[44] Diversity flows from the variability with which human beings undertake this practical task and that diversity conceals within itself a universal aspiration which does not permit diversity to be an end in itself. On the other hand, the fact that diversity is not an end in itself does not mean either that diversity is not real or that we should try to bring diversity to an end. Not only is it not possible to suppress diversity, it is undesirable to reject diversity. Diversity brings forth far more concrete experience of the possibilities of human well-being than could otherwise be possible or imaginable in the reflections of any human minds, or articulable in any actual regime.

In the midst of this diversity, the theorist must become transparent to himself. In our circumstances that will mean creating a dialogue between liberal rights theorists and exponents of the non-emaciated theory of good. Finnis believes this is possible because "the modern grammar of rights provides a way of expressing virtually all the requirements of practical reasonableness."[45] For Finnis, taking rights seriously establishes that an order can be known to be just only when participants can choose to assent. That choice carries with it duties of respect for the order which is to be secured through agreement. Finnis seeks to bring respect for rights into a recast Aristotelian perspective that is not restricted to a defense of individual or group liberty or authenticity:

> reference to rights…is simply a pointed expression of what is implicit in the term '*common* good', namely that *each* and everyone's well-being, in each of its basic aspects, must be considered and favoured at *all* times by those responsible for co-ordinating the common life.[46]

And,

> On the one hand, we should not say that human rights, or their exercise, are subject to the common good … On the other hand, we can appropriately say that most human rights are subject to or limited by each other and by other *aspects* of the common good, aspects which could probably be subsumed under a very broad conception of human rights but which are fittingly indicated (one could hardly say, *described*) by expressions such as 'public morality', 'public health', 'public order.'[47]

But then the problem of making this reciprocity specific in a particular order must be faced. Specificity is perpetually an uncertainty seeking certainty. Generally held notions of rights and duties in particular orders will potentially and actually vary in meaning in some measure from one person to the next. Orderliness cannot consist only in consensus. There must be a strong commitment to the continual resolution of conflicts as they arise. What is to guide conflict resolution? Finnis argues,

> There is, I think, no alternative but to hold in one's mind's eye some pattern, or range of patterns, of human character, conduct, and interaction in community, and then to choose such specifications of rights as tend to favour that pattern, or range of patterns. In other words, one needs some conception of human good, of individual flourishing in a form (or range of forms) of communal life that fosters rather than hinders such flourishing.[48]

There remains the possibility of conflict between the regard for every human being as a locus of flourishing and the necessities of policy which dictate that some goods and some individuals be preferred. Practical reasonableness requires only that we never intend to serve exclusively any one good or set of goods, or the good of any one or set of individuals to the exclusion of the others. Yet even if policymakers or statesmen accept all this, in the necessities of their position they may associate practical reasonableness with any ranking of the basic goods that fit their aims.

Finnis certainly wishes to take rights seriously. This means to him that every human being is entitled to consideration and respect, and that no one is permitted to pursue a policy in which someone or group may be destroyed as an end in itself. Nor, says Finnis, may anyone or group be destroyed as the means to some other possibly worthy end. One thinks of nuclear deterrence and the polarity between pacifism and the requirement of practical reasonableness to defend all the basic goods, not just life.

The aim of these dialectical arguments is clearly to moralize the use of power. It is easier to imagine this in the domestic society than in the international. It is easier to suppose that in the former some consensus on the range of patterns of permissible conduct might emerge effectively. It is also in the domestic realm that casuistry is less likely to be reduced to a cold logic of proportionality and intentionality, that rulers and ruled alike may be better able to act as if the basic values are not mere abstractions but "are aspects of the real well-being of flesh-and-blood individuals" and thus that judgments will be arrived at "by a steady determination to respect human good in one's own existence and the equivalent humanity or human rights of others."[49]

Nevertheless, the purpose of Finnis' arguments is to evoke a vision of the final reconciliation of rights and duties on a universal scale, without falling into mere apocalyptic moralizing. He intends to show the implicit universal striving of humanity and what, in principle, such striving would have to achieve in order to find final satisfaction. This is what he meant in saying that "the modern grammar of rights provides a way of expressing virtually all the requirements of practical reasonableness." The grammar is set out in the legal tradition which resists the separation of rights from duties. To understand the tradition of the rule of law is to understand the systematic effort to establish the technical requirements of human flourishing. To leave it at this, however, would be to obscure the motivating ends which this technical effort presupposes whether they are openly acknowledged or not.

The modern grammar of rights may provide a way for expressing the fact that all human beings are loci of flourishing, for recognizing a universal humanity. But it is also necessary to show that the comprehensive understanding of the basic goods is inherent in the experience of actual human beings prior to its philosophical expression. In seeing that the basic goods are not imposed upon, but are derived from, experience, the redemption of rights becomes possible.

The reconciliation between an ancient vision and a modern vocabulary is further constituted for Finnis in an outlook informed by reflection on the meaning of providence. The idea of absolute rights is an idiomatic formulation of an ancient philosophical and theological challenge to all forms of utilitarianism or consequentialism which Finnis chooses to refer to collectively as "proportionalism." The challenge is summed up in the principle: "There are some acts which cannot be justified by any end," or, as in the Pauline Epistles, "Evil may not be done for the sake of good."[50] In affirming these principles, the Judeo-Christian tradition affirms God's providence:

> We can see that the collision between proportionalism and Christianity has its origins in the proportionalist's implicit proposal to undertake the very responsibility that Christianity, like Judaism, ascribes to God Himself ... the proportionalist's imaginary perspective, as a God-like figure surveying possible worlds and choosing the world that embodies greater good or lesser evil, as in perspective that is simply not open to human practical reason.[51]

There are no "pre-moral choices" which then can be moralized or not according to later consequences. Implicated in the choices from the outset is a manifestation of the chooser's degree of illumination with respect to what the good requires.

Exemplary for Finnis is the Socratic principle that it is better to suffer wrong than to do it. To be able to say this is to understand that no matter what calculations of future outcomes may be entertained, the action is also a self-enactment, not a disembodied choice. The Socratic pattern would be one of those Finnis would include as part of the range of patterns of human flourishing.

Socrates' pronouncement that he spent his life trying to be good rather than seeming to be good means here that no states of affairs can be known to be coming to be which absolve him from the question of the rightness of his life.[52] The human world is a compendium of interactions the ramifications of which are so complex that it is impossible fully to evaluate the actual state of affairs. Politics is inevitably the pursuit of intimations, and all calculations are intimations too. Finnis denies that there can be a proportionalist ethic. In this respect, Finnis has surely departed from many features of contemporary thinking while yet seeking to come to terms with it.

On the other hand, political life is real and resists such arguments no matter how philosophically powerful. Thus, in identifying the *nature* of law, the experiential foundation from which all *concepts* of law arise, Finnis finds the reference point for testing the adequacy of concepts of law, and the basis for a potential reconciliation of natural or human rights with natural law. He evokes the ancient tension between politics and philosophy. His practical strategy is to challenge calculating qualifications to the acknowledgment of rights while holding back from postulating that their unqualified acknowledgment would be the prelude to an inevitable, final moral self-transformation in the human condition.

Such a transformation would require us to define an "aggregate collective good" that, as a concept, is incoherent since the common good of a community cannot be measured as an aggregate.[53] Individuals and societies may imagine that they can solve their problems by presupposing objectives which are taken to be sufficiently comprehensive of the common good as to produce the aggregate collective good when they are attained. But this will never be possible because there are no objectives of this character actually available to human beings. On the contrary, all objectives put forward to serve this purpose depend for their apparent unifying significance on suppressing other objectives of equal or greater significance in realizing human well-being. In the final analysis, the claims of certain knowledge that such efforts would have to sustain are a "cosmic impertinence."[54]

"Facts" and "norms" are only to be brought together in continuing acts of judgment. We must seek their reconciliation in the sense that it is always sought, believing that the seeking is the finding and thus akin to an end in itself. By the latter is meant that in seeking one is in conformity to what is good even if one is neither identical with goodness nor goodness fully incarnated.

NOTES

1. Ronald Dworkin, *Taking Rights Seriously* (Cambridge, MA: Harvard University Press, 1977), xi.
2. Ibid.
3. Ibid., 81.

4. Ibid., 84.
5. Ibid., 280.
6. Ibid., 87.
7. Ibid., 91.
8. Ibid., 91–92.
9. Ibid., 105ff.
10. Ibid., 123–24.
11. Ibid., 126.
12. Ibid., 128.
13. Ibid., 129.
14. Ibid., 130.
15. Michael Oakeshott, *On Human Conduct* (Oxford: Clarendon Press, 1975), 112–13.
16. Ibid., 118.
17. Ibid., 119.
18. Ibid., 119–21.
19. Ibid., 59.
20. Ibid., 60–61.
21. Ibid., 79.
22. Ibid., 88.
23. Ibid., 90.
24. Ibid., 104.
25. Ibid., 149.
26. Ibid., 109.
27. Ibid., 150.
28. Ibid., 153–54.
29. Ibid.
30. Ibid., 23–24.
31. Michael Oakeshott, "The Vocabulary of the Modern European State," *Political Studies* 23 (1975), 212–13.
32. Michael Oakeshott, "The Rule of Law," in *On History and Other Essays* (Totowa, NJ: Barnes and Noble Books, 1983), 144–46.
33. Ibid., 148.
34. John Finnis, *Natural Law and Natural Rights*, 2nd ed. (Oxford: Oxford University Press, 2011), 9.
35. Ibid., 14.
36. Ibid., 17.
37. Ibid.
38. Ibid., 18.
39. Ibid., 34.
40. John Finnis, *Fundamentals of Ethics* (Washington, DC: Georgetown University Press, 1983), 50–51.

41. Ibid., 48–49.
42. Ibid., 50.
43. Ibid.; see also Finnis, *Natural Law and Natural Rights*, 221–23.
44. Finnis, *Natural Law and Natural Rights*, 103.
45. Ibid., 198.
46. Ibid., 114.
47. Ibid., 218.
48. Ibid., 219–20.
49. Ibid., 225–26.
50. Finnis, *Fundamentals of Ethics*, 109–10.
51. Ibid., 111.
52. Plato, *Gorgias*, 527.
53. Finnis, *Natual Law and Natural Rights*, 253.
54. Ibid., 111–18.

CHAPTER 6

The Authority of the State and the Traditional Realm of Freedom

Carlos Marques de Almeida

I—Prologue

There is probably a long distance between the philosophical reflections of Charles Dickens and the political theory of Michael Oakeshott. Dickens opens his *A Tale of Two Cities* noting:

> It was the best of times, it was the worst of times, it was the age of wisdom, it was the age of foolishness, it was the epoch of belief, it was the epoch of incredulity, it was the season of Light, it was the season of Darkness, it was the spring of hope, it was the winter of despair, we had everything before us, we had nothing before us, we were all going direct to Heaven, we were all going direct the other way—in short, the period was so far like the present period, that some of its noisiest authorities insisted on its being received, for good or for evil, in the superlative degree of comparison only.

A close reading of the passage reveals a peculiar intimation of the complexity of the ideal character of a civil association and the moral value of

C. Marques de Almeida (✉)
Institute for Political Studies, Catholic University of Portugal, Lisboa, Portugal

© The Author(s) 2019
E. S. Kos (ed.), *Michael Oakeshott on Authority, Governance, and the State*, Palgrave Studies in Classical Liberalism,
https://doi.org/10.1007/978-3-030-17455-2_6

individual freedom. Turning to the normative and political side of *On Human Conduct*,[1] Oakeshott acknowledges that there are some general ideas ready to be invoked, although they do not all pull in the same direction, which means that a criterion of approval or disapproval untouched by contingency is necessarily absent. Moreover, demonstrative conclusions are necessarily impossible, final solutions and alternative ideal systems are persuasive evasions or corrupting delusions. In light of this argument, to choose what in this circumstantial flux should receive attention, to understand it in terms of its impact upon a practice of civil intercourse and political authority, and to deliberate the civil response to be made to it is the engagement of political intelligence. And although this engagement of caring for the conditions of a civil association may not seem at all demanding or exciting, it calls however for so exact a focus of attention and so uncommon self-restraint that it makes this mode of human relationship to be as rare as it is excellent. For Oakeshott, and as a mode of human intercourse, the civil association is an ideal character glimpsed here or there in the features of human goings-on, intimated in some choices and dispositions to choose and in some responses to actual situations, but it nowhere constitutes a premeditated design for human conduct.

From the account above, it is possible to perceive the presence of a state, eventually, to understand the exercise of an authority and, above all, to sense the enjoyment of a particular idea of freedom. Being so, the starting point of this essay is Michael Oakeshott's interpretation of the concept of civil association as the ideal of a limited state. According to Noël O'Sullivan,[2] the core of Oakeshott's conception of civil association is the characterization of it as the only appropriate *moral* response to the problem of reconciling authority with freedom in a modern Western political order. Following a little deeper the concerns of O'Sullivan, for Oakeshott the principal problem of European political thought since Hobbes has not merely been the technical one of securing order as effectively as possible in the newly emergent nation-states of the European world. It has been, rather, the normative one of how to constitute a state in conditions of cultural and social diversity without imposing coercive restrains on individual freedom.

The clarity of the statement immediately opens the political argument to a complex and persistent tension between the exercise of authority and the enjoyment of freedom. For Oakeshott, the reconciliation of these two opposite poles must in some way summon up, first, a certain "sentiment of solidarity" among individuals; second, a mutually shared sense by governors and governed of participation in a "public order" or "public concern." In the absence of this public concern, a state is devoid of a moral ground and is therefore indistinguishable from an instrument of domination or a bare and overwhelming exercise of power. At this bifurcation of political categories, the tension between the authority of the state and the enjoyment of freedom is notoriously profound enough to lead to a sharp divergence and ultimate collision of these two ideals. And, no doubt, different schools of thought return different answers to the same and only problem. The disagreement among modern political thinkers reflects, in the world of political theory, the practical puzzle of reconciling authority and freedom in the conditions of modern European politics. *Reconciling* is the appropriate word, because the tension is constitutive of the character of modern European politics, and therefore, it will never be an object of a theoretical solution or a practical eradication.

For the Argus-eyed observer of the philosophical and political itineration of Michael Oakeshott, such a tension has been the subject of several faces, faces translated in several dichotomies carefully scattered throughout his essays and reflections. To be more precise without being exhaustive, one can start by mentioning the tension between individualist and collectivist trends embedded in modern political thought.[3] At another time, the focus of Oakeshott's reflection is concerned with the tension between rationalism in politics and the understanding of politics as a tradition of behavior.[4] At yet another stage, the argument flows and the tension is perceived as the outcome between the politics of faith and the politics of skepticism.[5] Finally, in the Author's definitive statement expanded in *On Human Conduct*, the tension is lying between two modes of human association, namely civil association and enterprise association—civil association is an essentially formal and nonpurposive concept of the *respublica*; enterprise association seeks to create a public concern by imposing a substantive vision, a shared purpose, of the social good on all members of the society.

In short, Oakeshott's contention is that the modern European political consciousness is a "polarized consciousness."[6] The pole of civil association and the pole of enterprise association are its constitutive poles, and all other tensions are insignificant compared with the range, the scope, and the depth of these two historical, political, and theoretical categories.

Now, facing the world-picture of these attributes, the question that should immediately be asked is where one finds the moral and political argument for freedom. One can start the enquiry with enterprise associa-tion. The freedom inherent in enterprise association is that of the choice to be associated and the consequent capacity to dissociate if the pur-pose or the management of the pursuit of an enterprise is disapproved.[7] But where the association is a state, this freedom to exit is excluded by the logic of its constitution—allegiance here is to the common pur-pose. Each individual is the property of the association, an item of its capital resources. But when this freedom of association and dissociation is excluded, what remains? The freedom inherent in such a state is the condition of being released from every care in the world save one—the care not to be idle in fulfilling one's role in the enterprise, not to inhibit or prejudice that complete mobilization of resources which constitute the state, having then the enjoyment of an array of assured benefits. As Oakeshott writes bluntly, "freedom is warm, compensated servility."

Moving the enquiry toward civil association, the freedom inherent in this mode of human intercourse lies in the associates not being related to one another in the pursuit of any substantive purpose they have not chosen for themselves and from which they cannot extricate themselves by a choice of their one.[8] Moreover, in their actions and utterances the associates are not even officially noticed or noticeable in respect of their substantive character but solely in respect of the civil conditions to which they are required to subscribe. And it is a freedom to choose which is not only exercised in the performance of substantive actions but is also postulated in subscribing to the conditions of *respublica*: Laws cannot either specify actions or exhaustively define subscriptions to them. As Oakeshott writes assertively, the civil condition and a state understood in terms of civil association "postulates self-determined autonomous human beings,"[9] seeking the satisfaction of their wants in self-chosen transac-tions with others of their kind.

Michael Oakeshott is committing himself to a philosophical mindset where the framework of his political theory is definitely linked to a his-torical axis where authority and freedom are coupled together in an ines-capable tension. Only a *moral* perspective of this underlying tension can prevent the *nemesis* of authority (despotism) and the *nemesis* of freedom (anarchy).

In a less conventional approach, which implies keeping the central focus of the essay on the character of civil association, the important point is that the political drive and the philosophical procedure of the enquiry implies some sort of a theoretical twist, namely the analysis of the content of the authority of the state through the conceptual mirror of the moral value of individual freedom. Thus in order to fulfill the aim of the essay, it will be necessary to investigate three particular topics: the character of a modern European state, the authority of governments in a modern European state, and the understanding of an idea of freedom.

II—The Character of a Modern European State

Addressing the main features of this sort of political association which came to be called the state is addressing, in this particular context, the character of the inhabitants of a specific territory. What in modern Europe and elsewhere in the world is recognized as a "state" is, in the first place, a well-defined piece of territory. So, generally speaking, every man belongs to a state, and no man can belong to more than one state. And, for the most part, those who belong to a state live in its territory. But the human components of a modern European state have something to distinguish them besides normal residence within a certain area of territory. They enjoy what may be called a certain "sentiment of solidarity."[10] Now, the sentiment of solidarity in virtue of which the members of a modern European state compose a specific collectivity of human beings is much easier to detect than to define. And one of the great enterprises of modern European political thought has been concerned with attempts to understand and to interpret it. But three things may be said about the sentiment of solidarity enjoyed by the members of a modern European state. First, it is based neither on a belief in common blood, nor on a common language, nor on common religious beliefs, although any of these may be present and may contribute to it. It is less definite and less powerful than the sentiment of solidarity characteristic of a tribe, and it does not entail the same degree of homogeneity in those who share it. Second, it is a unique kind of sentiment of solidarity, it is one of the characteristics that most distinguishes these political associations from all others, and being a product of circumstances, each modern European state has achieved it in an idiom of its own. Third, all modern European states are greatly concerned with the promotion of this sentiment of solidarity among its members. Nevertheless, it is characteristic of modern European states that this solidarity has always remained limited, which is the equivalent of saying that each of these states has an internal variety that qualifies its solidarity. According to

Oakeshott's account, this internal variety is one of the inheritances of modern from medieval Europe, and it is the heart of modern politics.

For Oakeshott, then, the modern European state is, despite its other features, "an association of legally 'free' human beings, among whom a certain sentiment of solidarity had emerged."[11] Before elaborating a little further on the practical content of the internal variety distinctive of the sentiment of solidarity, it is quite relevant for the argument to realize the meaning of "free" in this particular historical context. Following the internal logic of Oakeshott's reasoning, the modern European state was never designed by anybody, never had the geometrical planning of a single architect.[12] Quite the opposite, the modern European state is the product of innumerable human choices and activities, it is to be understood as the net result of all the temporary and contingent enterprises, failures as well as successes, of these centuries of European politics—the path and direction of modern European political activity is neither more nor less than the footprints of those who engaged in politics.

And following the footprints of human choices and activities the argument returns to the internal variety that qualifies solidarity at the core of the modern European state and at the heart of modern politics. A modern European state has normally had a diverse population, some components of it often with memories of different allegiances or even of independence,[13] not to mention recollections of a different way of life. Every modern European state began, in respect of its population, with diversity. And the task of the rulers has been to consolidate its diverse population—to generate in it a sentiment of solidarity which was notably lacking. The most important diversities which stood in the way of this sentiment of solidarity have been those of local communities of various dimensions, often very ancient, and distinguished by various characteristics: race, religion, language, and social status. In this matter, and in modern European states, two opposed dispositions have been at work: the disposition to generate solidarity by *destroying* diversity, and the disposition to generate solidarity by *containing* diversity. These two dispositions run effectively through the whole of modern politics. The disposition to generate solidarity by destroying diversity has been pursued in processes of exclusion and suppression. And it is in this manner that the so-called nations of modern Europe have been created. But a disposition opposed to uniformity has also been unavoidably at work. Every European state began with diversities, and these diversities have promoted a belief that politics is an activity in which diversities are accommodated to one another, and that the necessary sentiment of solidarity may be achieved without any enforcement of suppression. This style of politics has always been difficult, but in spite of constant rejection, it has managed to survive. The fact remains that every modern European state is, and always has been, "plural" in respect of its population. Each, in some respect or other, is a barely stable balance of diversities. Overall, a modern European state, then, is to be recognized as an association of human beings which has been created out of the diverse materials of the European continent and throughout modern European history.

In Michael Oakeshott's narrative, the character of the modern European state is continuously driven by the observation of a sentiment of solidarity in perpetual tension with an historical diversity that reaches the apex of a condition of plurality embedded in the reality of time itself—diversity and plurality that point unequivocally toward a certain idea of freedom. And with an idea of freedom associated with the individual comes a certain concept of limitation linked to the character of the state. For its part, freedom arises as an outcome of human choices and activities in the works of negotiating the contingencies of the world. In Oakeshott's outlook, there is then a vision of a civilization in motion, a historical reality with profound and endogenous roots, a vision which may be regarded as the *matrix* of a conservative disposition. Moreover, intimations of freedom overlap intimations of a civil association, a moral mark pointing to the tentative reconciliation of the character of the modern European state with the enjoyment of freedom. In his *Dictionary*, Samuel Johnson did not include the word *civilization*; instead, the word printed for that effect is *civility*—definitely, an Oakeshottian gesture.

III—THE AUTHORITY OF GOVERNMENTS IN A MODERN EUROPEAN STATE

With regard to the authority inscribed in the modern European state, Oakeshott starts to acknowledge that the first incipient medieval beliefs on the authority of kings were in terms of authority derived from God and of authority derived from the consent of their subjects. And these beliefs were inherited and transferred in modern European political thought. They were beliefs about the authority of rulers obviously appropriate to a modern European state, because they recognized the ruled as free men—that is, as men not bound to their rulers by tenancies of land and services arising out of those tenancies.[14] Modern Europe, then, inherited the great achievement of medieval political thought—the idea of political authority distinguished from the authority of lordship. But it inherited also a sort of ruler who became the progenitor of modern governments. He was a ruler who, though he had become a king, had not quiet ceased to be a lord. He was a ruler in whose person the notion of authority of lordship had not yet been laid to rest. In the main, the great effort of modern European political thought has been directed to suppressing the relics of lordship in beliefs about the authority of modern governments.

Nevertheless, the belief in the authority of government as that of lordship did not perish. It survives, largely unrecognized, however, when a state is thought of as an estate (land and its inhabitants), and a government is thought of as the manager of the estate. Wherever a government acquires an extensive ownership of the land and resources over which it rules, and an extensive command over the activities of its subjects, it has been impossible to detach the authority attributed to it from being connected with these lordly rather than kingly characteristics. When Mme. De Staël said, in the eighteenth century: "Despotism is new, liberty is old," she referred to these two kinds of authority, lordly and kingly authority. And what she meant was that there had been a recrudescence of a belief in lordly authority after Europe had seemed to embrace the sort of authority which recognized its subjects as free men—namely kingly authority.

But there is an underlining query at the core of this perception of authority, namely the question that directly addresses the procedure or approved process through which a person or a government acquires the authority or the right to rule, and recognizing it as a symbol of some deeper beliefs emerging in the history of modern political thought. In accordance with Oakeshott's assessment and, as it first occurs, the question of authority is a "practical" question. There is, then, an approach to the problem less sophisticated than that of the philosophers, but also less fanciful and doctrinaire than the approach of those who thought evidence for the authority of government in the *origins* of governments.[15] The starting point of this line of enquiry is the admission that nothing is known specifically about the origins of government, but that at the same time, it is safe to assume that government begins in the exercise of power, force, and even violence. Nevertheless, to rule is to enjoy authority. Every ruler claims the right to rule, and authority is attributed to it by its subjects. Indeed, to recognize governments merely as seats of power is to recognize the subjects in relation to governments merely as "slaves." As a guide to perplexity, the question is obviously inevitable: "But how can 'authority' emerge from what begins as no more than 'power'?"[16] Oakeshott's statement points to the argument that the emergence of authority from power is a "historical process," but it is not a "historical event." The argument runs something like this: Many of the demands of the powerful are no doubt conceded because they are impossible to resist. And some of these demands may be supposed to be conceded because compliance carries with it some valuable *quid pro quo* or reward which makes it worthwhile to comply. Neither of these situations, however, turns the demands of the powerful into rightful demands or their power into authority. But it may be imagined that, in the course of time, some demands will acquire the force of custom. That is to say, they will be yielded to not under an express threat of harm, nor because to yield brings with it a valuable recompense, but because it has become "the done thing"—meaning to be a socially acceptable behavior. This done thing is still merely indicative and not imperative. But, imperceptibly, the done thing becomes recognized as a customary duty, and to recognize a duty is to have acknowledged an authority. Thus, authorization (meaning the recognition of authority) is not a historical event, nor is it a necessarily hypothetical act; "it is a process in which power is moralized."[17] The notion of a contract entered into is far too definite to represent what is going on. And even the notion of consent is too specific. It is much more like submission becoming acquiescence, and the absence of objection broadening down into customary recognition and the acknowledgment of demands rightfully made. So the gap between power and authority is bridged in a series of minimal steps, no one of which may be said to be itself the bridge. In short, the authority of rulers is like the rights of squatters. They begin in acts of power, they grow out of acquiescence and the absence of objection, and they are acquired, by prescription, when what was once a demand receives recognition as a rightful claim. Becoming prescriptive as the product of the lapse of time, the authority of the government is acquired by default, by a compliance that breeds a belief in right.

The progression of Oakeshott's argument addressing the question of authority in association with the character of a modern European state is quite revealing. Oakeshott's position rejects any philosophical contribution from both a foundationalist standing and a constructivist engagement. His account appeals to a moral and political imagination supported by an empirical and historical knowledge. Again, the method can be naturally associated with some sort of a conservative reflection. Furthermore, Oakeshott transforms the empirical and historical recognition of free men into a certain conception of what may be called a *pluralist individualism* associated with modernity. By starting the enquiry with a deliberate conservative presupposition, Oakeshott reaches a peculiar and definitely liberal outcome. Concerning the bridge between power and authority, Oakeshott's political device is to appeal to the action of time, to the unintended effect of actions that become uses and customs, finally, by prescription, acquiring the dignity and the morality of a tradition. Oakeshott is definitely upholding the importance of tradition in the establishment of political authority in the context of a modern European state. Authority, which is the outcome of a historical process, is then some hidden substance in the composition of power that can be transformed and extracted by the persistent action of morality. In a more unexpected and provocative way, the gap between compliance and freedom is once more bridged by the presence and the practice of a tradition—tradition is then an inescapable part of how individual agents act freely. Being a set of rules, that means that in the individual perspective, a tradition is essentially a tradition of behavior, not a set of commands in order to achieve a particular end. This is probably a reasonable way in which authority, morality, and freedom can be conciliated in an understanding of tradition as an open, complex, and plural reality. As such, freedom breathes the air of human performances as explorations of the resources of a range of traditions, and in this sense, it is quite natural to speak of a traditional realm of freedom.

IV—For the Understanding of an Idea of Freedom

Needless to say, Michael Oakeshott does not pretend to invent a political conception of freedom for himself. Quite the contrary, he is perfectly aware he belongs to a tradition. And in the mode of a disclaimer, Oakeshott writes:

> We must be clear, they say, about what we mean by 'freedom'. First, let us define it; and when we know what it is, it will be time enough to seek it out, to love it and to die for it. What is a free society? And with this

question (proposed abstractly) the door opens upon a night of endless quibble, lit only by the stars of sophistry. Like men born in prison, we are urged to dream of something we have never enjoyed (freedom from want) and to make that dream the foundation of our politics. We are instructed to distinguish between 'positive' and 'negative' freedom, between the 'old' and the 'new' freedom, between 'social', 'political', 'civil', 'economic' and 'personal' freedom; we are told that freedom is the 'recognition of necessity; we are taught that all that matters is 'inner freedom' and that this is to be identified with equality and with power: there is no end to the abuse we have suffered.[18]

Thus, the freedom which is the subject of the enquiry is neither an abstraction nor a dream, but actually a way of living. The purpose of Oakeshott's reflection is not to define a word, but to detect the key of what is actually the form and shape of freedom, which for Oakeshott has a political connotation that springs directly from a political experience. The question he raises might be read as follows: What are the characteristics of a society in respect of which freedom could be enjoyed? And the answer is that freedom lies in a coherence of mutually supported liberties, each of which amplifies the whole and none of which stands alone.[19] The most general condition of freedom, so general that all other conditions may be seen to be comprised within it, is the absence from the society of overwhelming concentrations of power. It first appears in a diffusion of authority between past, present, and future. A society is ruled by none of these exclusively. One can say that a society governed wholly by its past, or its present, or its future suffers under a kind of "despotism of superstition" which forbids freedom. The politics of a society is a "conversation" in which past, present, and future each has a voice; and though one or another of them may on occasion properly prevail, none permanently dominates, and on this account, freedom prevails. This condition of freedom can properly be called the Burkean Clause. Further, the second requirement of freedom is the dispersion of power among the multitude of interests and organizations that comprise society. The purpose is not to seek to suppress diversity of interest, but the enjoyment of freedom will be always imperfect so long as the dispersal of power among them is incomplete, and is threatened if any interest or combination of interests, even the interest of the majority acquires extraordinary power. Similarly, the conduct of government should involve a sharing of power, not only between the recognized organs of government, but also between the Administration and the Opposition. The exercise of freedom implies that no one in a society is allowed unlimited power. So, freedom emerges when power is diffused; diffused in the constitution of government and diffused among the variety of organizations that constitute the larger society. This condition of freedom can properly be called the Lockean Clause.

Moreover, one must be aware that the balance of such a society is always precarious. It might be thought that a society of this sort could be saved from disintegration only by the existence at its head of an overwhelming power capable of holding all other powers in check. But that is not the voice of experience. Normally, to perform its office, which is to prevent coercion, the government requires wielding only a power greater than that which is concentrated in any one other locus of power on any particular occasion.[20] But further, experience has disclosed a method of government remarkably economical in the use of power and consequently peculiarly fitted to preserve freedom—it is called the rule of law. A government by the rule of law, that is by means of the enforcement by prescribed methods of settled rules binding alike on governors and governed, while losing nothing in strength, is itself the emblem of that diffusion of power which it exists to promote and is therefore peculiarly appropriate to a free society. It is the method of government most economical in the use of power; it involves a partnership between past and present and between governors and governed which leaves no room for arbitrariness; it encourages a "tradition of resistance" to the growth of dangerous concentrations of power which is far more effective than any onslaught however crushing; it controls effectively, but without breaking the grand affirmative flow of things; and it gives a practical definition of the kind of limited but necessary service a society may expect from its government, restraining the individual from vain and dangerous expectations. Particular laws may fail to protect the freedom enjoyed in a society and may even be destructive of some of the parts of the apparatus of freedom—but the rule of law, by removing the fear of the power of government, is the greatest single condition for the enjoyment of freedom.

This outline of a free society will be thought to lack something important unless there is added to it a suggestion of the end or purpose which informs such a society.[21] However, it belongs to some other tradition to think of this purpose as the achievement of a premeditated utopia, as an abstract ideal or as a preordained and inevitable end. The purpose of this society, if indeed it may be said to have one, is not something put upon it from the outside, nor can it be stated in abstract terms without gross abridgment. A free society did not spring yesterday; a free society possesses already a defined character and recognized traditions of activity. In these circumstances, social achievement is to perceive the next step suggested by the character of the society in contact with changing conditions and to take it in such a manner that the society is not disrupted and that the prerogatives of future generations are not impaired. In place of a preconceived purpose, then, such a society will find its guide in a "principle of *continuity*," which is a diffusion of power between past, present, and future and in a "principle of *consensus*," which is a diffusion of power between the different legitimate interests of the present. A society may be called itself free because the pursuit of current desires does not deprive the individuals of a sympathy for what went before, which means that the society remains reconciled with the past. A free society, taking a view neither short nor long, is unwilling to sacrifice the present to a remote and incalculable future, or the immediate and foreseeable future to a transitory present. The individual can find freedom in a preference for slow, small changes which have behind them the voluntary consensus of opinion, and the ability to resist disintegration without suppressing opposition, and in the perception that it is more important for a society to move together than to move either fast or far. But, at any rate, there is no such thing as infallible decisions. Indeed since there is no external or absolute test of perfection, infallibility has no meaning. In this matter, a free society will find what it needs in a "principle of change" and in a "principle of identity," and in the perpetual necessity of striking a balance between two dissenting dispositions.

After going through the full argument of Oakeshott, it is now appropriate to return to the Burkean Clause and the Lockean Clause as two axes of an idea of freedom. In order to be precise and complete, the Burkean Clause is the aggregation of three elements—the diffusion of authority; the principle of continuity; and the principle of identity. Conversely, the Lockean Clause is also the aggregation of three elements—the dispersion of power; the principle of consensus; and the principle of change. A more accomplished reading of the present interpretation underlines the perception that the idea of freedom in Oakeshott's political understanding conveys a conservative perspective and a liberal outlook. To elaborate a little further on this position, one can say that in the background is always a conception of civil association as the only appropriate *moral* response to the problem of reconciling authority with freedom in a modern Western political order. In the foreground, through the Burkean Clause, freedom displays an explicitly political character and adopts a configuration associated with a particular way of life. Supported by the factual and the concrete side of politics, having the assurance of the rule of law, the reality of freedom is embedded in a time line, in history. This axis of freedom is projected as a conservative pattern. At the same time, through the Lockean Clause, freedom displays an explicitly political character adopting the prime goal of preventing coercion in the present time. This axis of freedom is projected as a liberal template. In a logical endeavor toward a conclusion, but certainly as the variation of a hypothesis, Oakeshott's idea of freedom seems to convey a conservative core and a liberal circle. And, metaphysical metaphors aside, common sense, prescribes that it is impossible to have an outer circle without an inner core.

Notes

1. Michael Oakeshott, *On Human Conduct* (Oxford: Clarendon Press, 1975), 178, 180–81.
2. Noël O'Sullivan, "Oakeshott on Civil Association," in *A Companion to Michael Oakeshott*, ed. Paul Franco and Leslie March (University Park, PA: The Pennsylvania State University Press, 2012), 290, 293–94.
3. Michael Oakeshott, "The Masses in Representative Democracy," in *Rationalism in Politics and Other Essays*, ed. Timothy Fuller (Indianapolis: Liberty Fund, 1990), 363–83.
4. Michael Oakeshott, "Rationalism in Politics," in *Rationalism in Politics and Other Essays*, 6–42.
5. Michael Oakeshott, *The Politics of Faith and the Politics of Scepticism*, ed. Timothy Fuller (New Haven and London: Yale University Press, 1996).
6. Oakeshott, *On Human Conduct*, 320.
7. Ibid., 316–17.
8. Ibid., 314–15.
9. Ibid., 315.
10. Michael Oakeshott, *Lectures in the History of Political Thought*, ed. Terry Nardin and Luke O'Sullivan (Exeter: Imprint Academic, 2006), 363–64.
11. Ibid., 373.
12. Ibid., 360.
13. Ibid., 378–80.
14. Ibid., 459–60.
15. Ibid., 465–68.

16. Ibid., 466.
17. Ibid.
18. Michael Oakeshott, "The Political Economy of Freedom," in *Rationalism in Politics and Other Essays*, 386–87.
19. Ibid., 388–89.
20. Ibid., 390–91.
21. Ibid., 396–97.

CHAPTER 7

Anarchic and Antinomian? Oakeshott and the Cambridge School on History, Philosophy, and Authority

Jordan Rudinsky

I—INTRODUCTION

This essay seeks to characterize Michael Oakeshott's relationship to that approach to the study of political thought that has been referred to as "contextualism" or the "Cambridge School" and has been chiefly associated with Quentin Skinner, John Dunn, and J. G. A. Pocock.[1] There seems to be an open question about this relationship. On the one hand, Terry Nardin can reasonably claim that "we can read [Oakeshott] as inspiring J. G. A. Pocock, Quentin Skinner, and other contributors to a revived discipline of historical studies of political thought by emphasizing the importance of languages of discourse as the context for reading political texts."[2] On the other hand, David Runciman is right in saying "the Cambridge School have, unsurprisingly, been critics of [Oakeshott] precisely because what he produced in his readings of the likes of Hobbes

J. Rudinsky (✉)
Department of Government, Harvard University, Cambridge, MA, USA
e-mail: rudinsky@g.harvard.edu

© The Author(s) 2019
E. S. Kos (ed.), *Michael Oakeshott on Authority, Governance, and the State*, Palgrave Studies in Classical Liberalism,
https://doi.org/10.1007/978-3-030-17455-2_7

was not history."[3] It is not too difficult to imagine how both *could* be true, but since that would require some speculation the question merits a closer look.

I address this question by considering Oakeshott's relationship specifically to Pocock and Skinner, for aside from being conventionally recognized as the chief exemplars of the Cambridge School they present the richest nexus with Oakeshott's thought. Oakeshott taught history at Cambridge from 1925 until 1949, around when Pocock started his Ph.D., and he interacted with Pocock and Skinner after settling into the London School of Economics in 1950.[4] More substantively, Pocock found in Oakeshott's writings on tradition useful imagery for understanding the task of historical inquiry, which he explored in depth in two early methodological essays and has occasionally invoked in his historical writings since then, as recently as *The Discovery of Islands* (2005).[5] The nexus between Oakeshott and Skinner is less obvious, as the most direct engagement either had with the other was Oakeshott's critical review of Skinner's *Foundations of Modern Political Thought* (1978).[6] However, while criticizing Skinner's assumption of a singular, Weberian concept of the modern state, Oakeshott invoked a claim he had made in *On Human Conduct* (1975): that a proper understanding of the history of modern political thought precludes such singularity and requires instead a pluralism according to which "the state" is simply the ongoing debate about what the state is or ought to be. Hence the two books can be seen in contrapuntal relationship, suggesting the appropriateness of a critical comparison of their arguments and the different directions they point for the history of political thought more broadly.[7]

These connections remain generally underexplored both in the bountiful literature devoted to Oakeshott's thought and in discussions of Skinner, Pocock, and the Cambridge School. Of the numerous books and articles on Oakeshott, only a few mention Skinner or Pocock[8]; still fewer include any close consideration of Skinner or Pocock in relation to Oakeshott.[9] With one exception, none of the contributions to either of the book-length companions to Oakeshott's thought considers this relationship.[10] The exception is one chapter by Martyn Thompson which includes an illuminating examination of Oakeshott and Skinner's disagreement of whether Hobbes' *Leviathan* should be read as philosophy or only ideological polemic.[11] Thompson's argument is different from but consistent with mine, although he does not compare their historical treatments of the modern European state as I do here. When we come to considerations of Pocock or Skinner, mentions of Oakeshott are likewise scarce. *Festschriften* for both Skinner and Pocock have appeared with no mention of Oakeshott.[12] However, James Alexander has discussed Oakeshott among many others in a recent attempt to contextualize the Cambridge School in the long history of studying politics at Cambridge since around 1875.[13] Alexander notices Pocock's debt to Oakeshott but does not examine it closely, and while his classification of Oakeshott as a philosopher whom Skinner is said "to trump" with history is helpful to a point, it precludes comparison of Oakeshott as an historian of the concept of the state alongside Skinner. The other two significant mentions of Oakeshott—Skinner's and Runciman's—are of particular importance to this essay, and I will consider both in the course of the essay.[14] What becomes clear is, despite the fact that Pocock could not accept Oakeshott's stringent, ultimately antiquarian conception of historical inquiry, Oakeshott's conceptualization of tradition attracted Pocock's early attention and left a clear mark on his subsequent scholarship. And although Oakeshott's *On Human Conduct* provides an intellectual history of the modern concept of the state like Skinner's *Foundations* and even shares emphases on Roman law and medieval circumstances, Oakeshott's theorization of the concept of the state can be seen as perhaps more historically sensitive. Finally, by way of a reinterpretation of Oakeshott's *On Human Conduct* in the light of his and Skinner's fundamental impasse over the possibility of philosophy, I suggest one way Oakeshott's approach points towards a new way of understanding the relationship of historical study to present concerns.

Throughout the essay, I am concerned not only to explain Oakeshott's relation to Pocock and Skinner but also to trace a specific line of inquiry into Oakeshott's thought. This line of inquiry concerns Oakeshott's theory of political authority and, by extension, his status as a liberal. One of Pocock's critiques of Oakeshott, as I demonstrate, was that with his denial of the practical relation of past to present he represented the "anarchic and antinomian strain in conservatism." It was in reference to Oakeshott's writings on the philosophy of history that Pocock made this critique, but I next consider it in reference to Oakeshott's theory of authority in *On Human Conduct*. Concluding that his theory of authority there bears no more relation to practical life than does history, on his account of history, I acknowledge that the charge of anarchism and antinomianism still stands. Shifting attention from Pocock to Skinner, I argue that Oakeshott's argument against Skinner that it is possible to do philosophy "above the battle" of politics should not be construed to mean that works of philosophy cannot bear any relation to practical life. Works of philosophy are not necessarily always written exclusively in the mode of philosophy. Consideration of Oakeshott's writings on Hobbes and Nietzsche suggests that works of philosophy can also incorporate the mode of art or poetry. I then suggest that the third, historical section of *On Human Conduct* should be understood as bi-modal in this way—both history and art—and that the aesthetic dimension of his discussion of the different "dispositions" informing theories of the state can be understood as the closest Oakeshott comes to bridging the gap between theory and practice, and thus the best answer to Pocock's charge of anarchism and antinomianism.

II—Oakeshott and Pocock: Historical Inquiry

Pocock's most direct engagement with Oakeshott's thought is found in two essays on methodology from the 1960s.[15] In both, Pocock considers Oakeshott's 1950 inaugural lecture at the London School of Economics.[16] Oakeshott's lecture is worth revisiting before considering Pocock's engagement with it. Oakeshott had proposed that political education involved three things: (1) the study of one's own political tradition, encompassing both political activity and thought, (2) the political traditions of other contemporary societies, and (3) the study of political philosophy, specifically in its historic dimension. This threefold concept Oakeshott had drawn from his characterization of political activity, which occupied the better part of the lecture. Political activity was said to be the attending to "general arrangements" by a collection of people who recognized certain "traditions of behaviour" which "intimate" various directions for change. For instance, one tradition of behaviour is law, and at law, Oakeshott observed, women at one time enjoyed a certain status composed of certain rights and duties which had in turn intimated other rights and duties not yet recognized by law. The political activity seeking "enfranchisement" of women was thus a "pursuit" of such intimations. Oakeshott's point was to refute the view of political activity as the practical application of "independently premeditated ideology."[17] This view itself was said to be the counterargument to the characterization of political activity as the pursuit of instinctive self-interest, a view Oakeshott labels "empiricism." The ideology–empiricism antagonism brings up an important contextual point. Oakeshott seems to have ascribed the ideological view to E. H. Carr when he quoted from Carr's *The Soviet Impact on the Western World* (1946): "Few people any longer contest the thesis that the child should be educated *in* the official ideology of his country."[18] Leaving aside the fact that in context Carr was describing Soviet Russia and not Britain, it is true that Carr would later mount a critique of the empirical school of history, as represented especially by Geoffrey Elton, and argue for the importance of ideology. This controversy is not only crucial context for Oakeshott but also for Pocock and Skinner's methodological interventions, as considered below. For Oakeshott, while it was unsatisfactory to discount ideology in political activity, it was crass to assume political activity flowed from ideology, for the reason that ideologies are demonstrably the *result* of political activity, "already intimated in a concrete manner of behaving."[19] Oakeshott's claim that ideologies are bound to contexts sounds much like the critiques Pocock and Skinner later advanced against any "history of ideas" that purported to narrate appearances of different forms of static ideas or "isms" across time and space.

Perhaps this resonance is what attracted Pocock's interest in Oakeshott's writings in the early 1960s. If so, as an attraction it must have existed alongside the simple fact that both in "Political Education" and other essays Oakeshott showed a keen interest in the nature of tradition and gave it a considered treatment that in some senses sounded not unlike Burke's notion of tradition, to which Pocock had already devoted considerable attention and frequently referred in his discussions of Oakeshott.[20] Either way, in both essays Pocock was primarily concerned not merely to understand Oakeshott but to put him to Pocock's own uses. In the "Methodological Inquiry," Pocock's purpose was to characterize the state of his discipline and offer a theoretical account of what historical study of political thought was. To do this, he adopted Oakeshott's schematic from "Political Education" as his starting point and proceeded to endow it with more detail. As he announced at the beginning, "I shall adopt the Burkean-Oakeshottian characterization of political theorizing as an activity of 'abstraction or abridgement from a tradition.'"[21] Moreover, Pocock proceeded also to use Oakeshott's distinction between different "levels of abstraction" at which reflection on politics may take place. One of the methodological errors Pocock was concerned to point out was that of tacitly treating all political utterances as though they had been uttered at a philosophical level of abstraction rather than a practical or ideological level. Likewise, Oakeshott had written:

> Reflection on political activity may take place at various levels: we may consider what resources our political tradition offers for dealing with a certain situation, or we may abridge our political experience into a doctrine, which may be used, as a scientist uses a hypothesis, to explore its intimations. But beyond these, and other manners of political thinking, there is a range of reflection the object of which is to consider the place of political activity itself on the map of our total experience.[22]

At the same time as Pocock borrowed these conceptual tools from Oakeshott in order to specify a theory of what historians of political thought do, his elaboration aligns fairly closely with Oakeshott's three prongs of political education. In fact, the latter half of Pocock's "Methodological Inquiry" is best understood as an elaboration or refinement of Oakeshott's idea of "getting to know" a tradition, an expression Pocock has often employed in his historical writings. For example, Pocock divided the historiography of political thought into the history "of action," which focuses on "what takes place when concepts are abstracted from a tradition of behaviour," and the history of thought, focusing on "what takes place when [such concepts] are employed in action within that tradition."[23] Likewise had Oakeshott distinguished the historical study of political activity as "a concrete manner of behaviour" from the study of "what people have thought and said about what happened: the history, not of political ideas, but of the manner of our political thinking."[24] Pocock elaborates this schema in greater detail than Oakeshott in his exploration of the composite nature of political tradition, which he says consists of many "languages" or "vocabularies" drawn from "different aspects of its social and cultural traditions." Pocock makes two points about these languages and vocabularies. First, languages may be more or less indiscriminately taken from their originating sub-traditions and applied in another context such as politics—we might talk about politics in terms of mechanics or natural law metaphysics. Second, there will likely be more abstract vocabularies designed to make sense of the chaotic intermingling of lower-level vocabularies, all the while keeping mindful of the limitation imposed by the important role played by "the unspoken in shaping the tradition on which thought is a commentary"—a mindfulness Pocock says is necessary for the historian "who wants to follow Oakeshott."[25]

What must be noticed is the close alignment of Pocock's elaborate framing of the activity of studying political thought with Oakeshott's framing. Pocock even seems to end his essay in the same way Oakeshott had ended his: by addressing the place of philosophy. For Oakeshott, as we saw, philosophic reflection on politics had an important place alongside but separate from the strictly historical study. Pocock concluded likewise, albeit with some hedging. In the event (which Pocock insists is rare) that, after patient analysis, the historian discerns her subject's language to be "specialized for use upon the highest attainable level of generality," then she must "abandon the role of a student of thought as the language of society, and become a student of thought as philosophy."[26] This is not to suggest that Pocock must be seen as a philosopher in the manner Oakeshott understood himself to be but that he carved out a place for political philosophy in his broader framing of the study of political thought. On this point, Pocock would seem to have more in common with Oakeshott than with Skinner, who would soon insist that all political utterance is ideological and has more recently presented this point as "the Nietzschean point of view" that "there is nothing but the battle" and hence "the idea of being above the battle makes little sense."[27] There thus appears to be a point on which one of the doyens of the Cambridge School is in greater agreement with Oakeshott than with Skinner. For his part, Oakeshott found little in Pocock's essay to take issue with while reviewing the collection in which it appeared. Aside from stating blandly that "Pocock observes most of the difficulties [facing the historian of ideas] very acutely and is not overcome with doubt," Oakeshott merely uses his short paragraph to restate the importance of sensitivity to "different levels of abstraction" and of combining the concerns of the philosopher and of the historian.[28]

So much for Pocock's agreement with Oakeshott. His more critical engagement with Oakeshott appeared, somewhat ironically, in a 1968 *Festschrift* for Oakeshott on the occasion of his retirement.[29] Here again, Pocock considered the nature of tradition—more specifically, the various ways in which a society imagines itself and its past and in which it interacts with these "self-images." Alongside "Political Education" hover the spectres of two other Oakeshott essays, "Rationalism in Politics" (1947) and "The Activity of Being an Historian" (1958). In the former Oakeshott had narrated the emergence of, and critiqued, what he termed the Rationalist style of politics, contrasting it with an understanding of political activity as a concrete "pattern of behaviour" which can be learned only over multiple generations through imitation and which is not completely, if at all, susceptible of "abridgement" into verbal teachings[30]. Oakeshott's concern in "The Activity of Being a Historian" in many ways rehashes his discussion of history in *Experience and Its Modes* (1933), where he insisted on the insuperable detachment of properly historical inquiry from present-day, or "practical" concerns. This admittedly "severe" manner of thinking thus precluded not only any attempt to extract "lessons" from the past but also such seemingly benign tasks as searching for "origins" of later phenomena—"reading the past backwards."[31] With characteristic penchant for vivid metaphor, Oakeshott described this style of historical inquiry as "obscene necromancy," for it forcibly resuscitates the past, presumed to be dead, and deals with it "as with a man, expecting it to talk sense and have something to say apposite to its plebian 'causes' and engagements."[32] Proper historical inquiry was said only to be "to discover the manner in which one concrete situation is mediated into another,"[33] and thus a proper historian, in Oakeshott's view, treats the past rather "as a mistress of whom he never tires and whom he never expects to talk sense."[34]

Pocock argues that Oakeshott's attitude towards history and historical inquiry must be understood as a strategic position adopted by a "conservative" to counter the historical claims advanced by "radicals." In this, it represents the third stage in a generic process that Pocock characterized in Oakeshott's language as a society "pursuing the intimations" of its traditions. Pocock thus accepted Oakeshott's image of society and tradition, but he took issue with Oakeshott's presumption that pursuing the intimations of tradition would be the simple "unfolding of a consistently traditional 'style' of either thinking or acting." Instead it "will involve us in conflict and contradiction" in which three successive attitudes towards the past can be discerned. First comes the "presumptive" attitude that insists on an unbroken chain of transmission between past and present and hence on the prescriptive authority of what has been inherited, in the manner of the common lawyers of the seventeenth century like Hale. Next comes the "radical" intervention, according to which the authoritative past is shown to be something different and thus to demand a radical change to the status quo. And finally in response to such appeals, the conservative finds it necessary to emphasize the complexity and consequent discontinuity between past and present, for if normative comparisons with the past cannot be made, radical appeals to some lost state of innocence are incoherent. It would seem at this point that the conservative has pulled the rug out from under himself, and hence Pocock calls this the "antinomian and anarchic strain in conservatism."[35] In this "strain," Pocock contextualizes Oakeshott's claim that politics is a concrete and inarticulate "pure style" of behaviour: "Because the intellect cannot grasp the full meaning of any act in the sequence of a tradition, it cannot grasp the whole meaning of the tradition."[36] This and the concomitant claim that the study of history can only be "for its own sake" and not in aid of present practical problems, Pocock further relativizes by claiming they are only possible in times and places of political stability. Various forms of this "antinomian" conservatism combine with various "radical" revisionisms to comprise for Pocock "a dialogue with and within tradition, out of which arises a constant discussion and redefinition of the modes of continuity and authority which link past to present and give the present its structure," making history not so much an Oakeshottian mistress as a wife: "an other self, perpetually explored."[37]

Considering Pocock's engagement with Oakeshott gives us a fuller contextualization of the earlier formation of some of Pocock's important guiding principles about the nature of historical study. Pocock found occasion to revisit Oakeshott's insistence on the gap between past and present at least twice in later years, and in both places advanced the critique first voiced in his 1968 essay.[38] And indeed on this point, in contrast with the earlier point about philosophy, Pocock's critique seems to resonate strongly with Skinner—specifically Skinner's critique of Elton's "cult of the fact."[39] On the other hand, an examination of Pocock's properly historical studies reveals that he continued to find Oakeshott's expressions and metaphors conducive to framing his various historical inquiries. For example, he has spoken in terms of Oakeshott's "conversation of mankind" in both *The Discovery of Islands* and *Barbarism and Religion* and in terms of "the pursuit of intimations" in *The Machiavellian Moment*.[40] In a certain sense, therefore, perhaps we can think of Pocock's voluminous historical writings as suggestive of what Oakeshott might have produced had he pursued the research of a "working historian," as Pocock has referred to himself, rather than the theoretical course his career took. If not, we are at least in a position to understand something of what Pocock meant when, speaking retrospectively in 2009, he mentioned his "deep if limited involvement with the thought of Michael Oakeshott, which I used for my own purposes in ways of which neither he nor his committed followers would have approved."[41]

Before turning to Skinner, I would like briefly to consider Pocock's characterization of Oakeshott as part of the "anarchic and antinomian strain in conservatism." It is certainly true that Oakeshott rejected appeals to historical reconstructions of the past as a justification for political authority. This is to transgress the modal divide between history and practice. You cannot look to the past to guide the present. This may amount to anarchism if Oakeshott does not replace history with an alternative basis for political authority, but in fact Oakeshott did have a theory of authority. Although he had written on the theory of political authority since at least 1929[42] and treated it at length in his 1946 introduction to Hobbes' *Leviathan*,[43] his most thoroughly elaborated theory comes in *On Human Conduct* (1975). There he articulates a version of Hobbes' theory of authority in a twofold manner: first by considering how authority could be determined within the system of laws itself, and second by considering how the authority of the system itself could be determined.[44] The first task was simple enough. Oakeshott explains how any legal system will contain procedural rules that can determine whether any given utterance by an office-holder is authoritative. One simply has to investigate whether the utterance accords with the constituting rules of the relevant office. But as to the authority of *those* rules Oakeshott has less to say. He writes:

> This authority cannot be acquired in a once-and-for-all endowment but only in the continuous acknowledgement of *cives* who are familiar with the distinction between recognizing a rule and subscribing to its conditions, discerning its utility, or giving approval to what it prescribes ... authority is the only conceivable attribute [civil association] could be indisputably acknowledged to have.[45]

The foundation of authority, then, is simply everyone's recognition of it. In response to Hanna Pitkin's critical review of *On Human Conduct*, Oakeshott elaborated this theory in plainer terms, noting that civil association did not require any particular constitution—monarchy, aristocracy, or democracy, for instance—because "this constitution will reflect contingent beliefs about what is to be recognized as authoritative... [civil association] does not postulate democratic participation, but then it does not postulate any particular procedure for making law."[46] So authority rests upon contingent beliefs, and any number of persons or institutions can bear it.

This, then, is Oakeshott's theory of authority. But does it exempt him from the charge of anarchism? Though a *theory* of authority, it is far from a *case* for authority. Consequently, one could still allege that Oakeshott leaves us with no good reason to acknowledge authority. Indeed, Oakeshott concedes as much in his reply to Pitkin: "I said nothing about why anyone should want to be related to others in this manner (that was no part of my business). But I gave reasons for thinking that if human beings were to be compulsorily related to one another, then this was the only kind of relationship that would not affront their moral autonomy."[47] So Oakeshott has no categorical but only a hypothetical case for authority: if you want to live in a civil association, then you must acknowledge an authority—no anarchism—but I am not telling you that you *should* want to live in a civil association. This forbearance on Oakeshott's part likely stems from his sharp distinction between theory and practice. If theory cannot be a guide to conduct, then there are no categorical cases for certain conduct to be made by someone speaking in the mode of history or philosophy. There are only conditional statements. If Oakeshott is an anarchist, then, it is not because he lacks a theory of authority, but because of this fundamental methodological assumption. In the following section, I will suggest that we must look to the third and final section of *On Human Conduct* to see how Oakeshott attempts to overcome this methodological stricture and thereby to avoid the charge of anarchism. The most fruitful way of introducing this section of text is by examining Oakeshott's exchange with Quentin Skinner on the latter's treatment of the modern European state in his *Foundations of Modern Political Thought*—a text which bears a certain relation to the third section of *On Human Conduct*, as I will now explain.

III—Oakeshott and Skinner: The Modern European State

There are two similarities and two differences worth noting between Oakeshott and Skinner. Considering them will suggest a certain interpretation of Oakeshott's attitude to the relation of history, philosophy, and practice and therewith a new approach to the question of history's relation to present concerns. First, Oakeshott and Skinner both emphasized the historical conditions giving rise to the theoretical reflections under their consideration in their historical work—for Skinner, the *Foundations*, for Oakeshott, the third section of *On Human Conduct*. In the preface to *Foundations,* Skinner had stated it as one of his three aims to "practise my own precepts"—to exemplify the method he had advocated in previous articles, which focused less on "leading theorists" than on "ideological superstructures" that formed part of "the more general social and intellectual matrix out of which their works arose."[48] Accordingly, Skinner focused not on canonical figures but on regional trends, with subdivisions not on "Machiavelli" but "The Italian Renaissance," not on "Erasmus" but "The Northern Renaissance," and so on. Likewise, alongside such recognizable names as Dante, Machiavelli, More, and Bodin appear Salutati, Patrizi, Jerome Barlow, William Roy, Mornay, La Noue, and others.

Oakeshott's approach is in a way similar. In his published *Lectures in the History of Political Thought*, parts of which reappear verbatim in *On Human Conduct* and out of which the latter likely grew, Oakeshott did not discuss theoretical reflections until after lecturing on "Medieval Political Experience," "Medieval Government," "Medieval Law," and "Medieval Parliaments" in that order. As he explained in the introductory lecture, it was to be "an historical study" in the sense of "trying to understand and account for these beliefs and ways of thinking by relating them to the circumstances of their appearance"—to understand "the significance of this event, or action, or belief in the context of events and beliefs in which it appears."[49] Indeed, in *On Human Conduct* he seems to spend more time explaining social, ecclesiastical, and political circumstances than he does considering theoretical texts. The elimination of the rival authorities of pope and empire from without and of nobility, customary law, and local government from within is said to "intimate" the concept of state as undivided and absolute sovereign. The extension of royal justice across the checkered legal landscapes of a realm, particularly in France and England, is said to intimate a notion of the state as guarantor of law and order. And both the assumption of spiritual authority by "godly princes" of the magisterial Reformation and frequent wars are said to intimate an understanding of the state as moral instructor of the people and leader of a collective enterprise.[50]

Second, Oakeshott and Skinner shared a concern to explain the modern by reference to the medieval.[51] By halfway through his first chapter, Skinner had already made one of his strongest claims about the state by crediting the jurist Bartolus of Saxoferrato (1314–1357) with the earliest clear intimation of the modern state. In his claim that Italian cities, not just the Emperor, should be recognized as holding in their territory the authority of *imperium* as specified in Roman law, Bartolus intimated the notion of a plurality of sovereigns.[52] Equalling Bartolus in importance for Skinner was another medieval thinker, Marsilius of Padua (1275–1342), who argued against the Church's claim to temporal jurisdiction, setting the "foundations" for its eradication and thus for the concept of sovereignty.[53] Likewise, Skinner was keen to emphasize the reliance of sixteenth-century Scottish and French Calvinist resistance theorists like Beza and Buchanan on fifteenth-century conciliarists like Gerson, as mediated by early sixteenth-century Jesuit Thomists like Suárez and Vitoria.[54] In this, he reiterated an argument that an earlier Cambridge historian, J. N. Figgis, had made, as Mark Goldie has pointed out.[55]

Oakeshott did not discuss conciliarism or Calvinist resistance theories, but he shared the general concern to emphasize the medieval roots of modern political thought, especially Roman law. He stated it as his contention that "the features of a state which evoked these understandings of its character were inherited from the realms and principalities of medieval Europe." Likewise, "it was in the medieval *civitas vel regnum* that [Modern European states'] common character was prefigured."[56] Hence, while the Reformation was important for removing the overlapping sovereignty of the Church, the earlier extension of royal adjudication across the patchwork of local customary law was equally important in fostering an understanding of the state in terms of legal relationships rather than the "undefined moral and prudential guardianships" of feudal lords—the notion of *lex facit regnum* found in thirteenth-century jurists Bracton and Beaumanoir.[57] And intimating a different but equally pervasive notion of the state was the Roman legal concept of corporation, or *universitas*. A "familiar feature of medieval life from the twelfth century," *universitas* intimated a notion of the state as "united in respect of a common purpose" which would reappear in certain later theories of the state, such as the Lutheran "godly prince."[58] Like Skinner, then, Oakeshott pinned the roots of the modern state in medieval jurists.[59]

Despite these similarities, Oakeshott reviewed Skinner's *Foundations* quite critically, centring around two main objections. The first was that Skinner assumed "a single 'recognizably modern concept of the state'" and retrospectively sought its "foundations" in the history he narrated.[60] Indeed, Skinner had offered little justification for adopting as his *telos* Weber's "famous definition" of the state as "the sole source of law and legitimate force within its own territory, and as the sole appropriate object of its citizens' allegiances."[61] By contrast, Oakeshott had concluded in *On Human Conduct* that historically speaking there was no concept of the state. The "state" was rather "an unresolved tension between the two irreconcilable dispositions represented by the words *societas* and *universitas*."[62] Concepts borrowed from Roman law, *societas* signified an association of individuals bound by common recognition of the authority of law understood as instrumental "conditions of conduct" in the custody and administration of a duly constituted government, while *universitas* signified association in terms of a common substantive purpose where law was instrumental towards that end.[63] Hence "the upshot of these centuries of political thought was not the emergence of a single 'recognizably modern concept of the State' but a variety of disparate conceptions, continuously resuscitated and reformulated in later times."[64] The state was thus "an ambivalent experience," "a polarized consciousness,"[65] an "interminable enterprise" distinguished by "the inconclusiveness of its outcome."[66] Skinner has since expressed regret about his approach, saying he was "wrong … in using a metaphor that virtually commits one to writing teleologically. My own book is far too much concerned with the origins of our present world when I ought to have been trying to represent the world I was examining in its own terms as far as possible."[67] It thus seems reasonable in this way to treat Oakeshott's conceptually fluid historical study in *On Human Conduct* as a very "Cambridge School" approach to the history of political thought. Imagining this history to be nothing more than a "conversation," as Oakeshott does, helps one avoid imposing any fictitious order on texts.[68]

So much for Oakeshott's first criticism. His second criticism reveals a starker difference between the two. Skinner went "too far" by suggesting that "the whole of 'political thought'" could be categorized as "ideological" writings concerned with "mere justification" of what rulers have done or what would-be rulers have claimed, because such categorization left out "philosophical reflexion."[69] As Pocock had considered and accepted, Oakeshott was insisting on the distinction between ideological political argument and properly philosophical reflection. Skinner's response is worth quoting:

> Michael Oakeshott was only the most distinguished of several hostile critics who berated me for failing to understand that 'genuine' political theory occupies an autonomous philosophical realm. (Nor was he the only critic to make things easier for himself by inserting his preferred conclusion into his premises.) Since then, however, times have changed; and very much for the better, I think. None of the contributors to the present volume seems

to find any difficulty with my cardinal assumption that, because in political argument there is nothing but the battle, the idea of being above the battle makes little sense.[70]

Skinner rightly observes that Oakeshott did not argue for so much as assert the possibility of "autonomous" political theory. However, aside from appealing to the handful of contributors to *Rethinking the Foundations* neither does Skinner make any attempt to justify his "essentially Nietzschean" "cardinal assumption," which here is also his conclusion, that "there is nothing but the battle." The two thus reach a fundamental impasse. Skinner was doubtless aware of what he was doing and that others, including perhaps most would-be contributors to a hypothetical similar volume on Oakeshott, could easily be found who would disagree with his cardinal assumption. It therefore seems appropriate to take Skinner as exemplifying his very point that "there is nothing but the battle." At a certain level of fundamentality, there can be no more reasoning—at the level of "cardinal assumptions" there is nothing but the battle, and the side with the larger or otherwise more intimidating army usually wins.

I wish to suggest that, notwithstanding his insistence on the "autonomy" of philosophy, Oakeshott actually shares this position with Skinner in a sense, and that once we understand this, we can understand what he is doing in *On Human Conduct* and, in conclusion, the direction it points the discipline of the history of political thought and the implication for political authority. Fittingly, Oakeshott's writings on Nietzsche are helpful for reaching this understanding, but before considering them, it is necessary to revisit *On Human Conduct*. In addition to the circumstantial factors such as law and war considered above, Oakeshott had sought to contextualize his history of political thought in terms of the psychological experience of modern man, which he mapped onto a spectrum of "moral dispositions." On one side is the disposition to "cultivate freedom" and "enjoy individuality," to understand life as "an adventure in personal self-enactment" which animates particularly those energized by the changed conditions of what would become understood as modernity. This is the disposition "of younger sons making their own way in a world which had little place for them, of foot-loose adventurers who left the land to take to trade, of town-dwellers who had emancipated themselves from the communal ties of the countryside, of vagabond scholars" and so on.[71] Such a disposition inclines towards a conception of the state that corresponds with *societas*. On the other side, inclining towards *universitas*, is the "individual *manqué*,"[72] characterized by "incapacity to sustain an individual life" and "longing for the shelter of a community."[73] Oakeshott acknowledges that such a person could perhaps not be "merely weak or insecure" but rather a victim of misfortune and aware of his own inability to "make good his loss" alone, but Oakeshott's seems more concerned to define this disposition in terms of "anxiety" and a "small seed of resentment" towards freedom.[74]

It is not difficult to guess which disposition Oakeshott favours. Indeed, he confirms one guess when he characterizes the "individual *manqué*" as "a relic of servility of which it is proper for European peoples to be profoundly ashamed,"[75] despite having just voiced a concern "not to prejudice the investigation" of *societas* and *universitas*.[76] The trouble is that he gives indications that his undertaking in *On Human Conduct* is to be classed as historical understanding and thus free of moral judgment. Referring to his possibly unsatisfying conclusion about the state he writes, "the temptation remains to seek a more general explanation of this ambivalence than a *historical understanding* can provide."[77] It seems unlikely that Oakeshott was oblivious to this tension. Indeed, he concluded the book by saying:

> In short if, somewhat improperly, something more were sought than a historical account of how the character of a modern European state and the office of its government came to be understood in terms of the diverse analogies of *societas* and *universitas* then perhaps it may be found in translating this divergence into the language of contingent human dispositions.[78]

This is his final word and he cryptically sneaks it in without elaboration. It seems to indicate that readers are meant to take the disquisition on dispositions, which formed a rather crucial part of the exploration of the character of a modern European state, as a "somewhat improper" appendix to the historical inquiry. How Oakeshott intended for it to be understood is unclear, but certain of his other writings might suggest an answer.

A possible explanation might involve Oakeshott's aestheticism. In *On Human Conduct,* Oakeshott had identified *Leviathan* as one of only a few masterpieces that attained the highest level of abstract thought, philosophy, by most successfully attempting to consider political experience on the "map of total experience" and "relatively undistracted by extraneous considerations."[79] Nonetheless, writing in 1947 he labelled it a "myth" that reached "the level of literature" with the consequence that "a more direct, less subtle consequence may be expected to spring ... not an access of imaginative power, but an increase of knowledge; it will prompt and it will instruct."[80] Specifically, *Leviathan* "recalls man to his littleness, his imperfection, his mortality, while at the same time recognizing his importance to himself."[81] Oakeshott understood Nietzsche's philosophical writings to have the same artistic quality: "if we are to understand Nietzsche," he wrote in 1948, "we must understand him as, in this sense, an artist." "In art, insight (diagnosis) is an end in itself. The remedy is not something that *follows*: if it is anywhere it lies in the diagnosis itself, in the removal of the corrupt consciousness."[82] So philosophy that rises to the level of art can be both "above the battle" and instructive.[83] The way Oakeshott would have us to understand *Leviathan* and Nietzsche, then, is as multi-vocal—written in the mode of philosophy as well as that of art.

We may now return to the interpretive problem in *On Human Conduct*. I wish to suggest that it may likewise be understood as multi-vocal, but written in the two modes of *history* and art rather than *philosophy* and art. It could be that alongside his historical goals Oakeshott harboured an artistic goal—to make a work of art which contained an oblique "diagnosis" of the inclination towards the individual *manqué* and which commended *societas* aesthetically by associating it with a certain disposition—the character of the heroic individual. On this reading, he would be, like Skinner has imagined himself, a present-minded archaeologist (though subtler, or more devious, for not acknowledging it so clearly).[84] For he had said elsewhere that the current categories of Left and Right "merely represent an insignificant squabble about the common purpose to be imposed upon a state already assumed to be a purposive association."[85] In other words, the consensus view of the state is that it is some sort of *universitas*; *societas* is the relic that needs to be unearthed and recommended, like republican freedom for Skinner.[86] Oakeshott commends it not as a "model" to "apply" or a "doctrine" to "follow" but as a work of art to behold. Perhaps he sought to move his readers on an aesthetic level—or what Aristotle, one of Oakeshott's favourite philosophers, would call the level of *ethos*. This is not to suggest that Oakeshott had a hidden agenda. He likely would have been content with an aesthetic accomplishment. But it's also fair to wager he would not have been disappointed if, being thus moved, his readers began to favour a conception of themselves as heroic individuals and consequently a conception of the state as *societas*. So, did Oakeshott really fancy himself to be "above the battle"? Yes and no. Part of *On Human Conduct* is strictly historical and in that sense unconcerned with practical affairs (though it is not always abundantly clear where history ends and mythologizing begins). What I have suggested is that Oakeshott's slips into the artistic mode may reasonably be understood as a modest punch thrown.

IV—CONCLUSION

I hope we can now see how both Nardin and Runciman were right in their characterizations of Oakeshott's relation to the Cambridge School. Saying we can read Oakeshott as "inspiring," Pocock and Skinner probably commits Nardin to too much, given that Pocock's interest in tradition and historiographical thought dates to his doctoral study, which he commenced before any of Oakeshott's relevant essays were published. Moreover, there's no evidence that Skinner took any cues from Oakeshott except what may have been mediated by Pocock. Nonetheless, Nardin was right in as much as Oakeshott's thought was and continues to be an important reference point for understanding Pocock's thought and can even be said to have shaped his historical imagination in some way.

Coming to Runciman, an attempt to connect the claims made in this essay to the broader "state of the discipline" must be made in closing. Runciman's characterization came in the context of his attempt to understand the "apparent turnaround" whereby the initial Cambridge School proscription of any attempt to take instruction from historical texts had since become used to recommend taking instruction from these new historians themselves.[87] Runciman seems to dismiss Peter Janssen's contribution to this turnaround on the grounds that Janssen relied on Oakeshott's sense of the artistic value (the "remedy" for the "corrupt consciousness") of reading certain texts but failed to note that on Oakeshott's own terms this cannot involve properly historical inquiry and hence is irrelevant to any consideration of the history of political thought. Indeed, it cannot. But as I have tried to illustrate, in *On Human Conduct* Oakeshott seems to have found a way, in spite of himself, to blend history with some sort of mythologizing, literary philosophy. The direction this would point the discipline is as follows. If a historian should wish to recommend, say, a neo-Roman concept of republican liberty, unearthed via proper historical scholarship, perhaps he should rely less on appeals to popular consensus or changing times and instead collaborate with, or become himself, a poet.[88]

To return finally to Pocock's allegation and the question of authority, it must be acknowledged that Oakeshott forbore from offering a justification of authority deduced from some universal first principle. He was too much of a philosophical sceptic and anti-foundationalist to do so. Where he could not appeal to a first principle of reason, he instead appealed to disposition. I think it is reasonable to read Oakeshott as avowing that the only possible "foundation" for philosophy is the disposition of the philosopher. Hence every part of his theory of civil association, including his theory of authority, will trace ultimately to the disposition associated with it, as opposed to that associated with enterprise association. One may still wish to assert that this amounts to anarchism and antinomianism, but the simple denial of practical appeals to history is insufficient grounds for such an assertion, once Oakeshott's theory of authority is considered in the way I have suggested. Finally, if Oakeshott is to be read as a liberal (and I think it is not unreasonable to understand his "civil association" as a species of liberal polity, justified explicitly in terms of "moral autonomy"), then his has to be a philosophically sceptical, anti-foundationalist liberalism rooted in a certain disposition, a certain character type of modern man which it is therefore proper to commend aesthetically.

Notes

1. See Mark Bevir, "The Contextual Approach," in *The Oxford Handbook of the History of Political Philosophy*, ed. George Klosko (Oxford: Oxford University Press, 2011), 11–23. The term Cambridge School can be misleading, since it signifies only general agreement among some but not all historians at Cambridge that the study of political thought should be primarily historical and since the various "members" of the school disagree about much else. Nonetheless, it has still been found useful as a term to represent the initial methodological intervention and the range of reinterpretations it prompted. For a nuanced recent assessment of the Cambridge School, see Richard Bourke, "Revising the Cambridge School: Republicanism Revisited," *Political Theory* 46, no. 3 (2016), 467–77.
2. Terry Nardin, *The Philosophy of Michael Oakeshott* (University Park, PA: Pennsylvania State University Press, 2001), 12. Paul Franco can likewise claim that "Oakeshott's critique of anticipations here anticipates (if I

may be excused the solecism) Q. Skinner's critique of the 'mythology of *prolepsis*.'" See Paul Franco, *The Political Philosophy of Michael Oakeshott* (New Haven: Yale University Press, 1990), 246n36.

3. David Runciman, "History of Political Thought: The State of the Discipline," *British Journal of Politics and International Relations* 3, no. 1 (2001), 89.

4. Kenneth Minogue, "The History of Political Thought Seminar," in *The Achievement of Michael Oakeshott*, ed. Jesse Norman (London: Duckworth, 1993), 88. Skinner is said to have presented an early version of "Meaning and Understanding" at the LSE political thought seminar convened by Oakeshott. Luke O'Sullivan, *Oakeshott on History* (Exeter: Imprint Academic, 2003), 170.

5. J.G.A. Pocock, *The Discovery of Islands: Essays in British History* (Cambridge: Cambridge University Press, 2005), 281.

6. Michael Oakeshott, "The Foundations of Modern Political Thought," *The Historical Journal* 23, no. 2 (1980), 449–53.

7. There is a further dimension to the nexus between Skinner and Oakeshott that is also underexplored but which I will have to omit for lack of space, and that is their shared interest in the philosophy of R.G. Collingwood. Skinner has more than once acknowledged his debt to Collingwood and has written somewhat extensively on him. Oakeshott's debt to Collingwood is well treated, but a comparison between Oakeshott and Skinner's historical epistemology as alternative appropriations of Collingwood could be illuminating.

8. See, e.g., Luke O'Sullivan, "Oakeshott on European Political History," *History of Political Thought* 21, no. 1 (2000), 132–51; Terry Nardin, *The Philosophy of Michael Oakeshott* (2001); David Boucher, "Oakeshott, Freedom and Republicanism," *British Journal of Politics and International Relations* 7 (2005), 81–96; and Eric Kos, *Michael Oakeshott, the Ancient Greeks, and the Philosophical Study of Politics* (Exeter: Imprint Academic, 2007), 124–36.

9. O'Sullivan and Nardin have a few scattered paragraphs on similarities and differences between Oakeshott, Skinner, and Pocock on the modern state, language, intentions, and the possibility of philosophy. Terry Nardin, "Rhetoric and Political Language," in *The Cambridge Companion to Oakeshott*, ed. Efraim Podoksik (Cambridge: Cambridge University Press, 2011), 178, 182; O'Sullivan, *Oakeshott on History* (2003), 231–33, 170–73.

10. Podoksik ed., *The Cambridge Companion to Oakeshott* (2011); Paul Franco and Leslie Marsh eds., *A Companion to Michael Oakeshott* (University Park, PA: Penn State University Press, 2012).

11. Martyn Thompson, "Michael Oakeshott on the History of Political Thought," in *A Companion to Michael Oakeshott*, eds. Franco and Marsh (2012), 197–216.

12. James Tully ed., *Meaning & Context: Quentin Skinner and His Critics* (Cambridge: Cambridge University Press, 1988); D.N. DeLuna ed., *The Political Imagination in History: Essays Concerning J.G.A. Pocock* (Baltimore: Owlworks, 2006).

13. James Alexander, "The Cambridge School, *c.*1875–*c.*1975," *History of Political Thought* 37, no. 2 (2016), 360–86. See also James Alexander, "An Essay on Historical, Philosophical, and Theological Attitudes to Modern Political Thought," *History of Political Thought* 25 (2004), 116–48.

14. Quentin Skinner, "Surveying the *Foundations*: A Retrospect and Reassessment," in *Rethinking the Foundations of Modern Political Thought*, eds. Annabel Brett and James Tully (Cambridge: Cambridge University Press, 2006), 244; David Runciman, "History of Political Thought" (2001).

15. J.G.A. Pocock, "The History of Political Thought: A Methodological Inquiry," in *Political Thought and History: Essays on Theory and Method* (Cambridge: Cambridge University Press, 2009), 3–19 (originally appeared in *Philosophy, Politics and Society* [Second Series], eds. Peter Laslett and W.G. Runciman [Oxford: Oxford University Press, 1962], 183–202); "Time, Institutions and Action: An Essay on Traditions and Their Understanding," in *Political Thought and History*, 187–216 (originally appeared in *Politics and Experience: Essays Presented to Professor Michael Oakeshott on the Occasion of His Retirement*, eds. P. King and B.C. Parekh [Cambridge: Cambridge University Press, 1968], 209–37).

16. Michael Oakeshott, "Political Education," in *Rationalism in Politics and Other Essays* (London: Methuen, 1962), 111–36.

17. Oakeshott, "Political Education," 118.

18. Ibid.

19. Ibid., 121.

20. See J.G.A. Pocock, *The Ancient Constitution and the Feudal Law: A Study of English Historical Thought in the Seventeenth Century* (Cambridge: Cambridge University Press, 1957); "Burke and the Ancient Constitution—A Problem in the History of Ideas," *The Historical Journal* 3, no. 2 (1960), 125–43. For consideration of Pocock and Oakeshott on tradition, see James Alexander, "Three Rival Views of Tradition (Arendt, Oakeshott and MacIntyre)," *Journal of the Philosophy of History* 6 (2012), 20–43; and "A Systematic Theory of Tradition," *Journal of the Philosophy of History* 10 (2016), 1–28.

21. Pocock, "The History of Political Thought: A Methodological Inquiry," 5.
22. Oakeshott, "Political Education," 132.
23. Pocock, "The History of Political Thought: A Methodological Inquiry," 12.
24. Oakeshott, "Political Education," 130.
25. Pocock, "The History of Political Thought: A Methodological Inquiry," 17.
26. Ibid., 18.
27. Quentin Skinner, "Meaning and Understanding in the History of Ideas," *History and Theory* 8, no. 1 (1969), 3–53; "Surveying the *Foundations*," 244.
28. Michael Oakeshott, Review of P. Laslett and W.G. Runciman, *Philosophy, Politics and Society* (Second Series), *The Philosophical Quarterly* 15, no. 60 (1965), 281–82.
29. Pocock, "Time, Institutions and Action" (see Note 14 above).
30. Oakeshott, "Rationalism in Politics," in *Rationalism in Politics*, 1–36.
31. Oakeshott, "The Activity of Being a Historian," in *Rationalism in Politics*, 160, 166.
32. Ibid., 166.
33. Ibid., 160.
34. Ibid., 166.
35. Pocock, "Time, Institutions and Action," 215.
36. Ibid.
37. Ibid., 216.
38. J.G.A. Pocock, Review of M. Oakeshott, *On History*, *Times Literary Supplement* (21 October 1983), 1155; "The Historian as Political Actor in Polity, Society and Academy," in *Political Thought and History*, 217.
39. Skinner, "The Practice of History and the Cult of the Fact," in *Visions of Politics* (Cambridge: Cambridge University Press, 2012), vol. I "Regarding Method," 8–26.
40. J.G.A. Pocock, *The Discovery of Islands* (2005), 281; *Barbarism and Religion* (Cambridge: Cambridge University Press, 2010), vol. 5, 304; *The Machiavellian Moment: Florentine Political Thought and the Atlantic Republican Tradition* (Princeton and Oxford: Princeton University Press, 2003 [1975]), viii.
41. Pocock, "Introduction," in *Political Thought and History* (2009), x.
42. Michael Oakeshott, "The Authority of the State," originally published in *The Modern Churchman* 19 (1929–1930), 313–27. Subsequently reprinted in *Religion, Politics and the Moral Life* (New Haven: Yale University Press, 2011).
43. Thomas Hobbes, *Leviathan*, ed. Michael Oakeshott (Oxford: Basil Blackwell, 1946).
44. Michael Oakeshott, *On Human Conduct* (Oxford: Oxford University Press, 1975), 149–54.

45. Ibid., 154.
46. Michael Oakeshott, "On Misunderstanding Human Conduct: A Reply to My Critics," *Political Theory* 4, no. 3 (1976), 355–56.
47. Ibid., 355.
48. Quentin Skinner, *The Foundations of Modern Political Thought*, 2 vols. (Cambridge: Cambridge University Press, 1978), I, x.
49. Michael Oakeshott, *Lectures in the History of Political Thought*, eds. Luke O'Sullivan and Terry Nardin (Exeter: Imprint Academic, 2006), 31.
50. Oakeshott, *On Human Conduct*, 206–24.
51. For the narratives of discontinuity that this approach targeted see Mark Goldie, "The Context of *The Foundations*," in *Rethinking the Foundations of Modern Political Thought*, eds. Annabel Brett and James Tully, 12–15.
52. Skinner, *The Foundations of Modern Political Thought*, I, 11.
53. Skinner, *The Foundations of Modern Political Thought*, I, 18–22.
54. Skinner, *The Foundations of Modern Political Thought*, II, 114–23.
55. Goldie, "The Context of *The Foundations*," 17.
56. Oakeshott, *On Human Conduct*, 206.
57. Ibid., 213.
58. Ibid., 215.
59. On the importance of the Roman tradition for Oakeshott more generally, see Boucher, "Oakeshott, Freedom, and Republicanism" (2005).
60. Oakeshott, "The Foundations of Modern Political Thought," 451–52.
61. Skinner, *The Foundations of Modern Political Thought*, I, x.
62. Oakeshott, *On Human Conduct*, 201.
63. Ibid., 201–6.
64. Oakeshott, "The Foundations of Modern Political Thought," 453.
65. Oakeshott, *On Human Conduct*, 320.
66. Ibid., 189.
67. See Goldie, "The Context of *The Foundations*," 12.
68. Perhaps this is why Pocock has occasionally invoked Oakeshott's metaphor of "conversation" (see Note 26 above). For Oakeshott on conversation, see "The Voice of Poetry in the Conversation of Mankind," in *Rationalism in Politics*, 197–247.
69. Oakeshott, "The Foundations of Modern Political Thought," 449–50.
70. Skinner, "Surveying *the Foundations*," 244.
71. Oakeshott, *On Human Conduct*, 239–41.
72. Ibid., 279.
73. Ibid., 276.
74. Ibid., 277.
75. Ibid., 321.
76. Ibid., 317.

77. Ibid., 323.
78. Ibid., 326.
79. See, e.g., Ibid., 109. It is important to note that, although *On Human Conduct* was written almost thirty years after "Leviathan: *A Myth*," Oakeshott still refers to *Leviathan* there as "a work of art," at 252, as he had in the earlier piece.
80. Oakeshott, "Leviathan: *A Myth*" [1947], in *Hobbes on Civil Association* (Oxford: Oxford University Press, 1974), 150–54.
81. Ibid., 154.
82. Oakeshott, Review of Janko Lavrin, *Nietzsche: An Approach* (London, 1948), in *The Concept of a Philosophical Jurisprudence: Essays and Reviews, 1926–51*, ed. Luke O'Sullivan (Exeter: Imprint Academic, 2007), 224–25.
83. It is unclear whether Oakeshott thought Nietzsche was "above the battle." Elsewhere he referred to him as a "profound philosophical thinker" yet "whose natural voice is that of the prophet rather than that of the philosopher." Ibid., 136.
84. Quentin Skinner, *Liberty Before Liberalism* (Cambridge: Cambridge University Press, 1998), x, 112.
85. Oakeshott, "Talking Politics," in *Rationalism in Politics and Other Essays* (Indianapolis: Liberty Fund Books, 1991), 459, as cited in Nardin, "Rhetoric and Political Language," 182.
86. Assuming Boucher is right to liken Oakeshott's *societas* to Skinner's republicanism, then this claim would support his. See Boucher, "Surveying the *Foundations*, Freedom, and Republicanism" (2005).
87. Runciman, "History of Political Thought," 88.
88. See Sophie Smith, "The Nature of Politics. Political Science in Early Modern England," Lecture, Quentin Skinner Lecture and Colloquium 2017, Cambridge University, Cambridge, UK, June 9, 2017, for a similar critique of John Rawls drawing from a reading of Hobbes in the light of contemporary rhetoric and drama.

CHAPTER 8

Michael Oakeshott's Political Realism

Gülşen Seven

The daemon of Socrates, according to the Apology, would sometimes hold him back, but it never urged him forward.[1]

I

Most of us, most of the time, find the attempt to understand politics both hard and unrewarding. We are usually content to respond to immediate practical necessities as they arise, using the means at hand as effectively as we can. When our myopic understanding of politics produces catastrophic results, however, we might feel the need "to stand back from the pressing concerns of immediate political practice and ask how the toolbox can be improved."[2] Political theorists do this by reflecting on the state of their art. Discussions concerning moralism and realism in political theory is one of the most recent forms such reflection has taken on how to do political theory, so it can lead to better political understanding.

G. Seven (✉)
Department of Political Science and International Relations,
TED University, Ankara, Turkey
e-mail: gulsen.seven@tedu.edu.tr

© The Author(s) 2019
E. S. Kos (ed.), *Michael Oakeshott on Authority, Governance, and the State*, Palgrave Studies in Classical Liberalism,
https://doi.org/10.1007/978-3-030-17455-2_8

Bernard Williams and Raymond Geuss, to whom we owe the renewed interest in the term realism, originally utilized it as a yardstick to judge the state of much of contemporary political theory.[3] They raised forceful objections to the dominant political philosophy's failure to engage with the real world of politics and political practice in a satisfactory manner. Instead of models of political theory that attempt to understand politics on the basis of the priority of the moral to the political and treat politics "something like an applied morality," they insisted on approaches to political theory that will give "greater autonomy to distinctively political thought."[4] Many diverse thinkers, since then, have expressed sympathy for their judgement that political theory, if it is to aid political understanding, should begin to develop an understanding of politics not with an external specification of moral ideals that are to regulate the political realm, but from within political practice itself.[5] It should *be* political, instead of attempting to "displace" or "abolish" politics.[6] This entails, above all, bridging the increasingly widening gap between political philosophy and the "real world," making political theory more attentive to the realities of politics and reconsidering political theory's relationship to political practice and context. This general call for a reorientation of political theory and a reconceptualization of the relationship between political theory and political practice constitutes the minimum agreement among the realists. It has been interpreted in a myriad of different ways in relation to variety of theoretical positions which are supposed to be compatible with realism to various degrees.[7] Consequently, the literature on political realism has grown exponentially.

Substantially, the literature has focused on debates on the degree of autonomy the political sphere does and can enjoy (the two extreme positions being that politics is completely autonomous from any other field and that, despite some distinctiveness, politics is still related to other fields)[8]; on the very meaning of the autonomy of the political[9]; on possible opposites of realism (including discussions on ideal and non-ideal theory as well as utopianism and anti-utopianism)[10]; on the moods, especially optimism and pessimism, that accompany each form of political theorizing[11]; on the need to emphasize allegedly fundamental, ineradicable features of politics that any realist theory should take into account (including political disagreement, conflict, and centrality of power) and the concomitant need to reorient political theory away from justice to concerns with legitimacy and away from entertaining the prospects of finding a well-ordered society to accepting *modus vivendi* arrangements as the only attainable practical possibility[12]; on how to conceive the real (factually? empirically? normatively? affectively?) and how it bears on political theorizing (desirability concerns and feasibility constraints)[13]; on the centrality of political understanding and judgement to realistic political theory[14]; on action-guiding aspects and prospects of political theory; on the critical purchase of realism on politics[15]; on realism's ideological nature (liberal, socialist, radical, conservative)[16]; and on realism's prospects as a coherent affirmative and substantive political position as opposed to being just a critical outlook or a set of methodological tools.[17]

These diverse positions and approaches compatible with political realism have themselves been subject to several scholarly analyses.[18] Some of these, attempting to do full justice to the heterogeneity of the movement, have provided rival realist topographies, which disagree about what exactly characterizes realism, while others have sought to impose some kind of order on the basis of some specifiable criteria of classification.[19] Of the latter type, many allude to an incompatibility between realism's critical implications and its action-guiding aspirations.[20] In particular, they identify a tension between realism's general scepticism about the role of theory in the world of real politics and its own desire to be more relevant. They resolve this tension by dividing the realisms on offer in contemporary political theory into two categories, depending on whether they aspire to interpret the world correctly or to change it. I think, for truly realistic approaches, such as those of John Dunn and Raymond Geuss, this is a false dichotomy. In order to show this, in the second part of the essay, I provide yet another typology of political realism, by taking its action-guiding aspiration as its constitutive component. Instead of two, I argue that three categories of realistic approaches are identifiable: those that see no relationship between theory and practice, assuming like Michael Oakeshott that the world can only be interpreted *theoretically* (or separately, *practically*); those that consider the relationship between theory and practice to be simple, such as non-ideal theories, which trust that right theory can change the world, and, finally, those of John Dunn and Raymond Geuss, who emphasize the centrality of political judgement in politics, and hold that understanding the world and changing the world are not necessarily mutually exclusive *theoretical* ambitions. Since my overall aim is to suggest that only those who transcend the understanding/changing dichotomy are truly realistic thinkers, in the third part of the essay, I reflect on Michael Oakeshott's realism and consider the challenge his strict separation between theory and practice poses to the likes of Dunn and Geuss. If Oakeshott's challenge is compelling, then realistic political theory should not, perhaps, aspire to be action-guiding.[21] I argue, nevertheless, that Oakeshott's position is closer to that of Dunn and Geuss than it seems to be at the outset. A lot, however, hangs on what we take "change," "prescription" and "action-guidance" to be.

II

According to realists, moralism encompasses theoretical positions premised on the assumption that it is in principle possible to fashion ourselves, as human agents, and the world we live in, using a model of what ideally ought to be the case.[22] What ought to be the case can be discovered by appeal to the supposedly autonomous field of ethics containing pure moral precepts allegedly unsullied by the vagaries of historical reality. Observance of these pre-historical and pre-political ethical injunctions in conducting ourselves and in fashioning the institutions through which we must act in real historical circumstances would ensure better outcomes in our collective political life.

Realism, in contrast, starts with the recognition that any attempt to provide guidance to human beings must take them as historically located agents in their historically contingent circumstances. In other words, it must start with what "is" the case as opposed to what "ought to be" the case both in relation to human agency and to the causal properties of the environment within which they must act. This entails recognizing that the desires, beliefs, values, motivations and interests they hold, as well as the institutional structures through which they must act to realize these, vary historically. Any realist theoretical construct aiming to guide human actions must reflect and respond to this dynamism and historical variation. The first step towards this is acknowledging the stark truth that there are no grand recipes for guiding human actions within the political domain. All there is, is historical individuals creating historical realities through their actions at all times. Realism, thus understood, is all about the importance of history as well as centrality of human agency for politics.[23]

Such a broad view of realism makes it compatible with various non-moralising positions.[24] In this section, I offer a classificatory scheme based on different conceptualizations of the relationship between political theory and political practice. For my analysis of how different strands of realism conceive of this relationship, I study what they consider as politics, political practice or the real in general terms and how they understand the real to bear on political theory or the practice of political theorising. The combined question I use to classify various realisms on offer in contemporary political theory, then, is: "How does the real require us to answer the question 'What is to be done?'" Three answers, I suggest, can be distinguished, analytically. These are answers associated with what I shall call paralysing, neutral and activist realisms.[25] For paralysing realists, the real is a constant reminder that political theory, rather unfortunately, cannot do much to influence political practice despite all good intentions, hence their desperation in the face of reality; for neutral realists, the real is a limiting factor on what can be achieved theoretically and politically; and finally, for activist realists, the real is the only hope we have for improving our political theory and concomitantly our political practice by taking it seriously and developing a better perspective of the relationship between political theory and political practice.

I shall briefly say something about each of these variants of realism.

Paralysing realism is the antithesis of activist realism and conceives the human world as largely impervious to individual agency. Paralysing realists are usually pessimists who hold that people simply act the way they do for a variety of different reasons in a variety of different circumstances and nothing much can be done about it. More specifically, there is a denial that society could ever be improved in some substantial way. A strong version of this view is based on a denial of the possibility that people can be educated to form wiser political judgements that would enhance the outcomes of their collective actions. A weak version denies specifically that political *theory* can be of any help to educate people to form better judgements. What inhibits paralysing realists from entertaining this possibility is the solid and impermeable nature of some fundamental constraints on human political aspirations and on the collective action necessary to bring them about. While different theories that fall within the bounds of this type of realism may identify and emphasise as significant different set of constraints, the ones most alluded to can be grouped into two depending on whether the emphasis is on the structural properties of the causal world within which humans need to act, or on human failure itself due to some of the natural, psychological, or motivational aspects of human agency. The first group of theories usually appeal to the inevitable intractability of the world as one of the greatest obstacles towards educating people to form better political judgements.

Put simply, these theories claim that the world is too complex to be understood by any individual, no matter how impressive one's cognitive and intellectual powers are. The world is simply beyond our epistemic grasp. The second group of theories place the emphasis on what they take to be unalterable historical universals and deficiencies of humans as expressed, for instance, in the Hobbesian perception that human beings are capable of great cruelty or in the judgement that conflict is a permanent feature of the world.[26] A persistent theme of this view is that encounter with the real is an encounter with the bleakest causal features of the political world and their primary source, human agency itself. A recognition of this should act as a constraint on political ambitions, hopes and aspirations and, in particular, on what people consider to be politically possible. Such a narrowly conceived scope of political possibility leads paralysed realists to endorse the preservation of order, the promotion of stability and *modus vivendi* political arrangements as our highest possible political aspirations.[27] The encounter with the real, in other words, leads to pessimism and paralysis. Such paralysis consists, to be sure, of a degree of apprehension about the fate of humanity, but, more (or perhaps less!) consequentially, it leaves one without sober interest in political philosophy and politics.[28] It gives rise to the politics of resignation.[29] Paralysed theories are, therefore, not very directive at all. They warn us against what perhaps most of us, most of the time, have good reason to fear and be wary of, but they do not provide us with "a steady intellectual instrument for the ultimate understanding of what is really going on politically at any time, or of how we would be wisest to respond to this."[30]

Neutral realism encompasses theoretical articulations that respond to the accusations that political theory is too detached from the real world. This is the sort of realism that has been thrown up by the ideal and non-ideal theory debate.[31] Accepting most of the major premises of the mainstream liberal political paradigm, this family of approaches aims to bring normative political theory of a familiar Rawlsian type closer to the real world by engaging in fact-sensitive normative theorizing, that is, by improving ideal theory through incorporating real features of the world into the act of political theorising itself.[32] Such theories, it is argued, are more likely to be practicable and politically relevant (i.e., capable of being implemented in practice), since they build upon descriptive accounts of the real that are free of philosophical or ideological presuppositions. The very possibility of purely descriptive accounts of the real, is, of course, a highly contested issue among philosophers. For that matter, neutral realism should be understood to encompass a range of more or less realistic political theories. In general, the more fact-sensitive a theory is, the more realistic it is assumed to be. Furthermore, the more relevant the facts about the world are that a political theory incorporates, the more "capable it will be of effectively criticising political circumstances and guide action in the real world."[33]

According to this allegedly scientific understanding of realism, which encourages the empirical study of politics, what is desirable is that political theorists be neutral especially with respect to any evaluative standpoints or normative positions. In a way, it claims to present detached experts' objective reflections on politics and hence is non-committal in respect to their implications for action, except for the kind of actions the empirical facts themselves are taken to recommend. The empirical facts, on this view, are taken to speak for themselves and to determine what is doable in practice. The weak version of neutral realism recommends doing only those things that are doable, while the stronger version suggests one should aspire to do only those things that are doable and act as a constraint on one's aspirations. It, thus, involves chastening the ambitions of normative political theory with the feasibility constraints reality presents political theorists with. This is why this form of realism is considered anti-utopian, though it is hopeful about political reform.[34]

We have seen so far that for both paralysing and neutral realisms the real world is relevant, but only as a potential source of constraint.[35] To a large extent, the difference between the two is the sentiment that accompanies an encounter with the real, which, inevitably, translates into how much influence one expects a theory to exert on political practice. A thorough sense of pessimism and concomitantly high degree of political conservatism characterises paralysing realists, while neutral realists appear to be neither pessimistic nor optimistic in the face of reality. For them, the real world of facts is neither a source of despair nor of hope. Facts are facts, hard and faceless. In this understanding, unlike that of paralysing realism, what leads to political conservatism and a status-quo bias is not an attitude of resignation, but an attitude of neutrality with regard to the real (i.e., facts), if the facts point that way.[36] On the other hand, there is room for reform and incremental change within the existing paradigm, to the extent it is ordained by the empirical realities of the world.

Activist realism, of the three, is perhaps the only one that takes seriously the centrality of human agency in politics and the importance of history for political understanding. A historical perspective is a fundamental prerequisite for understanding politics, because the agents, institutions and discourses which are the subjects of political understanding cannot be separated from their historical context, and, as such, are all historically and contextually variable.[37] It is only at the expense of ignoring this that political theorists, such as paralysing realists, build their theories upon what they claim to be permanent features of the world or fixed universal traits of human beings. Any historically informed political theory cannot afford to take anything as permanently fixed. While it might be difficult to argue against certain propositions regarding our social and political life, such as the inevitability of conflict, historical sensitivity requires us not to absolutise them.[38] In a similar vein, it necessitates recognising and registering that human capacities, motivations and hence actions are extremely varied so that what happens in politics depends, to a large extent, on which one of them will be employed when.[39] Activist realism, for that matter, develops an understanding of politics from the perspective of those who participate in it, that is, from the perspective of the political agents, rather than that of political experts as in neutral realism.[40] It recognises that what happens in politics, in the end, depends on the political judgements of real actors.

With regard to the relationship between political theory and political practice, activist realists subscribe to the view that although there might not be grand, once and for all solutions to political problems and hence, a single, clearly specifiable guide to human action within the political domain, there are many things that can be done at any given time, place and condition to secure better outcomes, or, at least, prevent worse ones. Whether the many things that can be done, will in fact get done in reality and what outcomes they will bring about depend, to a great extent, on what human agents judge to be possible, permissible and desirable in given historical circumstances and how they would choose to act on those judgements. The real, factual or empirical features of the world do not, in this understanding, speak for themselves and ordain certain courses of action. They are always interpreted by human agents as enabling them to realise or preventing them from realising their desires, hopes and aspirations. Our judgements of what is possible, permissible and desirable are, in other words, affected by our interpretation of existing circumstances. This expresses how political judgement is closely related to political innovation and political imagination.[41] A political theory capable of shedding new light on existing circumstances through a reinterpretation of prevailing interpretations or through conceptual innovation, far from supporting the status quo, can, in fact, lead to radical change.[42] While political theory cannot designate a single principle or recipe to alleviate the burden of judgement for human agents, it can help to specify the minimal conditions that a realistically informed political judgement requires. Activist realism, within this framework, should be seen as an attempt to specify conditions for arriving at better political judgements in relation to the question "What is to be done?" in full cognizance of the fact that there are no permanent solutions in politics.

Paralysing, neutral and activist realism are ideal types. Of these, I believe, only activist realism gives us a sketch of a truly realistic theory, because only it invites a realistic reflection on political theory's role *vis-à-vis* political practice and eschews the dichotomy between understanding the world and changing it. If this is true, it seems hard to think of Oakeshott, who adamantly kept theory and practice apart, as a realist. At best, he might be considered a paralysing one, who thought nothing can be done *theoretically* to influence practice. In the next section, I argue, however, that Oakeshott is more at home with the activist realists, like John Dunn and Raymond Geuss than he might at first appear to be, though he would probably not be so much at ease with some of their deliberately polemical vocabulary.

III

For some time, there has been a debate about what would be the most suitable label to characterise Michael Oakeshott. In terms of his political leanings, he has been labelled a liberal, a conservative, or some qualified version of the two such as a "moderate conservative," "sceptical conservative" or a "cold war liberal"[43]; philosophically, he has of course been associated with Idealism[44]; in addition, he has been called a sceptic[45] and, most recently, a realist. The literature on contemporary political realism is, however, remarkably unclear on the subject of Michael Oakeshott's political realism. The few studies that mention Oakeshott as a realist, or as an unacknowledged influence on contemporary realists, agree that what makes him suitable for the label is his disdain for a rationalistic understanding of politics.[46] Among dedicated Oakeshott scholars, the few who call him a realist do so for not so dissimilar reasons.[47] Of these, Terry Nardin, who calls him "a sceptical realist," has developed the most elaborate justification for the suitability of the label and, admirably, attempted to relate his own account to that of the "new realists."[48] According to him, contemporary political realism is basically anti-Rationalism, which, nevertheless, lacks Oakeshottian refinements, especially the political disengagement which comes as a consequence of Oakeshott's insistence on the conceptual separation of theory and practice.[49] Oakeshott, in other words, shares with contemporary realists a critical outlook and an ambition to understand the world rightly (or, at least, less wrongly), but does not share the hope to influence it. Oakeshott insists that understanding the world and changing it are different and separate things, while for contemporary realists the dichotomy between understanding and changing the world is a false one, especially if change is understood realistically. If Nardin is right, then, in order to adjudicate between these rival conceptions of realism, we would have to conclude either that contemporary political realism is terribly confused and should abandon the ambition to be action-guiding, or that Oakeshott can, and does, in fact, qualify as an "activist realist," a category, which, I suggested before, is the only truly realistic one.[50] Since most Oakeshottians are highly likely to find my choice of vocabulary to refer to truly realistic political theory rather unpleasant, let me offer an Oakeshottian rendering of the classificatory scheme I have developed. Then we will be in a better position to evaluate whether and how he fits into the scheme.

An Oakeshottian interpretation of the classificatory scheme of contemporary political realisms would entail, to begin with, reducing the tripartite division into two, since Oakeshott was very fond of dualities, as is evident especially in his postwar writings. Some of the lesser known of these, in relation to moral and political life, are found scattered through *Rationalism in Politics*. These include the distinctions between technical reason or knowledge and practical reason or knowledge[51]; between moral life as "a habit of reflective *thought*" and moral life as "a habit of *affection* and *conduct*;"[52] between reflective morality and customary morality; between a situated, contextual or abstract understanding of rationality and a concrete understanding of rationality.[53] These distinctions resemble the more famous distinctions between faith and scepticism in *The Politics of Faith and Politics of Scepticism*,[54] and between "enterprise association" and "civil association" or *universitas* and *societas* in *On Human Conduct*.[55] There are, as should be obvious, too many of them for us to think that the dyadic pattern is unintentional. Indeed, it is not. Neither the dichotomies, nor the works in question, are unrelated. In his essay "Rationalism in Politics," Oakeshott is at his best as a critic of "the most remarkable intellectual fashion of post-Renaissance Europe," which reduces almost everything in the human world, but especially morality and politics, "to a simple, abstract (and manageable) plot."[56] Oakeshott refers to it as Rationalism. The posthumously published *The Politics of Faith and Politics of Scepticism*, believed to have been written around 1952, is "an attempt to organize into a single expression the diverse arguments of Oakeshott's essays of the 1950s."[57] In it, the politics of faith assumes "almost all the characteristics of rationalism in earlier writings."[58] This time, however, Oakeshott's one-sided polemics against rationalism gives way to a balanced consideration of the value and place of everything the modern predicament has offered the people of Western societies, including rationalism itself, which is now referred to as faith, alongside its counterpart, scepticism. Oakeshott's decisively stated preference for politics of moderation in this work should be seen as a consequence of his philosophical understanding of the modern political predicament. One of the most significant aspects of modern predicament, for Oakeshott, is its complexity. This complexity manifests itself in the ambivalence of our activity and the ambiguity of our vocabulary.[59] Neither the ambivalence nor the ambiguity is beyond our comprehension. There is a pattern, or a character, as Oakeshott prefers to call it, that they both exhibit.[60] The characteristic ambiguity is a product of "the principal polarity of our politics: for the politics of modern Europe the relevant horizons are faith and scepticism."[61] Our political activity, he supposes, oscillates between the extremes of the politics of faith (or rationalism in politics), and the politics of scepticism. The vocabulary we use to make sense of it is similarly "double-tongued, because it serves two masters."[62] This must be one of the principal reasons for Oakeshott's rather unusual, yet careful, choice of terminology in *On Human Conduct*, where he presents *universitas*, or the purposeful association of human beings and *societas* or civil and lawful association of human beings, as two contradictory, yet indispensable, parts of the character of the modern European state.[63]

The identification of ambiguity as a constitutive feature of our moral and political vocabulary is one of the most important Oakeshottian insights, which, if taken seriously, is primarily a warning against the temptation to treat political language as "a tool of inquiry" rather than as "something to be investigated" itself.[64] For Oakeshott, such investigation takes the form of recognising the pull of forces of faith and scepticism, "the principal polarity of our politics," on our language.[65] If we are to understand contemporary political realism in an Oakeshottian spirit, thus, we must consider it in light of the force of these two extremes of our political activity. The politics of faith, for Oakeshott, is characterised by an overoptimistic faith in human perfectibility, through human powers and effort.[66] The organization and direction of the pursuit of perfection is primarily, from this pole, the responsibility of government.[67] The politics of scepticism, on the other hand, originates from the Hobbesian insight about the centrality of conflict among human beings, who live in close proximity to one another, and the concomitant transitoriness of human achievement, especially of social and political order, which is always under threat of decay and even termination.[68] The activity of governing, from the sceptical pole, thus, involves the preservation of this great human achievement of order rather than the pursuit of perfection.[69]

Oakeshott's distinction between faith and scepticism is primarily about politics or, strictly speaking, the activities associated with government and the thoughts which compose our understanding of these activities.[70] If we take political philosophy to be an ordered understanding of our political activity, the realisms on offer in contemporary political theory can be grouped into two depending on whether they are inclined toward faith or scepticism. Let us call these extremes dogmatic realism and sceptical realism, respectively. Dogmatic realism comprises realistic approaches to political theory which are premised on the assumption that political theory can be perfected to such extent that it can guide political practice. What is required for political theory to achieve such perfection is an awareness of relative constraints "the real" places on the ambitions of theory. If these constraints are taken into account by political theorists while developing their normative recommendations or by practitioners of politics while applying abstract normative recommendations to concrete cases, then theory and practice can be brought very close together. For dogmatic realists, now revealed to be identical with neutral realists, the relationship between theory and practice is simple. Some neutral realists might object to my classification on the grounds that they are not believers in perfection, but in improvement. Interestingly, in this regard, Oakeshott does consider the distinction between improvement and perfection only to dismiss it on the grounds that it is impossible to maintain. The real issue here is not about how much improvement they think it is possible but the fact that there is a *telos*. Improvers, he argues, usually deny utopian pretensions. Yet, "those who already know the direction of the 'better' are utopians whether they deny it or not."[71] The issue is that they do not have any hesitation about the direction in which the improvement is to be sought. So, for Oakeshott "the word perfection and its synonyms such as improvement denotes a single, comprehensive condition of human circumstances."[72]

Sceptical realism includes realistic approaches to political theory which express uncertainty about the prospects of improving either theory or practice. It is therefore potentially compatible with both paralysing and activist realisms. For paralysing realists, just as for neutral realists, the real acts as a limitation on the aspirations of political theory, but the limitation it places on it is absolute. There is, they suppose, nothing that can be done *theoretically*, except perhaps expressing a sentiment of despair, defeat and resignation in the face of reality. This is hardly directive of political practice at all. The relationship between theory and practice, thus, is non-existent, just as Oakeshott thought. The real for activist realists, like John Dunn and Raymond Geuss, on the other hand, is as much a source of hope as it is of despair. It is not necessarily constraining. It can, in some cases, be enabling. Which one of the two in practice it will actually be can only be decided in *practice* through the political judgements and actions of political agents. The relationship between theory and practice is complicated, because bridging the gap between the two involves a lot more than simply formulating or applying a set of rules. It involves an attempt to influence the judgements of real political actors.

Oakeshott's determination to argue that theory has *nothing* to offer to real politics seems to set him apart from other sceptical realists like Dunn and Geuss, who believe that theory has *something* to offer, though what it offers might not be conclusive. There are, however, I think, strong reasons against considering Oakeshott a paralysing realist and for considering him closer to Dunn and Geuss than might appear at first. The most important of these is his extremely refined historical sensibility, which he shares with Dunn and Geuss and which underlies their scepticism.[73]

Oakeshott's historical sensibility is strongly expressed in one of the most remarkable aspects of his dyadic understanding of the modern predicament, which is his insistence on the necessity and value of recognising the polarity within which our politics move, without attempting to supersede it. This does not mean that Oakeshott is equidistant to faith and scepticism or *universitas* and *societas*. On more than one occasion, he states his preference for the latter terms in those pairs. He forcefully argues, though, that they are not alternatives to one another, but poles of a single activity, of modern politics.[74] Historical investigation reveals that in practice we find them in different combinations, but never alone. Philosophical investigation of their postulates discloses how, if their excesses are not trimmed by the countervailing effects of the other, they are to end up in self-destruction. The totality of our political experience, therefore, is to be found in *concordia discors* or the discordant harmony between these two poles, rather than in the dogmatic vindication of one at the expense of the other.[75] The harmony is to be found, for Oakeshott, in a moderation of extremes, which is not an exercise in reaching a fixed point, but always a matter of judgement.[76] Here, we could adapt the slogan of another sceptic and realist, John Dunn: "Neither fatalism, nor voluntarism: political understanding." For Oakeshott, the argument would be: "Neither faith, nor scepticism: political judgement."[77]

Oakeshott's anti-absolutism does not only manifest itself in his endorsement of Rationalism or the politics of faith as the so-called necessary evil or in his insistence that the mean in action is not a fixed point, but a matter of judgement, but also in his consideration of the whole framework he provides us with for understanding modern politics as historically contingent. The two poles of our political activity, which give us the circumscribed field of movement within which we must *now* act, are themselves products of past human actions. The limits they set, therefore, are historic rather than absolute.[78] In politics, where everything is dependent on human actions, though not on human design, there is no place for absolutes.[79]

These deeply sceptical remarks about the character of our political predicament quite decisively indicate, I think, that it would be injudicious to consider Oakeshott to be a paralysing realist. They also reveal the resemblance of his position to that of contemporary sceptical realists like Dunn and Geuss, who, similarly, emphasise the centrality of political judgement in politics.[80] They obviously disagree, however, as I suggested earlier, about the role political theory should have in relation to political practice. Unless we can argue that both Oakeshott's position and Dunn and Geuss's position are equally cogent, we have to ask which of these positions is more properly sceptical when it comes to considering the relationship between theory and practice. There is the possibility that both suspend scepticism at this point, in which case all we can say is that the way one conceives the relationship between theory and practice is a matter of one's temperament or one's politics.[81] But there is also the possibility that we can vindicate one of the positions as being more sceptical and realistic.

Let me first clearly state both positions with respect to the role of political theory in relation to practice. Oakeshott's separation of theory and practice goes back to one of his earliest works, *Experience and Its Modes*, where he distinguishes between philosophy, science, history and practice as different modes of understanding experience.[82] These modes, according to Oakeshott, are autonomous in themselves, and, though they all have valuable things to say from their respective perspectives, their conclusions are non-transferable. It is this categorical indifference of each mode of understanding to the other which prompted "the distinctively Oakeshottian gulf between theory and practice."[83] Oakeshott retained this distinction in all his works and expressed it with vigour in *On Human Conduct*, where he, this time, separated theorising from doing.[84] Those who fail to distinguish the two, he argued, confuse the process and the product, that is, confuse the process of theorising and some sort of theory as end result. Theorising is a continual process of criticism, of examination of the presuppositions of every achieved understanding, including one's own, whereas doing, which aims at action, requires suspension of criticism. The two, thus, cannot coexist. Since an understanding cannot be interrogated and used at the same time, one is *either* engaged in understanding the world *or* in changing it. The first activity requires the detached calmness of an observer, and the second one the engaged passion of a participant. This suggests that a theorist *qua* theorist cannot direct practice. If he or she attempts to do so, he or she ceases to be a theorist and becomes a "theoretician."[85]

For Dunn and Geuss, the relationship between theory and practice is much more organic and intertwined than this. Geuss, argues, for instance, that "propounding a theory, introducing a concept, passing on a piece of information, even, sometimes, entertaining a possibility, are all actions."[86] Dunn, in a similar fashion, holds that thinking is action, a form of activity, and that authors are agents.[87] He goes even further, when he implies that not only are theorists agents, but we all are theorists of some sort: most of us amateur theorists, some of us official theorists and, last but not least, referring to academics, some of us professional theorists.[88] It seems to me that what both Dunn and Geuss want to draw attention to by speaking of theories as actions is their consequentiality. Theorising, for them, is a consequential activity, and sometimes, though not always, its consequences might be politically significant. Whether they will or will not be significant is a matter of practice and cannot be decided theoretically. But political theorists, when they are theorising, should act responsibly, as if their theories will have consequences, some of which might be practical. Theories are not just a theoretical matter, as Oakeshott supposed. Oakeshott thought that when one *uses* a theory, one ceases to be a theorist, because one steps outside the theoretical realm and enters the realm of practice. This sounds *theoretically* reasonable, but whether "philosophical disengagement is either possible or sincere" in *practice*, is highly questionable.[89] The problem with Oakeshott's view of the relation between the ivory tower and the outside world is that it is not sceptical at all. It is a once and for all, absolute theoretical answer. Oakeshott offers us a sceptical inclination hardened into a dogmatic assertion that a certain line should not be crossed, whereas Dunn and Geuss, who maintain that the nature of the relation between theory and practice *can only be resolved in practice*, offer us a far more realistic and sceptical response.

It might be objected that Dunn and Geuss suspend scepticism, when they demand political theory to be action-guiding, unlike Oakeshott, for whom political philosophy aims at understanding. When stated in terms of a rigid dichotomy between offering a description or a prescription, their views in relation to the purpose of theorising seem to be more incongruent than they actually are. The tension dissolves, I believe, once it is seen that for Oakeshott understanding does not quite leave the world as it is, as Wittgenstein famously asserted, and that action-guidance for Dunn and Geuss does not consist in determinate, conclusive sort of guidance.[90]

The Politics of Faith and the Politics of Scepticism is perhaps the best of Oakeshott's works to focus on in order to gauge what role he thinks *understanding* might play in relation to the practical activity of politics, since "it is as close to a book of advice for the practice of modern politics as Oakeshott ever produced."[91] It offers a powerful, historically sensitive, philosophical depiction of our modern political predicament and contains Oakeshott's clearest statement on the value of this task for politics. The framework he proposes is based on his conception of politics as a deeply structured realm of human action.[92] As a realm of human action, it is hard to consider politics as unresponsive to our wills, wishes and desires. Yet, at any given time, it also confronts us as a highly structured field of activity circumscribed by what appear to be relatively fixed features. These relatively permanent arrangements of our politics demarcate the historic limits of political possibility, and govern, though not in any absolute sense, what is thinkable and doable in the circumstances in which we happen to find ourselves. Political theory, which offers us a way of thinking about our politics, is useful "as a guide for political reasoning."[93] Its claim to usefulness, nevertheless, is modest.[94] It provides us with a sketch of our situation, "of its limits and possibilities," but certainly does not provide us with a repository of conclusive solutions to our problems.[95] Since limits are relatively easier to ascertain than possibilities, "the only appropriate ambition" for such a theory of political reasoning is "not to be deceived" and "to find oneself a little less perplexed and a little more understanding of even the unpleasing surface of politics."[96]

John Dunn has been lamenting our lack of political understanding for over five decades.[97] In a way that is highly reminiscent of Oakeshott, he takes one of the greatest obstacles to developing a proper political understanding to be related to the nature of politics, which is both a field of human agency and, to quite a large extent, structurally determined. Understanding this field requires a continuous conversation between the perspective of an external observer and the perspective of an agent, which Dunn believes, if not impossible, is extremely difficult to achieve, because the two perspectives, on their own, produce two incommensurable and clashing styles of the fatalist and the voluntarist.[98] While the fatalist conceives the world as deeply impervious to human agency, the voluntarist perceives history as a stream of continually achieved purposes. In the same way that Oakeshott thought that the politics of faith had become too dominant as a style of thinking about politics, so Dunn thinks that most contemporary political theory is in the grip of voluntarist vision. In a similar spirit, Geuss has forcefully argued against modern philosophy's deceptive message that the world is fully intelligible to us and receptive to our desires.[99] This message, which has come to dominate much of mainstream philosophy since Kant, he claims, is a form of collective wishful thinking, a fantasy, which, nevertheless, has eminently real consequences.[100]

Neither Geuss nor Dunn, however, takes this sorry state of modern political theory to be a reason for despair or a reason for abstaining from the effort to try and understand the setting of our lives as best as we can. Geuss argues that we should fight the widely shared forms of wishful thinking and illusions of our era with the help of a historically informed philosophy.[101] Dunn's conviction is not only that we should try harder to attain some kind of political understanding, but also that the history of political theory still offers the most valuable starting point for proper political understanding.[102] Nobody should think about the history of political theory as a potential guide to the deepest questions of life. But it does provide us with a frame to answer some of the most significant questions related to politics and answer them for ourselves.[103]

Where does this leave us with respect to Oakeshott's political realism and realism's capacity to provide guidance to our actions? If I am right, then, in contrast to the common belief, Oakeshott's dogmatic assertion of a gulf between theory and practice is one of the least realistic and sceptical elements of his thought. Fortunately, his own practice is testimony to the relevance of a historically informed philosophical sensibility for generating a proper political understanding of our modern predicament. Political understanding of the sort advocated by sceptical realists like Oakeshott, Dunn and Geuss, remains the best guide for action, at least for those who do not confuse possession of it with any sort of Platonic political epiphany. It forcefully registers that in politics, any change for the better, barring happy accident, will always be matter of practice, prudence and good judgement.

NOTES

1. Michael Oakeshott, *Notebooks 1922–1986*, ed. Luke O'Sullivan (Exeter: Imprint Academic, 2014), 448.
2. Raymond Geuss, *History and Illusion in Politics* (Cambridge: Cambridge University Press, 2001), 160.
3. Representative works are: Bernard Williams, *In the Beginning Was the Deed: Realism and Moralism in Political Argument*, ed. Geoffrey Hawthorn (Princeton: Princeton University Press, 2005); Raymond Geuss, *Philosophy and Real Politics* (Princeton: Princeton University Press, 2008).
4. Williams, *In the Beginning Was the Deed*, 1, 3.
5. Glen Newey, "Two Dogmas of Liberalism," *European Journal of Political Theory* 9, no. 4 (October 2010), 449–65; Enzo Rossi, "Justice, Legitimacy and (Normative) Authority for Political Realists," *Critical Review of International Social and Political Philosophy* 15, no. 2 (2012), 149–64; Andrea Sangiovanni, "Justice and the Priority of Politics to Morality," *Journal of Political Philosophy* 16, no. 2 (2008), 137–64; and Marc Stears, "Liberalism and the Politics of Compulsion," *British Journal of Political Science* 37, no. 3 (2007), 533–53.

6. Bonnie Honig, *Political Theory and the Displacement of Politics* (New York: Cornell University Press, 1993), 1–17; John Gray, *Enlightenment's Wake* (London: Routledge, 1995), 76; and Lorna Finlayson, *The Political Is Political: Conformity and the Illusion of Dissent in Contemporary Political Philosophy* (London and New York: Rowman and Littlefield, 2015), 3–4.

7. Matt Sleat ed., *Politics Recovered: Realist Thought in Theory and Practice* (Columbia: Columbia University Press, 2018), 8.

8. Eva Erman and Niklas Möller, "Three Failed Charges Against Ideal Theory," *Social Theory and Practice* 39, no. 1 (2013), 19–44; Mark Philp, *Political Conduct* (London: Harvard University Press, 2007); Mark Philp, "Realism Without Illusions," *Political Theory* 40, no. 5 (2012), 629–49; Matt Sleat, *Liberal Realism: A Realist Theory of Liberal Politics* (Manchester: Manchester University Press, 2013); and Matt Sleat, "Legitimacy in Realist Thought: Between Moralism and *Realpolitik*," *Political Theory* 42, no. 3 (2014), 314–37.

9. William Galston, "Realism in Political Theory," *European Journal of Political Theory* 9, no. 4 (2010), 390–93.

10. Michael Freeden, "Interpretive and Prescriptive Realism," *Journal of Political Ideologies* 19, no. 1 (2012), 1–14; Galston, "Realism in Political Theory," 394–95; Alan Hamlin and Zofia Stemplowska, "Theory, Ideal Theory and the Theory of Ideals," *Political Studies Review* 10, no. 1 (2012), 48–62; Robert Jubb, "Tragedies of Non-ideal Theory," *European Journal of Political Theory* 11, no. 3 (July 2012), 229–46; Enzo Rossi and Matt Sleat, "Realism in Normative Political Theory," *Philosophy Compass* 9, no. 10 (2014), 689–701; Sleat, *Liberal Realism*; Matt Sleat, "Realism, Liberalism and Non-ideal Theory Or, Are There Two Ways to Do Realistic Political Theory?" *Political Studies* 64, no. 1 (March 2016), 27–41; Zofia Stemplowska, "What's Ideal About Ideal Theory?" *Social Theory and Practice* 34, no. 3 (2008), 319–40; Adam Swift, "The Value of Philosophy in Non-ideal Circumstances," *Social Theory and Practice* 34, no. 3 (2008), 363–87; Laura Valentini, "Ideal vs. Non-iIdeal Theory: A Conceptual Map," *Philosophy Compass* 7, no. 9 (2012), 654–64; and Federico Zuolo, "Realism and Idealism," in *A Companion to Political Philosophy: Methods, Tools, Topics*, ed. Antonella Besussi (Farnham: Ashgate, 2012), 65–75.

11. Joshua Foa Dienstag, "Pessimistic Realism and Realistic Pessimism," in *Political Thought and International Relations: Variations on a Realist Theme*, ed. Duncan Bell (Oxford: Oxford University Press, 2009), 159–76; Lorna Finlayson, "With Radicals Like These Who Needs Conservatives? Doom, Gloom and Realism in Political Theory," *European Journal of Political Theory* 16, no. 3 (July 2017), 1–19; Finlayson, *The Political Is Political*, 121–30; Raymond Geuss, *Outside Ethics* (Princeton and Oxford: Princeton University Press, 2005), 219–33; and Bonnie

Honig and Marc Stears, "The New Realism: From Modus Vivendi to Justice," in *Political Philosophy Versus History? Contextualism and Real Politics in Contemporary Political Thought*, eds. Jonathan Floyd and Marc Stears (Cambridge: Cambridge University Press, 2011), 177–205.

12. Alex Bavister-Gould, "Bernard Williams: Political Realism and the Limits of Legitimacy," *European Journal of Philosophy* 21, no. 4 (2013), 593–610; Emanuela Ceva and Enzo Rossi, *Justice, Legitimacy and Diversity: Political Authority Between Realism and Moralism* (London: Routledge, 2012); Erman and Möller, "Three Failed Charges," 19–44; Edward Hall, "Political Realism and Fact-Sensitivity," *Res Publica* 19, no. 2 (2013), 173–81; John Horton, "Realism, Liberal Moralism and a Political Theory of Modus Vivendi," *European Journal of Political Theory* 9, no. 4 (October 2010), 431–48; Charles Larmore, "What Is Political Philosophy?" *Journal of Moral Philosophy* 10, no. 3 (2013), 276–306; David MacCabe, *Modus Vivendi Liberalism* (Cambridge: Cambridge University Press, 2010); Newey, "Two Dogmas of Liberalism," 449–65; Rossi, "Justice, Legitimacy and (Normative) Authority for Political Realists," 149–64; Hans-Jörg Sigwart, "The Logic of Legitimacy: Ethics in Political Realism," *The Review of Politics* 75, no. 3 (2013), 407–32; Matt Sleat, "Bernard Williams and the Possibility of a Realist Political Theory," *European Journal of Political Theory* 9, no. 4 (October 2010), 485–503; Matt Sleat "Liberal Realism: A Liberal Response to the Realist Challenge," *The Review of Politics* 73, no. 3 (Summer 2011), 469–96; and Williams, *In the Beginning Was the Deed*, 1–17.

13. Francesca Pasquali, *Virtuous Imbalance: Political Philosophy Between Desirability and Feasibility* (Surrey: Ashgate, 2012).

14. Richard Bourke and Raymond Geuss, *Political Judgement: Essays for John Dunn* (Cambridge: Cambridge University Press, 2009); John Dunn, *Interpreting Political Responsibility: Essays 1981–1989* (Princeton: Princeton University Press, 1990); and John Dunn, *The Cunning of Unreason: Making Sense of Politics* (HarperCollins, 2000).

15. Geuss, *Real Politics*; Janosch Prinz, "'Raymond Geuss' Radicalization of Realism in Political Theory," *Philosophy & Social Criticism* 42, no. 8 (2016), 777–96; and Janosch Prinz and Enzo Rossi, "Political Realism as Ideology Critique," *Critical Review of International Social and Political Philosophy* 20, no. 3 (2017), 348–65.

16. Finlayson, "With Radicals Like These," 1–19; Finlayson, *The Political Is Political*.

17. Galston, "Realism," 385–411; Finlayson, "With Radicals Like These," 1–19; Finlayson, *The Political Is Political*; Enzo Rossi, "Can Realism Move Beyond a Methodenstreit?" *Political Theory* 44, no. 3 (2016), 410–20; and Adam Swift and Stuart White, "Political Theory, Social

Science and Real Politics," in *Political Theory: Methods and Approaches*, eds. David Leopold and Marc Stears (Oxford: Oxford University Press, 2008), 49–69.

18. Galston, "Realism in Political Theory," 385–411; Rossi and Sleat, "Realism in Normative Political Theory," 689–701; David Runciman, "What Is Realistic Philosophy?" *Metaphilosophy* 43, no. 1–2 (2012), 58–70; Stears, "Liberalism and the Politics of Compulsion," 533–53; Freeden, "Interpretative and Prescriptive Realism," 1–14; Alice Baderin, "Two Forms of Realism in Political Theory," *European Journal of Political Theory* 13, no. 2 (2014), 132–53; and Sigwart, "The Logic of Legitimacy," 407–32.

19. Sleat, *Politics Recovered*, 10.

20. Baderin, "Two Forms of Realism," 132–53; Freeden, "Interpretive and Prescriptive Realism," 1–14.

21. For an example of this line of thought see John Horton, "What Might It Mean for Political Theory to Be More Realistic?" *Philosophia* 45 (2017), 487–501, 489.

22. Having a model of what ideally ought to be the case does not require one be able to fashion oneself in accordance with the model. The model might function as an ideal to approximate or give orientation, even if it cannot be fully realised right now. But this does not change my main point.

23. Bourke and Geuss, *Political Judgement*, 2–3.

24. Raymond Geuss, "Realism and the Relativity of Judgement," *International Relations* 29, no. 1 (2015), 3–22.

25. The term "activist" realism has recently been utilised by Lea Ypi to describe an approach to political theory, which, while acknowledging the force of some of the realist critiques, is, I think, rather close to political moralists' concern with justice. See, Lea Ypi, "From Realism to Activism: A Critique of Resignation in Political Theory," in *The Trouble with Democracy: Political Modernity in the XXIst Century*, eds. Gerard Rosich and Peter Wagner (Edinburgh: Edinburgh University Press, 2015), 233–48. My use of the term bears no relation to hers. For another rather different account of activist realism see David Owen, "Activist Political Theory and the Question of Power," *Ethics and Global Politics* 6, no. 2 (2013), 85–91.

26. Dunn, *The Cunning of Unreason*, 40; Finlayson, "With Radicals Like These," 1–19.

27. Finlayson, *The Political Is Political*, 5–6.

28. Ibid., 130.

29. Ypi, "From Realism to Activism," 1, 10.

30. Dunn, *The Cunning of Unreason*, 41.

172 G. SEVEN

31. David Estlund, "Human Nature and the Limits (If Any) of Political Philosophy," *Philosophy and Public Affairs* 39, no. 3 (2011), 207–36; Colin Farrelly, "Justice in Ideal Theory: A Refutation," *Political Studies* 55 (2007), 844–64; Finlayson, *The Political Is Political*, 121–35; Hamlin and Stemplowska, "Theory, Ideal Theory and the Theory of Ideals," 48–62; Jubb, "Tragedies of Non-ideal Theory," 229–46; Holly Lawford-Smith, "Debate: Ideal Theory—A Reply to Valentini," *The Journal of Political Philosophy* 18, no. 3 (July 2010), 357–68; Pasquali, *Virtuous Imbalance*; Ingrid Robeyns, "Ideal Theory in Theory and Practice," *Social Theory and Practice* 34, no. 3 (July 2008), 341–62; Enzo Rossi, "Facts, Principles, and (Real) Politics," *Ethical Theory and Moral Practice* 19, no. 2 (2016), 505–20; Sleat, "Legitimacy in Realist Thought," 314–37; Stemplowska, "What's Ideal About Ideal Theory?" 319–40; and Valentini, "Ideal vs. Non-ideal Theory," 654–64.
32. Sleat, "Legitimacy in Realist Thought," 314–37.
33. Valentini, "Ideal vs. Non-ideal Theory," 654–64, 659.
34. Galston, "Realism in Political Theory," 394.
35. Finlayson, *The Political is Political*, 124.
36. Ibid., 111–35; Rossi, "Facts, Principles, and (Real) Politics," 505–20.
37. Bourke and Geuss, *Political Judgement*, 4.
38. Finlayson, *The Political Is Political*, 128.
39. Dunn, *The Cunning of Unreason*, 40.
40. Bourke and Geuss, *Political Judgement*, 1–26.
41. Ibid., 7; Geuss, *Philosophy and Real Politics*, 42–50; and Raymond Geuss, *Politics and the Imagination* (Princeton: Princeton University Press, 2009), i–xiii.
42. Some realist scholars argue, for this reason, that the opposite of activist realism is not utopianism. In fact, they suggest, activist realism is perfectly compatible with the 1968 slogan: "Be realistic. Demand the impossible." See, for instance, Rossi and Sleat, "Realism in Normative Political Theory," 691.
43. Edmund Neill, "The Nature of Oakeshott's Conservatism," in *The Place of Michael Oakeshott in Contemporary Western and Non-Western Thought*, ed. Noel O'Sullivan (Exeter: Imprint Academic, 2017), 90–106; Paul Franco, *The Political Philosophy of Michael Oakeshott* (New Haven and London, 1990), 140–56; and Terry Nardin, *Michael Oakeshott's Cold War Liberalism* (Palgrave Macmillan, 2015).
44. David Boucher, "The Idealism of Michael Oakeshott," *Collingwood and British Idealism Studies*, 8 (2001), 73–98; David Boucher, "Oakeshott in the context of British Idealism?" in *The Cambridge Companion to Michael Oakeshott*, ed. Efraim Podoksik (Cambridge: Cambridge University Press, 2012), 247–73; and Terry Nardin, *The Philosophy of Michael Oakeshott* (Pennsylvania: Pennsylvania State University Press, 2001).

45. Steven Anthony Gerencser, *The Skeptic's Oakeshott* (Basingstoke: Macmillan, 2000); and Roy Tseng, *The Sceptical Idealist: Michael Oakeshott as a Critic of the Enlightenment* (Exeter: Imprint Academic, 2003).

46. Edward Hall, "The Limits of Bernard Williams's Critique of Political Moralism," *Ethical Perspectives* 20, no. 2 (2013), 237; Horton, "What Might It Mean?" 499; David Owen, "Realistically," *Radical Philosophy*, 154 (2009), 60; and Sigwart, "The Logic of Legitimacy," 418.

47. Kenneth Minogue, *Conservative Realism: New Essays on Conservatism* (London: HarperCollins, 1996), 1–6; Nehal Bhuta, "The Mystery of the State: State Concept, State Theory and State Making in Schmitt and Oakeshott," in *Law, Liberty and the State: Oakeshott, Hayek and Schmitt on the Rule of Law*, eds. David Dyzenhaus and Thomas Poole (Cambridge: Cambridge University Press, 2015), 10; Nardin, *Michael Oakeshott's Cold War Liberalism*, 8, 24; Terry Nardin, "Rationality in Politics and Its Limits," *Global Discourse* 5, no. 2 (2015), 179; Terry Nardin, "Oakeshott on Theory and Practice," *Global Discourse* 5, no. 2 (2015), 310–22; Terry Nardin, "Oakeshott as a Moralist," in *The Place of Michael Oakeshott in Contemporary Western and Non-Western Thought*, ed. Noel O'Sullivan (Exeter: Imprint Academic, 2017), 66; and Terry Nardin, "The New Realism and the Old," *Critical Review of International Social and Political Philosophy* 20, no. 3 (2017), 314–30. Luke O'Sullivan, *en passant*, refers to Oakeshott's Hobbesian realism about power in Michael Oakeshott, *What Is History? And Other Essays*, ed. Luke O'Sullivan (Exeter: Imprint Academic, 2004), 33.

48. Nardin, *Oakeshott's Cold War Liberalism*, 8–9, 34; Nardin, "The New Realism and the Old," 314.

49. Nardin, *Oakeshott's Cold War Liberalism*, 32, 34; Nardin, "Oakeshott on Theory and Practice," 315.

50. Horton, "What Might It Mean?" 489.

51. Michael Oakeshott, *Rationalism in Politics* (Indianapolis: Liberty Press, 1991), 5–42.

52. Ibid., 465–87.

53. Ibid., 99–131.

54. Michael Oakeshott, *The Politics of Faith and the Politics of Scepticism*, ed. Timothy Fuller (New Haven and London: Yale University Press, 1996).

55. Michael Oakeshott, *On Human Conduct* (Oxford: Clarendon Press, 1975), 199.

56. Oakeshott, *Rationalism in Politics*, 5; Kenneth Minogue, "The Fate of Rationalism in Oakeshott's Thought," in *A Companion to Michael Oakeshott*, eds. Paul Franco and Leslie Marsh (University Park, PA: Pennsylvania State University Press, 2012), 232.

57. Timothy Fuller, "Editor's Introduction," in *The Politics of Faith and the Politics of Scepticism*, x.
58. Minogue, "The Fate of Rationalism," 237.
59. Oakeshott, *The Politics of Faith and the Politics of Scepticism*, 12.
60. Ibid., 118.
61. Ibid., 125.
62. Ibid., 13, 21.
63. Oakeshott, *On Human Conduct*, 199.
64. Nardin, "The New Realism and the Old," 316.
65. Oakeshott, *The Politics of Faith and Scepticism*, 125.
66. Ibid., 23–4.
67. Ibid., 25.
68. Ibid., 32.
69. Ibid., 32–4.
70. Ibid., 4.
71. Ibid., 25.
72. Ibid., 26.
73. For the importance of history for scepticism see James Alexander, "A Genealogy of Political Theory: A Polemic," *Contemporary Political Theory* (November 2018), 15. https://doi.org/10.1057/s41296-018-0275-7.
74. Oakeshott, *The Politics of Faith and the Politics of Scepticism*, 91, 118.
75. Ibid., 80, 118.
76. Ibid., 121.
77. Dunn, *Interpreting Political Responsibility*, 143.
78. Oakeshott, *The Politics of Faith and the Politics of Scepticism*, 116.
79. Ibid., 20.
80. Dunn, *The Cunning of Unreason*; Raymond Geuss, "What Is Political Judgement?" in *Political Judgement*, eds. Richard Bourke and Raymond Geuss (Cambridge: Cambridge University Press, 2009), 29–46; Geuss, *Politics and the Imagination*, 1–16; and Geuss, "Realism and the Relativity of Judgement," 3–22.
81. For the view that the difference between the two positions is a matter of ideology, see James Alexander, "A Sketch of a System of Theory and Practice," *Political Studies Review* 13 (2015), 485–93.
82. Michael Oakeshott, *Experience and Its Modes* (Cambridge: Cambridge University Press, 1933).
83. Franco, *The Political Philosophy of Michael Oakeshott*, 161.
84. Oakeshott, *On Human Conduct*, 33–5, 88–91.
85. Ibid., 26, 30.
86. Geuss, *Philosophy and Real Politics*, 11.

87. John Dunn, *Rethinking Modern Political Theory* (Cambridge: Cambridge University Press, 1985), 17.
88. Ibid., 8; Dunn, *Interpreting Political Responsibility*, 8, 202–3.
89. Nardin, "Oakeshott as a Moralist," 66.
90. Ludwig Wittgenstein, *Philosophical Investigations*, trans. G. E. M. Anscombe (Oxford: Blackwell, 1958), 49.
91. Fuller, "Editor's Introduction," x.
92. Oakeshott, *The Politics of Faith and the Politics of Scepticism*, 20.
93. Ibid., 125.
94. Minogue, "The Fate of Rationalism," 246.
95. Oakeshott, *The Politics of Faith and the Politics of Scepticism*, 125.
96. Ibid., 20.
97. Dunn, *Interpreting Political Responsibility*, 8; John Dunn, *Western Political Theory in the Face of the Future* (Cambridge: Cambridge University Press, 1993), xii, 136; and John Dunn, *The History of Political Theory and Other Essays* (Cambridge: Cambridge University Press, 1996), 1–2.
98. Dunn, *The Cunning of Unreason*, 344–55.
99. Geuss, *Outside Ethics*, 131–52.
100. Raymond Geuss, "Realismus, Wunschdenken, Utopie" *Deutsche Zeitschrift für Philosophie*, 58, no. 3 (2010), 419–29; Raymond Geuss, *A World Without Why* (New Jersey: Princeton University Press, 2014), 22–44, 135–43, 175–94 and 205–06.
101. Geuss, *History and Illusion; Geuss, Outside Ethics*, 153–60.
102. Dunn, *Interpreting Political Responsibility*, 8; Dunn, *Western Political Theory in the Face of the Future*, xii, 136; and Dunn, *The History of Political Theory and Other Essays*, 1–2.
103. Dunn, *The Cunning of Unreason*, ix.

CHAPTER 9

Government as a British Conservative Understands It: Comments on Oakeshott's Views on Government

Ferenc Hörcher

I

This essay is to shed light on Oakeshott's idea of what government in a conservative key means. It will rely on two of Oakeshott's works based on his lectures. First, the essay looks at the conceptual differentiation in his "History of Political Thought" between teleocratic and nomocratic activity. While the first one means to "impose a single end or purpose upon its subjects and their activities",[1] the second one stands for an activity "which provides rules … which do not themselves impose any single and premeditated end or purpose upon that conduct".[2] Obviously, Oakeshott prefers the second one, even if he does not admit it in the lecture course directly.

F. Hörcher (✉)
Research Institute of Politics and Government,
National University of Public Service, Budapest, Hungary
e-mail: horcher.ferenc@uni-nke.hu

Institute of Philosophy, Hungarian Academy of Sciences, Budapest, Hungary
e-mail: horcher.ferenc@btk.mta.hu

© The Author(s) 2019
E. S. Kos (ed.), *Michael Oakeshott on Authority, Governance,*
and the State, Palgrave Studies in Classical Liberalism,
https://doi.org/10.1007/978-3-030-17455-2_9

Next, it looks at his explanation of how a conservative regards government in his essay "On Being Conservative".[3] Here, the main point is a criticism of the progressivist hubris of government as the realisation of a vision of a better future. As opposed to his opponent, the conservative in this account is satisfied if things do not deteriorate in a dramatic fashion.

The essay is to show that Oakeshott's notion of nomocratic government should be interpreted together with his description of the limits of government as the conservative would expect it, based on his account of human nature.

II

Conservatives in the British tradition tend to receive with some suspicion any signs of the activism of government. This phenomenon has its very good reasons. The British idea of liberty is defined as a "negative", personal liberty, freedom from any authority whatsoever. Furthermore, the twentieth century witnessed an unparalleled overextension of the powers of the state. Although the legislative has grown rapidly, it is especially the executive branch that tends to exaggerate its role and function and which tends to become oversized. Generally speaking, when British conservatives are highly critical of this recent development of the government, they mean the whole political machinery of the state.

Oakeshott is no exception to this. One of his most frequently returning themes is the potential threat of an oversized or simply overambitious state. This essay cannot take all the works of Oakeshott referring to this theme on board. It will limit itself to two specific loci, where Oakeshott faces the problem. First, it looks at the last part of his posthumously published notes of his "Lectures in the History of Political Thought". Here, he presents a less elaborate version of the famous distinction between the enterprise state and the understanding of the state as civil association which will return in a more sophisticated way in his final work.[4] Although this earlier one is a less detailed and less stylish account of the distinction, it allows us to have a clearer sight of the original intentions behind this conceptual pair. Also, given the fact that this analysis can be found in an afterword to his course on the history of political thought, here, he provides the historical context of the distinction too. This essay is built on the assumption, that in case of political philosophical concepts it is significant to see the historical origins of them, to see the raison d'etre of these ideal types. It needs to be pointed out in connection with these phrases that their description fits both a (classical) liberal and a conservative paradigm. This is not surprising in the British tradition where these two ideologies developed side by side.

In the second part of the essay, I shall deal with the essay "On Being Conservative" written a good decade earlier. I shall look at those arguments of Oakeshott that serve to substantiate the conceptual distinction's conservative philosophical foundation. Although Oakeshott starts out from a non-political interpretation of conservatism in the essay, in its second part, he arrives at the explication of political conservatism based on a sceptical, conservative account of human nature. I argue that the later conceptual opposition relies on this conservative philosophical anthropology, and that to fully appreciate Oakeshott's views on government, we should read his formalist account of a minimal state together with his views on human nature.

III

Oakeshott's "Lectures in the History of Political Thought" published posthumously by Terry Nardin and Luke O'Sullivan were originally given at the London School of Economics "during the late 1960s".[5] This is the last version of a course that he gave annually at the university, and during which the lecture hall was "packed with students from all disciplines" across the LSE.[6] This last version ends with an exposition of the authority of government, followed by two condensed lectures on what he calls "The office of government".[7] It is in this context that he presents his conceptual pair of *telocracy* and *nomocracy*. These concepts etymologically derive from the following two classical concepts: *telos* (appr. ultimate aim) and *nomos* (appr. law, norms governing social conduct). Telocracy refers to a political regime where "the proper business of governing" is "understood as the organisation of the energies and activities of its subjects, and of the resources of its territory, for the achievement of a single, premeditated end".[8] Its role is that of the "guardian or organizer" of the affairs of the community, to arrange it so as to reach the object previously defined. Education, art, the media, all the potentials of the community should serve the very same aim, which is "understood as a substantive condition of life".[9]

While his description itself is certainly very critical of this regime, Oakeshott makes it clear, that in the early modern political context it was quite adequate. What is more, he suggested that it was inevitable that this type of government had appeared on the historical stage at a certain moment of modernity. This is an important point because it suggests that perhaps the validity of his two prototypes is historically conditioned. After all if regimes of government depend on their historical context, how can they be conceptualised as eternal concepts. Of course, Oakeshott himself does not want to relativize political values. On the other hand, however, he keeps suggesting that his "ideal type" is specifically a response to the modern conditions. Let us have a glance at the particular historical examples he offered and then return to the conceptual analysis.

The first type of a historically conditioned teleocratic regime appeared in what he calls the "religious idiom".[10] According to his historical narrative, it surfaced in the "Geneva of Calvin and Beza, the Zurich of Zwingli"[11] as well as in Cromwell's England. In Oakeshott's interpretation, all of these specific sociopolitical and religious cultures aimed at the creation of a "righteous community".[12] While to unite these religious autocracies or even tyrannies under one label is historically perhaps not absolutely precise, Oakeshott's search is for an ideal type in the Weberian sense of the word. What he wants to pinpoint by covering all these historical accidents by one term is the supposed mechanism which he claims to be responsible for the birth of these regimes and which seemed to him similar in each of these cases. One can of course contradict this claim, arguing that the case of the Swiss early protestant city states can be easily distinguished from the Cromwellian episode of the English monarchy about a century later. And yet Oakeshott has a point supposing that there is something shared by all three cases: they were the experimental workshops of the relation of Church and State in the protestant Christian idiom. However, Oakeshott's choice of examples is ironic and exaggerated. All the three examples are radical versions of the State–Church relationship while both the Swiss and the British state are going to be much more relaxed in this respect in the long run. The later English development's liberality will be admitted by Oakeshott's own list of authors presented at the end of his account of the alternative phrase, that of the nomocratic regime, including the major protagonists of the liberal canon. We shall return to this problem when discussing the second phrase.

But let us remain for one more moment at the first concept, *telocracy*. The second example is quite the opposite of the one mentioned. While the first one was an exaggeration of the religious idiom, this one, the idiom of the Enlightenment, is a denial of it. While the first one was an exaggeration of the worldly power of divine authority, the second one is an exaggeration of the power of the secular authority, called Enlightened absolutism. Importantly, Oakeshott emphasises that this is the German and the French Enlightenment (the tradition of Frederick the Great and Louis XIV), and has nothing to do with the British context.

Surprisingly, the two regimes (the religious and the enlightened idiom) are claimed to have had a common feature: both of them regard power as far above the heads of the subjects, who are destined to accept political rule without much questioning of its legitimacy, so long as they work for the common telos, which was righteousness in the first case and an early form of "welfarism" in the second case. Oakeshott's list includes here the German cameralists (Justi, Sonnenfels, Wolff and Frederick the Great, among others), as well as the French ancient regime as described by Tocqueville. An important characteristic of this new version of *telocracy* is that it looks at governance as a kind of "social engineering", a "scientific operation" run by professional administrators.[13] They are the only agents of government, as in their vision "the mass of ordinary people were ignorant, helpless, 'unenlightened' canaille", "children", and the field of politics, therefore, a "clean sheet" on which to write required professional bureaucratic efficiency and educated leadership.[14]

His third example seems to be the utopian philosophical version of the Enlightened rule, embodied by Francis Bacon, the philosopher. "[I]n the Baconian version of *teleocratic* belief, a 'state' is understood as an 'economy', the managing director of which is the government".[15] This sounds like a reference to Bacon's incomplete utopian work, *New Atlantis*, even if it were published posthumously in 1627, while Oakeshott refers to Bacon as a sixteenth-century author, due to the fact that most of his life was spent in that century. Bacon's utopianism is followed by what seems to be a description of Marxism, where *telocracy* aims at a just distribution of goods in a society, the key values of which are acclaimed to be "equality" and "security".[16]

Two final points about Oakeshott on *telocracy*: firstly, even in the twentieth-century context, he seems to imply that this theory of the "office" of government can be appropriate—arguing for this position with reference to the world wars, to the increased size of populations as well as to new techniques of administration (presumably those of the mass media). And secondly, he has a very short and cryptic reference to the connection between *telocracy* and democracy, which is far from explicit, but which seems to suggest Oakeshott's own disdain of certain features of contemporary forms of democracy ("that is, government constituted in a certain manner").

On the whole, however, we need to know Oakeshott's whole philosophy to fully appreciate the critical undertone of his historically embedded and otherwise moderate and balanced description of *telocracy*. To be able to fully apprehend it, we need the other part of the story, i.e. his description of *nomocracy*. Here is the definition he provides: "government understood as the rule of its subjects by means of law".[17] In this form, it does not seem to be much more than the conventional description of the "rule of law". However, he breaks it down into the following two points: the government's office is to make sure that the subjects may "pursue their own chosen ends",[18] and also to defend "the interests of the association".[19] In other words, a priority is given to the defence of individual rights (and duties). To be sure, on a secondary level, group-interest (i.e. the properly political dimension) is also a key issue for him. The question is, if we keep to this order of priorities, whether it results in a system which can be sustained on the long run. For it is rather difficult, as a republican would argue, to imagine that an individualist regime (that *nomocracy* in this description seems to be) can mobilise enough people with enough zeal to defend the country in emergency situations. In other words, the system might run smoothly until subjects follow suit, however, when a foreign enemy wants to wage war with this political community, it might turn out to be unable to defend itself properly. One can certainly appeal for a professional army, but it might not be enough if the enemy is too zealous, as was the case in the Second World War, when Germany managed to occupy large parts of continental Europe and it found no army to defend its country properly (except for Russia and Churchill's Britain).

Here again, Oakeshott tries to substantiate his theoretical claim with references to historical examples. One of the more interesting ones is that he claims that in modern Europe *nomocracy* "antedates a belief in *telocracy*".[20] Unfortunately, he does not provide historical proofs for this claim, which makes his point sound less convincing (it is true, that at a later point he identifies the *politiques* of sixteenth-century France, and the England of the restoration period as believers in *nomocracy*, however, these examples are examples of subjects turning against the already existing *teleocratic* tendencies). Oakeshott's effort seems to aim at avoiding an obviously teleological, Whig historical metanarrative, where an uncivilised earlier form of *telocracy* would be overcome historically by the more refined and more humane form of *nomocracy*. However, he does not fully succeed with this effort. At a later point, he returns to the competition of the two forms, and claims, that *nomocracy* won where enough subjects joined to "resist the teleocratic tendency", and as a result, "ruling was turned in a nomocratic direction".[21]

Oakeshott tries to work out a whole dogmatic of *nomocracy* when he analyses it in seven points. We do not have here, however, enough space here to go into the details of it. Rather, I would like to pick out a formulation that sounds typically Oakeshottian: "for the believer in *nomocracy*, *how* a government acts is a more important consideration than *what* it does".[22] This reminds his readers of his distinction—when talking about political knowledge—between the *know-how* of politics and the *know what*.[23] And this is one of the strongest points of Oakeshott's legacy, where his politics of moderation is the most radical. While most political philosophies concentrate on the content of the relevant thought-experiment, Oakeshott is so modest as to limit his efforts to point at the relevance of the know-how.

Let me finish this overview of Oakeshott's presentation of *nomocracy* with two final points. First of all, perhaps the most astonishing part of the whole text is the shortlist of thinkers Oakeshott discusses in connection with *nomocracy*. First of all, his top runner is Kant. Although there is an obvious reason for this choice—that Kant gives a very strong philosophical underpinning to the notion of man as a morally autonomous being—one should not forget that Kant neither belongs to the British, nor to the conservative tradition. He was a thinker from Königsberg, whose ideas of rule following had a strong influence on the birth of the *Rechtsstaat*, but he was no believer in the rule of law as such. As for the other two protagonists of Oakeshott's story, Smith and Bentham, they at least are part of the British political culture—even if they are a bit far away from a pronounced conservative stance. In fact Bentham is not less than a philosophical radical, whose political ideas were sometimes also quite radical. All in all, the list of Kant, Smith and Bentham does not seem to fit very well the picture of Oakeshott as a conservative legend.

The second point I would like to make is that there was an obvious potential in Oakeshott's term of *nomocracy* that he seems to have missed. Compared to the Romans, who had a civilisation in which law played a major role, the Greeks did not have an autonomous realm of law in their social life. The term *nomos* therefore does not simply translate into the modern English idiom of the law. Its meaning was much less well defined than the present day English term: it included all kinds of social norms, from customary law to manners and morals. In fact, it could have been interpreted to refer to socially transferred traditions, including the commonly held and cherished values in the most general sense of the word. And this interpretation—quite in line with the Burkean interpretation of the common law and the ancient constitution[24]—could have been used by Oakeshott to show the conservative-tradition-based dimension of the notion of *nomocracy*.

This opportunity has been left out here, and one could easily argue at this point that this is because Oakeshott's own point of view is less conservative; it is closer to a classical liberal one. My argument would not go that far. Although I do not think that in the British tradition these two standpoints are so far away, I tend to think that Oakeshott is much closer to the conservative pole. To defend this view, this I turn now to Oakeshott's famous essay.

IV

On Being Conservative was first presented in 1956 as a talk at the University of Swansea, and its first written version appeared in the original edition of the collection of essays entitled *Rationalism in Politics* (1962). This volume served to position Oakeshott in the forefront of post-war British conservatism. And therefore, this essay is of crucial relevance in that volume and in Oakeshott's whole oeuvre.

The British political thinker is cautious enough to make it clear at the very beginning of the paper that his "theme is not a creed or a doctrine"[25]; in other words, it is not about the meaning of political conservatism. This is, however, to a large extent only a rhetorical strategy, dictated perhaps partly by the given (academic) political context of the lecture. Parts three and four of the essay are directly addressing the issues of political conservatism. And perhaps we are not surprised—after having seen that his lecture series on the history of political thought ended with his remarks on government—to find that he approaches political conservatism through examining its "beliefs about the activity of governing".[26] He states that in his view conservatism should not claim a natural law basis for politics. This way of thinking is not much more than "the observation of our current manner of living" together with the belief

that "governing is ... the provision and custody of general rules of conduct, which are understood, not as plans for imposing substantive activities, but as instruments enabling people to pursue the activities of their
own choice with the minimum frustration".[27] This is remarkably close to
the definition of *nomocracy* in the lecture series. This can be seen from
the overlap of the two vocabularies (custody, rules, substantive activities,
pursue). And even more importantly from the fact, that in both cases
priority is given to the individual's preferences over anything else. The
most interesting point, however, is the fact that this description is applied
here not simply to a specific form of government, but to political conservatism as such. The argument here—which substantiates that such a
form of government is rightly called conservative—is rather shortcut:
as these rules of conduct are the instruments securing individual freedom of choice, they are entitled to be conserved. And yet this typically
English, common sense and sober account is quite convincing exactly
because of its sobriety. In line with the Humean and Burkean criticism
of philosophical politics, Oakeshott is quite ready to admit that he can
offer only a minimalist account of governing (he claims, e.g., that "the
inclinations of government are to be found in ritual, not in religion or
philosophy"[28]). He is, as we have seen in the Lectures, aware of more
sublime accounts of it, including dreamy visions of a better future, but
he finds them rather shaky. This is because they do not fit our "current
condition of human circumstances",[29] which he described in the first two
parts of the essay under the term of the conservative disposition. But
why exactly should we prefer the current circumstances? First of all, he
provides a sceptical argument about human leadership potentials: "it is
beyond human experience to suppose that those who rule are endowed
with a superior wisdom ... which gives them authority to impose upon
their subjects a quite different manner of life".[30] In his view, they can
have only very limited roles to play. And yet these roles are necessary,
even essential: "to resolve some of the collisions ... to preserve peace ...
by enforcing general rules of procedure upon all subjects alike".[31] To
preserve peace is to preserve present conditions—this is an obvious way
to argue for the conservative disposition in the operations of a political
government. Most of the time there is no need to innovate to preserve
peace, in this sense governing differs from enterprise. With some exaggeration, he claims that the only thing to do is to make parties interested in keeping peace, by enforcing laws of procedure, i.e. "to provide a

vinculum juris", "a bond of law", [32] which secures for the association the authority established by the self-government of the individual members.

To be sure, Oakeshott does not seem to be a traditionalist conservative even here (a point which will be relevant when we see his critical remark on Burke). Rather, he sounds like a "status quo conservative", if one needs a label to identify him. And even the status quo can be given up in his view, if there is a need for that to preserve peace and avoid greater collisions. He is ready to allow the government to innovate. Here, his only point is to prefer common law-like "small adjustments"[33] as opposed to grand-scale transformations. Innovation should only reflect the external circumstances (beliefs and activities) and never simply impose change. Caution is required in every act of governing, as it can easily "inflame and direct desire".[34] The outburst of emotions in politics can cause serious problems, as humans are already too passionate without the direct involvement of government, and therefore, this latter should rather direct its efforts to moderate existing passions instead of raising new ones: "to restrain, to deflate, to pacify and to reconcile; not to stoke the fires of desire, but to damp them down".[35] This is an avowedly anti-activist, and even more an anti-populist vision of the office of government, one that is aware that the risks are much higher to cause serious social calamities by a progressivist, hyper-active attitude than the hopes of certain advantages gained by it. In fact, this consideration can be seen as Oakeshott's own critique of a populist kind of conservatism. The subjects, if they think on the long run, will receive the merits provided by this government with "loyalty ... respect and some suspicion, not love or devotion or affection".[36]

All these cautious remarks sound traditionally British. Both the suspicion against political passion and desire, a returning theme of British political thought in the long eighteenth century, due to the experience of the chaos and internal disorder of the seventeenth century, and the philosophically underpinned caution towards the deeper, metaphysical aims and expectations of politics, expressed by an advocacy of humour and irony instead—reminding us of the writings of the Third Earl of Shaftesbury.[37] The phrases used by Oakeshott in connection with this latter point sound very Shaftesburian: irony, raillery, mockery, inertia, and scepticism. These two aspects (to avoid strong passions and to inject humour into politics) are once again stylishly summarised in the following succinct formulation: "the conjunction of dreaming and ruling generates tyranny".[38]

V

By now, I hope it is clear, how this essay suggests interpreting the counter-concepts of *telocracy* versus *nomocracy*. At first sight, it might seem to be not much more than a reworking of Isaiah Berlin's distinction between negative and positive liberty, a vindication of liberalism in the Kantian (and for that matter, Rawlsian) paradigm. However, if we read it with *On Being Conservative* in the background, we see that its minimalism is not simply an overestimation of a neutral state and a simple-minded focus on individual rights. Rather, it is drawing the reasonable political conclusion from a rather sceptical account of human nature, provided in *On Being Conservative*. To illustrate this philosophical choice of a sceptical account of human nature his list of preferred authors in *On Being Conservative* seems rather different from the ones listed above: "there is more to be learnt about this disposition from Montaigne, Pascal, Hobbes and Hume than from Burke or Bentham".[39]

As we see, here Bentham is not an idol, as he is in the description of *nomocracy*. This difference might be explained by the fact that here Oakeshott's view of man is the key issue, and there he wants to present the British nineteenth-century hero of the rule of law. On the other hand, it is more surprising to find that Burke is a counterexample here. After all, if someone were sceptical about human nature, Burke indeed was. If one searches for an explanation of Oakeshott's criticism of Burke, an explanation might be that Burke's views of human nature can be interpreted as still belonging to the natural law tradition, which is highly problematic for Oakeshott.[40] His tradition is a secular scepticism, based on historical contingencies, and not a scholastic-dogmatic type, or an orthodox traditionalist one.

But even if we have problems to explain his counterexamples, Oakeshott's favourites in *On Being Conservative* (Montaigne, Pascal, Hobbes and Hume) circumscribe a very well defined view of the human condition, which helps us to make sense of his less explicit account of the concept of *nomocracy* in the other lecture series. If we compare the two lists (Kant, Smith, Bentham versus Montaigne, Pascal, Hobbes and Hume) they do seem to be a bit contradictory. But they serve different functions. One is strictly about the office of government, while the other one is about Oakeshott's views of human nature, and perhaps the two lists together (as the two lectures together) might give a better account of Oakeshott's complex political philosophy than either of them alone. These themes will come together in his last masterpiece, *On Human Conduct* (1975).

Notes

1. Michael Oakeshott, *Lectures in the History of Political Thought,* eds. Terry Nardin and Luke O'Sullivan (Exeter: Imprint Academic, 2006), 471.
2. Oakeshott, *Lectures,* 471.
3. Michael Oakeshott, *Rationalism in Politics and Other Essays* (Indianapolis: Liberty Press, 1991), 407–37.
4. Michael Oakeshott, *On Human Conduct* (Oxford: Oxford University Press, 1975).
5. Oakeshott, *Lectures,* vii.
6. Robert Grant, *Oakeshott* (London: Claridge Press, 1990), 19.
7. Ibid., 469.
8. Ibid., 471.
9. Ibid., 473.
10. Ibid., 475.
11. Ibid., 475.
12. Ibid., 475–76.
13. Ibid., 478.
14. Ibid., 479–80.
15. Ibid., 480.
16. Note, that security is not directly important in the Marxist theorem, while it plays a crucial role in the Grand Inquisitor's narrative of Dostoyevsky, which is a biting criticism of socialist doctrines.
17. Oakeshott, *Lectures,* 483.
18. One should note the reference to the historical expression "the pursuit of happiness".
19. Michael Oakeshott, *Lectures,* 483–84.
20. Ibid., 484.
21. Ibid., 490.
22. Ibid., 484.
23. Michael Oakeshott, *Rationalism in Politics,* 12.
24. See J.G.A. Pocock, *The Ancient Constitution and the Feudal Law: A Study of English Historical Thought in the Seventeenth Century,* Reissue with a Retrospect (Cambridge: Cambridge University Press, 2009).
25. Oakeshott, *Rationalism in Politics,* 407.
26. Ibid., 423.
27. Ibid., 424.
28. Ibid., 428.
29. Ibid., 426.
30. Ibid., 427.
31. Ibid., 428.
32. Ibid., 429.

33. Ibid., 430.
34. Ibid., 432.
35. Ibid., 432.
36. Ibid., 433.
37. Third Earl of Shaftesbury, "Sensus Communis: An Essay on the Freedom of Wit and Humour," in *Shaftesbury: Characteristicks of Men, Manners, Opinions, Times* (1711) (Indianapolis: Liberty Fund, 2001, I–III) vol. I, 37–94.
38. Oakeshott, *Rationalism in Politics*, 434.
39. Ibid., 435.
40. For this interpretation of Burke see Peter J. Stanlis, *Edmund Burke and the Natural Law* (Ann Arbor, MI: University of Michigan Press, 1958).

CHAPTER 10

Global Governance and the "Clandestine Revolution": From the Legal State to the Judicial State

Agostino Carrino

I

Recently both the use and the theory of "governance" entered a new phase that might indicate the exhaustion of this idea's evocative force and of its explanatory might for real processes. Out of date is now the work of political analysts, economists, sociologists, and jurists, who in the first twenty years of the past century tried to explain the differences between the various types of "governance" and the new path of social organization that marked the entrance of mankind in the "global" world. This new world was intended as a place where the old concepts of politics and law, State and sovereignty, authority and decision, power and government gave way to a progressive, peaceful, and rational universe in which human rights would rule over the actions of individuals and the

A. Carrino (✉)
University of Naples Federico II, Naples, Italy
e-mail: agocar@tin.it

© The Author(s) 2019
E. S. Kos (ed.), *Michael Oakeshott on Authority, Governance, and the State*, Palgrave Studies in Classical Liberalism,
https://doi.org/10.1007/978-3-030-17455-2_10

institutions empowered with managing the relationship between individuals and groups. This was in the light of a new liberal revolution according to which history had reached its end.

Global governance was presented as the alternative of a renewed, "humanitarian," and "democratic" enlightenment to every form of authoritarianism. As the French sociologist André-Jean Arnaud, an enthusiastic observer of this phenomenon, wrote,

> parler de gouvernance, c'est en finir avec le type de gestion pyramidal et autoritaire, c'est y introduire tous ceux qui sont concernés, c'est faire prévaloir les compromis sur le conflit, entre acteurs ayant des intérêts divergents. C'est remplacer, dans les relations entre pays, au niveau global, une logique de relations internationales qui nous vient de la philosophie politique et juridique du 18ᵉ siècle, par une approche complexe de prise de décision démocratique permettant une participation de tous les intéressés aux affaires internationales. Le développement d'une gouvernance globale ne serait plus le résultat d'un processus de prise de décision top-down, mais plutôt d'un projet commun.[1]

What is implied here, as one can ascertain from this definition, is a plain ideology, a new form of anti-political utopia, which, as with every utopian ideology, conceals in itself projects and purposes whose nature is anything but abstract. Quite the contrary, they are often very tangible. There is no need to suspect the good faith of the theorists of the cosmopolitan and participatory democracy à la Held, Beck, Archibugi, etc. One might view this as a narrative that transforms real processes from wishful thinking and misinterprets actual socioeconomic transformations as having normative purposes which often coincide with the interests of financial élites engaged in world business. Utopia should replace history and its harsh replies. But history is not ended; new and more serious dangers threaten the modern man struggling with an unprecedented crisis, not only economic ones, but also ones impacting civilization itself.

History has restarted its engines and the illusions of the bleeding hearts, one after the other, are miserably collapsing. Anyway, it would be a serious mistake not realizing the damages that this recent anti-political humanitarianism, based on the so-called *values* of the "human rights," globalization and governance, has created. It is indeed an error of judgment to consider governance as a process, on some level, neutral, according to the suggestions of certain sociologists. One among the major scholars in this vein, R.A.W. Rhodes, offered a definition of the phenomenon: "Governance refers to self-organizing, interorganizational networks characterized by interdependence, resource-exchange, rules of the game and significant autonomy from the State."[2] Autonomy from the State, or rather the refusal of the State, of this magnificent construction of the post-Renaissance European civilization (and as such endowed of a plain political character), is an undeniable element of this new form of rationalistic ideology, whose purpose is world government and perpetual peace—a kind of ideology of which Oakeshott was rightly suspicious. Not at random did he criticized rationalism and ideologies, as Timothy Fuller observed, but because he thought that they "promoted … a philosophically mistaken understanding of human reason and how it works, and derivatively because he thought [they] magnified the dangers of political misjudgment in assuming that we can know where we are going and how to get there, what he called the pursuit of perfection as the crow flies."[3]

At the same time, it has also been observed that governance represents an overcoming of the classical distinction between State and civil society: Acting at a private level, the State loses its character of a sovereign entity, whereas the private citizens lose their quality of holders of private interests. This has led to a confusion that, for now, has caused no more than pure and simple self-referential, sociological hypothesis; anyway, its purpose is to legitimate the cancellation of what has been the essential character of Western civilization from ancient times until now, namely the distinction between what is "political" and what is not.[4]

The rationalism identified by Oakeshott as distinctive of a certain mode of modern politics, or rather of its last phase, finds, however, a practical tool that is as dangerous as it is effective. We could say that the ideology of the global governance is the postmodern translation of the legal cosmopolitanism that considers judges—for example, the judge of Hans Kelsen's *civitas maxima*, a sort of *Weltstaat*—empowered with the capacity to produce a radical disillusionment of the world in the name of "technique." This practical tool is offered by the increasingly political (but basically anti-political) office of the courts, national, supranational (like the Court of Justice or the European Court of Human Rights) and international.

II

Since I am a lawyer, I will restrict myself to pointing out how the idea of governance, along with its armed branch (the courts) endangers the fundamental principles of rule of law. The rhetoric of governance, which had to supplant State and government, has begun to crumble, but still remains the concrete effect of governance qua ideology, a bad ideology. Governance has two historical foundations: from one side, the real crisis of the welfare State beginning with the 1970s; from the other side, the policy of the World Bank, to whose officials we own the early elaboration of the concept of governance.

Beforehand, in order to avoid a misunderstanding, I have to remark that neither "governance" nor judicial activism can be interpreted as a postmodern form of "civil association." In fact, contrary to Oakeshott's idea of civil association, governance implies an entrepreneurship which aims, through the fading of all the traditional, "vertical" relationships of power and the forms of its regulation (rule of law) to an "horizontal" organization[5] endowed with the task of cancelling the classical differences between political associations or "*societates*": In other words, "governance" is the "post-modern" form of the politics of faith deprived of any politics of skepticism. Not by random, as one reads in the *Report* by the UN Commission on Global Governance (*Our Global Neighborhood*, 1995), "There is no alternative to working together and using collective power to create a better world," a better world which seems to me to be the clear manifestation of what Oakeshott termed the politics of faith, transplanted now on a global scale. In fact, it's also written in the *Report*, "the development of global governance is part of the evolution of human efforts to organize life on the planet, and that process will always be going." Governance is nothing else than the organization of human life according to principles that someone considers to be the best for mankind. Its justification is that governance is to be seen as founded on consensus, while government on command; An idea quite wrong, since no government could act legitimately without a certain amount of citizen consensus. But government implies exactly authority, i.e., the maintenance of a political relationship, since politics is an ontological dimension rooted in every man. Through abolishment of national governments, the ideologists of globalization and its governance plan to abolish a constitutive part of humans as participants in a civil association.

So, governance means the attack brought to an essential part of Western civilization that is to the political dimension of being human. And, this in particular, if one considers that what seems to be only formal (the rules of the rule of law) are never really only "formal," but always also substantial; as has been noted as far as Oakeshott's civil condition is concerned—a condition that the English philosopher wants to be "formal, not substantive," in which *cives* are related "solely in terms of their common recognition of the rules which constitute a practice of civility."[6] This relationship (hence Mr. Bhuta's criticism),

> is formal only in the sense that it is distinguished from a relationship entered into in order to attain a particular satisfaction or common good (the enterprise association). It is my contention that the relationship has (considerable) substance in the same sense that all practices have substances, emerging as they do from particular ways of life, traditions, vernaculars of social and political being and a ceaseless flow of antecedent historical events. The common recognition of the rules is also at the same time a common and unconditional acknowledgement of the authority of the *respublica* and the obligations it imposes and can enforce.[7]

In other words, what governance is questioning is the very existence of a public sphere that is legitimate as such, i.e., of a legal system which is politically legitimate thanks to its intrinsic morality; actors of global governance not only are not interested in this, but *civitas* is to them, from many points of view, a foe.[8] Global governance appears to be the postmodern ideological form of a process of neutralization and de-politicization that finds exactly in the Judicial State both its tool and its end. It is a double-sided ideology: from one part the refusal of the verticality of government, from the other the primacy of *Richterrecht*, of the law created by courts.

What is under criticism, from the theorists of global governance and of the so-called legal interpretivism justified through principles, as argumented for instance by Ronald Dworkin, is not only the procedural justification of the validity of a legal system, but also the political foundation—what Carl Schmitt would call the fundamental political decision—that in a more general meaning a law must possess in order to be the valid law of a given society endowed with its own *jus*, its intrinsic righteousness or legitimacy. From this point of view, I can easily envision that Oakeshott, who already had the opportunity to criticize the

Dworkin judge, a judge who "usurps the office of legislator,"[9] would be a harsh critic of the judges' legislative power and also the power of the so-called independent administrative authorities, a power which represents an effacement of the very foundations of the separation of powers. It is better if the authority inheres in the proper offices, specifically that of the legislator, which has to be a sovereign one in order that the rule of law be kept alive. Even though in Oakeshott's thought *lex* and *jus* are concepts not always completely clear, I think that the spirit of his philosophy as far as law and politics are concerned would turn today to a path absolutely contrary to each form of rights-based judicial activism, which represents the contrary of that association's mode that we call rule of law: "And what it has no room for is either a so-called Bill of Rights (that is, alleged unconditional principles of *jus* masquerading as themselves law), or an independent office and apparatus charged with considering the *jus* of a law and authorized to declare a law to be inauthentic if it were found to be 'unjust.'"[10]

As Stephen Turner rightly comments: "The Rule of law has no place ... for courts applying the principles of Natural Law to determine whether a law is just, or conforms with the will of God, or even one concerned with what one would now call 'social justice.'"[11] And what are the principles of the Dworkin's judge if not natural law interpreted according the "values" proper to a specific ideology, the "liberal" and "humanitarian" one based upon continuously new and more and more crowdy "bills of rights"? We are witnessing to a series of usurpations of functions—a parliament which pretends to administrate instead of legislate, courts which are not limited to implement laws but create new laws, a government which is no more able to govern—that endanger the very foundations of the historical process that brought to the birth of the modern State, the tension between *societas* and *universitas*. The outcome is the final lost of State authority, a fact that has until now allowed the creation of several narratives about the "death" of the State.

This project of dismantling of the classical forms of Western politics, on one side always in tension between faith and skepticism, on the other founded on the separation of powers and the rule of law, grows significantly through the strengthening of the judicial power. When one talks about governance, a phenomenon tightly bound with the concept of globalization, so much that normally one talks about *global* governance, the focus is often on the economic aspects. Yet, there is another side which is worth mention: the phenomenon of the so-called global judiciary network, which implies exactly a kind of "governance": By the judicial power through an office that, while globalizing, pretends to be the ultimately decision maker on important sides of peoples' and individuals' lives in the name of, for instance, human rights and world peace. In particular, Anne-Marie Slaughter[12] has stressed the role played by courts in this new world order, a role that looks specially relevant as far the European law is concerned, where the Court of Justice not only has been, in the past decades, the real engine of the integration process, attributing to the treaties the role of a constitution, but also has been recognized *expressis verbis* (in the Lisbon Treaty) as having a control function that can also reach an *ultra vires* activity. This is read for example in the Art. 263 TFUE (ex. Art. 230 TEC):

> The Court of Justice of the European Union shall review the legality of legislative acts, of acts of the Council, of the Commission and of the European Central Bank, other than recommendations and opinions, and of acts of the European Parliament and of the European Council intended to produce legal effects vis-à-vis third parties. It shall also review the legality of acts of bodies, offices or agencies of the Union intended to produce legal effects vis-à-vis third parties.

This means that European "governance" keeps a control function in the Court of Justice, which is by now the legal source of the European law, a "soft," mobile law, which can be continuously "upgraded" according to the court's policy.

III

The courts' power at the "regional" and world levels is anyway only the transposition of a process self-evident already at national level. This is clear in the civil law countries, but also in those originally of common law, as the USA. It is a common problem, well known under the label of "judicial activism." The overwhelming power of the so-called judge of the laws can be criticized from several points of view: In this field, it is instructive to consider the attitude of a US constitutional lawyer, Robert Bork, who was an advocate of the originalist interpretation of the constitution and a theorist of the judge as a "neutral" office. In his books, especially *Coercing Virtue*,[13] Bork tirelessly exhorts courts to stay true to the original meaning of the US Constitution and to leave policy-making to legislators.

Bork's book presents a strategic limit. In fact, inter alia, Bork condemns the judicial imperialism especially because judges want to bend things politically in a socialist perspective. They appear as the expression of a liberal conspiracy, as representatives of a left intellectual class who aim at changing the existing social relationship with the purpose of imposing a special political consideration imbued with values which do not belong to most people. In this way, the judge becomes a legislator on the basis of his own subjective feelings; he does not enforce the existing law, but creates a new one, politically oriented according to his own prejudices.

But it is also true that if today one can say that often judges act as progressive politicians, this does not mean they will act the same way also in the future, for in the past they acted politically in a conservative and a reactionary mode, as during the Weimar Republic in Germany, or when the US Supreme Court defended the rights of enterprises against workers.

In fact, the problem of the Judicial State is a *structural* problem of the Legal State: The advent of the Judicial State is at the moment an unavoidable process written in the contradictory origins of the modern State. Bork, too, admits that the real problem consists in the fact that "we have so far found no way to retrieve constitutional law from the exclusive control of judges and to restore it to democratic legitimacy. Such action would require that judges conform their rule to principles actually found within the constitutions they apply and, in turn, practice republican virtue."[14] Not by random, in Bork's books one detects not so much anger as resignation. Judicial "imperialism" and justices as "moral teachers": This seems to be our fate.[15]

There is a gap produced by a loss of authority of the State, under attack by non-political ideologies and also owing to what Oakeshott defined "politics of faith." It is in this void between legality and legitimacy that the judicial power finds its strength, not only exercising a substitute role, but also pretending a power of its own, self-founded and no more cooperative with others in the framework of the State's unity. This new judicial power doesn't aim at enforcing the existing law, it is a fundamentally autonomous power that cancels the limits between the powers in the name of higher "charters of rights"; what had to be done by governments is today left in part to the so-called independent authorities, endangering in a substantial way the enforcement of the rule of law.[16] It is a process that in the West found its most significant phase in the USA during the years of the Warren Court and the practice of this Chief Justice to "choose fundamental values" at his discretion when deciding cases. "No argument," says Bork again, in a prescient essay, "that is both coherent and respectable can be made supporting a Supreme Court that 'chooses fundamental values' because a court that makes rather than implements value choices cannot be squared with the presuppositions of a democratic society."[17]

The process of neutralization and depoliticization, emphasized by Carl Schmitt and with whom I believe Oakeshott could fundamentally agree, has been showed by Duncan Kelly in a recent essay to have experienced an acceleration in the shifting of constitutional Legal State toward the Judicial State.[18] It is an objective process which finds its argumentation in the ideology of global governance and in the "positive" law of the charters of rights. They try to give a justification which is, in my opinion, a counter-justification insofar as what really matters in a well-ordered society are duties and obligations on which also rights have to be found. As Timothy Fuller observed talking about the rule of law, "[i]n this respect, Oakeshott was skeptical of appeals to Bills of Rights and to Natural Law arguments insofar as they encourage appeals to substantive considerations above and beyond the law."[19]

IV

From one side, we can agree with the fact that the (modern) State is not dead and that is good it is not; from the other side, it is evident that the State is undergoing a phase of deep crisis, that is depriving it of the authority it in the past had been able to prove it had, whether that be the liberal Legal State, the Napoleonic State, the authoritarian State of Bismarck, the fascist State or the so-called welfare State.[20] The State loses its authority not only when, as in the worst period of the welfare State in Europe, it intervenes deeply in social and economic relationships, coming to be owner and producer of cars, ships or foodstuffs (French President Macron is doing something similar in this time). The State also loses its authority—that is, its legitimacy—when one of its powers overwhelms the others breaking an equilibrium, which is in the Legal State always fragile and precarious based on the division of powers. The present-day judicial activism represents, from this point of view, the most serious danger for the authority of the State based on the rule of law. Global governance and human rights imperialism hold out a new form of *universitas* which limits more and more the individual's freedom.

Ultimately, global governance represents the ideological attempt to imagine a human community at a worldwide level kept together by rights valid everywhere as they are "discovered" by judges and scholars of a certain political bent independent from any national empowerment, without the need of general and abstract rules enhanced at a national level. This project can be described as a teleocracy focused on the progressive effacement of every cultural and historical difference. Here, we assist in a radical reversal of the premises which led to the birth of the modern State: An attempt to rationalize all human relationship. Hence the courts, be them constitutional, supranational or international, represent a fundamental element and tool of a humanitarian and moralist project based on the idea to impose a *pensée unique* everywhere for all peoples and individuals. Men don't deserve an equal treatment on the basis of their own individual rights (be they "natural" or enhanced by the State) and as human beings anymore; the courts have the moral duty to treat everybody in all circumstances as equals, in the sense that the judge's moral "compassion" must lead him to favor people considered at a disadvantage for belonging to a certain group—blacks, homosexuals, workers, immigrants, and so on—because that particular group has the scars of having been persecuted, discriminated, and mistreated.

From this perspective, judicial activism seems to be the final outcome of rationalism as described by Oakeshott. The definition of the rationalist can apply to the new "wise" judge who knows the secrets of the moral law: He "never doubts the power of his 'reason' ... to determine the worth of a thing, the truth of an opinion or the propriety of an action. Moreover, he is fortified by a belief in a 'reason' common to all mankind, a common power of rational consideration."[21]

The postmodern judge, exponent of this universal reason, no longer needs the positive rules or the common law or the constitutions: He already knows the "truths" at the basis of every "rational" activity. The judicial interpretation based on principles and values as defended by Ronald Dworkin, Robert Alexy, and others needs only the judge's reason, that grasps in the tables of universal values the "truth" carved on them, or rather the universal reason as it appears to its interpreters who more than anyone else are provided with the moral knowledge needed to pronounce morally and rationally legitimate sentences. The activist approach is wanting to be authorized by the constitutions, and it's the only authorization that judges accept from a positive legal text. Judges, Roger Scruton wrote criticizing Dworkin, "must call on principles that have a different authority from that of the rule issued by the legislature. Those principles are permanent features of the judicial process, invoked in the application of law even to central and unproblematic cases."[22]

Judges act, having in mind two premeditated goals (values): justice and equality. But justice and equality are concepts, values, principles, that are extremely vague and also self-contradictory; when left to the judicial discretion, they become powerful ideological weapons in the service of a determinate political ideology, this independently from the fact that judges are not aware of that. So, the Judicial State is a form of practice tied to the "politics of faith." What is more and more serious is the fact that the "politics of faith" as it has been put in practice by courts is no longer a single pole in tension with another. Quite the contrary, it has become a one-directional movement toward a higher and undisputable goal: "discovery" and protection of new rights of man. What I mean is that in the history of the modern State, politics has always been in tension between the two poles of "politics of faith" and "politics of skepticism." Even though sometimes the "politics of faith" was a necessary choice (for example in war periods), the movement has always alternated, while now the pendulum has stopped on one of the two poles: "politics of faith." Only a few today dare to put in doubt the civilizing and progressive function of "human rights" rhetoric and humanitarian cosmopolitism. Besides, Supreme Courts are ultimately decision-makers, that is to say, sovereign. Their judgments are final.

V

The Judicial State seems to be the final outcome of the modern State's ambiguities and the contradictions that affect the concept of rule of law, too.[23] Oakeshott did not omit to stress the ambiguities of the modern State and modern politics, that is why he can be helpful in the criticism of this intellectual deviation, particularly if we understand and try to solve some of the difficulties in Oakeshott's thought on the law, since sometimes he too seems to run into a form of utopianism when the refusal of purposiveness gets too harsh. The rule of law must go down in the contradictions of the actual experience, where no practice is ever "pure" in itself but always ambiguous and characterized by polar tendencies; it is the only way for the rule of law to be realized and not just hypothetical. Oakeshott appears to have a purely internal point of view of the rule of law, to speak in Hart's terms (something similar can be said of Professor Allan recent book, *The Sovereignty of Law*[24]). But the sole internal point of view isn't enough. It is also necessary to have an external point of view, be it political or sociological, which accepts that dose of teleocracy needed in order to avoid some offices in the institutional order, for example, the judicial branch, claiming for themselves powers that don't belong to them. As pointed out by David Dyzenhaus:

> since neither Oakeshott nor Hayek, and certainly not Hobbes, thought that judges could legitimately strike down valid laws on the basis that the laws lacked the attributes of *jus*, all three seem to concede that a democratic legislature has the authority to use the form of *lex* to create an administrative State dedicated to redistribution. Such a State might lack the attributes of *lex* on Oakeshott's list from *On Human Conduct* and thus be an affront to the rule of law, but its laws would still have authority.[25]

In fact, the new situation of power on a global level dictates a number of considerations in order to envisage the need to rescue, so to speak, the rule of law from itself, or better to rescue it from the danger of becoming, clandestinely, rule *by* law. Oakeshott stresses that the rule of law implies that the courts' business has to be "that of declaring the meaning of a law in respect of a contingent occurrence." However, the fact that the procedure's rules "cannot themselves announce such conclusion, any more than a law can itself declare its meaning in respect of a contingent occurrence,"[26] lets the judge have a wide margin of discretion; the extent of this judicial discretion and its keeping within the limits of the rule of law depends on the ability of the other State offices performing their own functions. The present-day crisis of the State has allowed the courts to overstep more and more their borders, going against the civil association's rules (and therefore those of the rule of law and of the separation of powers) and moved the courts toward an activity more functional for a teleological conception of the law. The courts—the constitutional courts in particular—have no interest in the *jus* of the *lex*, if this *jus* is a set of formalities guarding for the "prevailing educated moral sensibility." Rather, I would say that this "sensibility" cannot prevail over that "sensibility" which is specific to the activist judge, who stands for a "universal mind" founded on values and principles—better, "independent principles," quoting Oakeshott—and on the human rights rhetoric. Courts, in the ideological argumentations of intellectuals like Dworkin, are after all the only subjects capable of rightly interpreting principles, rights, and statutes and making them compulsory. In fact, "his 'political morality' consists almost entirely of rights and claims and makes little room for the ideas of duty and obedience."[27]

So, the judicial activist is for sure not an ignorant or a corrupt agent, but exactly a kind of modern *"philosophe"* who, to use once more Oakeshott's ironical words, has "a gift of inestimable value to mankind: a definitive understanding and language to supersede and to take the place of all other understandings and languages."[28]

Even though the activist judge as a new *philosophe* was probably not in Oakeshott's mind, because his idea of the rule of law keeps the courts as a central office in the maintenance of the ideal of a government not of men, but of laws, it is nevertheless true that, in his words: "doing is an understanding, and undeniably in all understanding there is doing."[29] So, when a judge interprets a statute, he is doing something, i.e., he is creating something. Without a limit to this creation, the courts become the creators of the law, but on whose authority? Where is the legitimacy's foundation for this activity? When a judge takes a decision applying precedents or interpreting a statute, his deliberation is a decision; his ruling doesn't have to persuade anybody of its righteousness. But when the basis on which he builds is no longer a precedent or even a legal text enacted by an elected legislature, but instead a principle or a precept that the judge alone considers binding for his jurist's conscience, his sentence won't be merely a decision that demands obedience, but a decision that, aside from obedience, pretends also to be believed based on its universal and logical validity; even if, as a matter of fact, it is *a* possible choice among several possible choices. Therefore, the argumentation in favor of the decision will probably be of a "persuasive" sort: The judge will first of all search for other judges' support, then the support of public opinion and last the support by a certain kind of politics.

But, what is a "persuasive" argument? Oakeshott says:

> In short, persuasive argument even as an auxiliary to action is itself action; it is the diagnosis of a situation (the task of persuading another to perform a chosen action), deliberation about what will persuade (namely, about the beliefs and opinions and perhaps the interests of an audience in relation to an action), the choice of an utterance related to an imagined and wished-for outcome (these others persuaded) and the resolve to make the

utterance. It was in virtue of these considerations that Plato identified persuasive discourse as inherently corrupting utterance, especially where the
audience is large and miscellaneous, and conduct (of which persuasion is a
postulate) as an inherently corrupting engagement.[30]

His definition is convincing and, even if it represents a general view, I
consider it fruitful to use in the case of judicial power.

I am not saying that the so-called activist judges are corruptors of the
public opinion, but if those who decide on the basis of their beliefs and
principles are convinced of their own choices, they will try to do their
best to convince, in a persuasive way, the others. Oakeshott notices fittingly that: "there is nothing whatever to correspond with the corrupt and corrupting expressions, 'collective understanding' and 'social
learning.'"[31]

The judge can act properly only if he complies with what justice and
the rule of law require; these are already given in a society seen as a practice of agents who produced, in history, a given structure or form of the
action that can't be changed by a judge's will, in particular if this change
is attempted on the basis of abstract principles, such as man or society:
"Man has no moral or intellectual stature, Society has no moral or intellectual worth."[32]

It is no coincidence that the activist judge attempts to give voice to
a "social consciousness" that doesn't exist and, in the end, is only that
particular judge's conscience, that dictates his own personal interpretation on what is right and what is wrong, a decision which then the judge
imposes on others. Judicial activism, from this point of view, is only
the outcome of the lost of authority of the modern State, a casualty of
the crisis of politics already stressed by Carl Schmitt in his works of the
1920s and 1930s of the last century. "Reason," in its postmodern forms,
seems to have prevailed on history and historical reasons. It is exactly in
this loss of historicity that modern constitutions lose their legitimacy. As
has been pointed out:

Legitimacy ... rests on believing in a story about the political system:
where it has been and where it should be going ... [F]or this reason judgments of legitimacy require that members of the political community be
able to see themselves as part of a political project that extends over time
... Legitimacy requires an ability to see both the past and the present as
part of a collective undertaking that begins in the past and extends out-
ward into the future.[33]

This collective undertaking takes place within a debate, a controversy, a political conflict on how to understand our own system, our own political constitution. The constitution, in fact, is nothing more than the common symbolic space within which political conflict moves: "The task for democratic theorists and politicians should be to envisage the creation of a vibrant 'agonistic' public sphere of contestation where different political projects can be confronted."[34]

It is unlikely that this process can be stopped, but, at least, scholars have the duty to mark the limit beyond which the non-compliance with these rules opens up the road to the practice "of what has been called 'a sovereign prerogative of arbitrary choice.'" We are looking at an ongoing until now more or less "clandestine" revolution,[35] that is leading toward a Judicial State; a revolution which attempts to overcome the "unresolved tension" of the modern State between *societas* and *universitas*, shifting it toward *universitas*, that is the realm of utopia, of blind faith. However, if this Judicial State is an inevitable outcome, a State where judges make their decisions on the basis only of what *they* regard, from their moral point of view, as the "higher law," we have at least the moral duty to understand and expose what is going on.

Notes

1. André-Jean Arnaud, *La gouvernance: Un outil de participation* (Paris: LGDJ, 2014), 79–80. Cf. the essays collected in Gunnar Folke Schuppert (Hrsg.), *Governance-Forschung: Vergewisserung über Stand und Entwicklungslinien* (Baden-Baden: Nomos, 2005), especially Renate Mayntz, *Governance-Theory als fortentwickelte Steuerungstheorie?*, 11–20. In the perspective of a favorable reconstruction of "governance" see Gunnar Folke Schuppert, *Governance und Rechtsetzung: Grundfragen einer modernen Regelungswissenschaft* (Baden-Baden: Nomos, 2011).
2. R.A.W. Rhodes, *Understanding Governance: Policy Networks, Governance, Reflexivity and Accountability* (Buckingham: Open University Press, 1997), 15.
3. Timothy Fuller, "Jacques Maritain and Michael Oakeshott on the Modern State," in *Reassessing the Liberal State: Reading Maritain's "Man and the State"*, eds. Timothy Fuller and John P. Hittinger (Washington, DC: American Maritain Association, 2004), 30.
4. "[D]i.e. abendländische Sozialordnung seit der Antike bis in unsere Zeit hinein bestimmt wird durch die Unterscheidung von Politischem und Nichtpolitischem," Wilhelm Hennis, *Demokratisierung—Zur Problematik eines Begriffs* (Köln und Opladen: Westdeutscher Verlag, 1970), 24.

5. Cf. Lawrence M. Friedman, *The Horizontal Society* (New Haven: Yale University Press, 1999).

6. Michael Oakeshott, *On Human Conduct* (Oxford: Clarendon Press, 1975), 121, 128.

7. N. Bhuta, "The Mystery of the State," in *Law, Liberty and State. Oakeshott, Hayek and Schmitt on the Rule of Law*, eds. D. Dyzenhaus and T. Poole (Cambridge: Cambridge University Press, 2015), 20.

8. "En fait, avec la globalisation des échanges, la gouvernance globale a opéré une sorte de transgression sauvage—eu égard à la tradition juridique—et brutale, de tous les espaces, non seulement économiques et financiers, mais aussi politiques, culturels et juridiques. Dorénavant, ce sont souvent les firmes transnationales et non pas les Etats ou les institutions internationales qui décident des contraintes opérationnelles pesant sur elles, par exemple en matière de droits sociaux fondamentaux." Arnaud, *La gouvernance: Un outil de participation*, 104.

9. Michael Oakeshott, "The Rule of Law" (1983), in *On History and Other Essays*, ed. Timothy Fuller (Indianapolis: Liberty Fund, 1999), 157.

10. Ibid., 156.

11. Stephen Turner, "Oakeshott on the Rule of Law: A Defense," *Cosmos and Taxis* 1, no. 3 (2014), 78.

12. Anne-Marie Slaughter, "A Global Community of Courts," *Harvard International Law Journal* 44 (2004), 191–219; and *A New World Order* (Princeton: Princeton University Press, 2004).

13. Robert H. Bork, *Coercing Virtue: The Worldwide Rule of Judges* (Washington, DC: The AEI Press, 2003). Cf. also *The Tempting of America: The Political Seduction of Law* (New York: Touchstone, 1991).

14. Ibid., 138.

15. "Activist courts accomplish their ends by a combination of coercion and moral persuasion. Courts inevitably assume the role of moral teachers." Ibid., 12.

16. "There is a fundamental difference between human rights and human rights law. The importance of human rights in moral thought and political deliberation does not necessarily entail any particular institutional arrangement. Still, the traditional separation of powers is an intelligent way to make provision for government that is capable of securing rights, is disciplined by law, and realises democratic self-rule. The rule of law and self-government are requirements of justice in constitutional design. Statutory bills of rights tend to fail to meet these requirements. They expand the scope and significance of judicial discretion and introduce considerable uncertainty into the law, which risks undermining executive action, the legal effect of statutes and the freedom of a representative assembly to decide what should be done." Richard Ekins, "Human

Rights and the Separation of Powers," *University of Queensland Law Journal* 34 (2015), 238.

17. Robert H. Bork, "Neutral Principles and Some First Amendments Problems," *Indiana Law Journal* 47, no. 1 (1971), 6.

18. Duncan Kelly, "Reconfiguring Reason of State in Response to Political Crisis," in *Law, Liberty, and State: Oakeshott, Hayek, and Schmitt on the Rule of Law*, eds. David Dyzenhaus and Thomas Poole (Cambridge: Cambridge University Press, 2014).

19. Timothy Fuller, "Michael Oakeshott on the Rule of Law and the Liberal Order," *Law and Liberty*, Liberty Fund, Inc., September 2, 2012, https://www.lawliberty.org/liberty-forum/michael-oakeshott-on-the-rule-of-law-and-the-liberal-order/.

20. Cf. Philip Bobbitt, *The Shield of Achilles: War, Peace, and the Course of History* (New York: Norton, 2002).

21. Michael Oakeshott, *Rationalism in Politics and Other Essays*, New and Expanded edition (Indianapolis: Liberty Press, 1991), 6.

22. Roger Scruton. *Fools, Frauds and Firebrands: Thinkers of the New Left* (London and Oxford: Bloomsbury Publishing, 2015), 79.

23. "[T]he rule of law *cannot*, without qualification, characterize a modern European State." Oakeshott, "The Rule of Law," 168. Timothy Fuller rightly comments: "This is so because the emergence of the rule of law in modern times retained a connection to ideas of a higher law. There is an ambiguity in the ideas of the rule of law we have inherited: On the one hand, appeals to a higher law may suggest that there is a set of substantive social arrangements prescribed by that higher law which is the task of humanly made law to implement. On the other hand, the higher law may be taken to be a set of precepts or maxims which express background conditions for identifying what law properly so called is, and for making laws of the sort Oakeshott has been describing. Appeals to Natural Law, for instance, may be appeals to a description of the formal character of law as such, or appeals to a substantive prescription for how we ought to live. Needless to say, this ambiguity must affect the ambivalence we experience as to the function or the purpose of the modern State." Fuller, "Michael Oakeshott on the Rule of Law and the Liberal Order."

24. T.R.S. Allan, *The Sovereignty of Law. Freedom, Constitution, and Common Law* (Oxford: Oxford University Press, 2013).

25. David Dyzenhaus, "Dreaming the Rule of Law, Law, Liberty and the State," in *Law, Liberty and the State*, eds. David Dyzenhaus and Thomas Poole (Cambridge: Cambridge University Press, 2015), 256–57.

26. Oakeshott, "The Rule of Law," 157.

27. Scruton, *Fools, Frauds and Firebrands: Thinkers of the New Left*, 67.

28. Oakeshott, *On Human Conduct*, 29.

29. Ibid., 34.
30. Ibid., 49.
31. Ibid., 87.
32. Ibid., 87.
33. Jack M. Balkin, *Constitutional Redemption: Political Faith in an Unjust World* (Cambridge, MA and London, UK: Harvard University Press, 2011), 44–45.
34. Chantal Mouffe, *On the Political* (London: Routledge, 2005), 3.
35. See Bernd Rüthers, *Die heimliche Revolution vom Rechtsstaat zum Richterstaat* (Tübingen: Mohr Siebeck, 2014).

CHAPTER 11

Three Different Critiques of Rationalism: Friedrich Hayek, James Scott and Michael Oakeshott

Shekhar Singh

I

The rationalist imposition of doctrines from above has been regarded as a serious concern for liberalism and has also posed a general threat to human freedoms. Even though it is recognized as a threat, a substantial response to rationalist imagination is yet to be agreed upon. While two responses to rationalist plans offered by Friedrich Hayek and James Scott have been influential in certain academic circles, a closer look at these approaches exposes their limitations. It is in this context that a study of Michael Oakeshott's unique critique of rationalism gains relevance.

This chapter proposes that the comprehensive nature of Oakeshott's critique of rationalism sets it apart from other critiques of doctrinal

S. Singh (✉)
Department of International Relations and Governance Studies,
School of the Humanities and Social Sciences, Shiv Nadar University,
Greater Noida, India
e-mail: shekhar.singh@snu.edu.in

© The Author(s) 2019
E. S. Kos (ed.), *Michael Oakeshott on Authority, Governance,
and the State*, Palgrave Studies in Classical Liberalism,
https://doi.org/10.1007/978-3-030-17455-2_11

rationalist thinking. Oakeshott's comprehensiveness stems from it being located in a wider philosophical understanding that is skeptical of doctrinal interventions in practical activity. Unlike Hayek's and Scott's critique of rationalism, which share an anti-doctrinal orientation but tend to become doctrinal in numerous ways, Oakeshott manages to be comprehensively anti-doctrinal by offering a critique of rationalism as a part of a wider philosophical position that separates practice from theory, science, poetry and other engagements. Oakeshott's critique of rational interventions in practical conduct is presented with the awareness that the practical worldview has limitations.

In his work *Political Philosophy of Michael Oakeshott*, Paul Franco provides a comparison between Michael Oakeshott's and Hayek's ideas on rationalism, freedom and a limited state.[1] This chapter draws from the argument put forth by Franco and extends the argument to include James Scott's work, which perhaps provides a more nuanced analysis of statecraft than Friedrich Hayek's.

This approach is likely to be criticized on the grounds that these thinkers are discussing different issues—for instance, Hayek critiques "central planning" and Scott's focus is on "high modernist plans"—and hence, a comparison of the three is comparing the incomparable. Here, however, I suggest that although Hayek, Scott and Oakeshott use different terms and phrases, a common question runs across their work— the imposition of rational plans from above. All three of them, albeit differently, have argued that simplified plans are incapable of capturing the rich practical life, a practical life that is a repository of knowledge that evolves over a period of time. They share a common concern of defending the rich practical life against doctrinal thinking, and thus, it is not implausible to look at all three thinkers as responding to rationalism, even though Oakeshott is the only one among them using the term "rationalism" in his works. Hence, this chapter uses "central planning," "high modernism" and "rationalism" interchangeably.

The chapter will first discuss central arguments found in Friedrich Hayek's and James Scott's critiques of rationalism and then argue how these critiques tend to become doctrinal. This discussion, however, will be limited to highlighting the problems that their arguments run into. The focus of this chapter will be the wider philosophical imagination employed by Oakeshott in his critique of rationalism and its uniqueness.

II—Limitations of the Hayekian Critique
of Central Planning/Rationalism

In *The Constitution of Liberty*, as the title suggests, Friedrich Hayek focuses on the legal regime that fits well with a free market economy, while his *The Road to Serfdom* is a broadside against those who believe that political freedom and centrally planned economies can cohabitate.

In *The Road to Serfdom*, Hayek makes two kinds of arguments about central planning. His first argument relates to difficulties surrounding planning complex societies. Hayek maintains that the attempt to plan complex societies from above will fail due to the unavailability of information required for executing such a plan. Human interactions involve various factors, and Hayek argues that it is impossible for one person or even a team of people to record and understand these diverse elements. He writes,

> There would be no difficulty about efficient control or planning were conditions so simple that a single person or board could effectively survey all the relevant facts. It is only as the factors which have to be taken into account become so numerous that it is impossible to gain a synoptic view of them, that decentralisation becomes imperative.[2]

Without recording and understanding this information, planning cannot proceed and a plan based on unrepresentative information is bound to fail. In his work, Hayek tries to draw distinctions between different forms of planning. Hayek's arguments are not against all kinds of planning and he is not suggesting that human societies should flourish organically, unhindered by any conscious ordering of interactions.

There is a distinction, Hayek argues, between planning one's own individual life and planning bigger and complex societies. We usually build plans for our own lives—what occupation should one choose, how much should one spend, etc.; this kind of ordering of our lives is essential. The difference between this kind of planning of one's life and the planning of complex societies by a team or a leader from above are numerous and, for Hayek, too dangerous to be missed. Plans are often prone to failure, and while in our individual lives we would readily take up the responsibility for that failure, it is not clear how failure has to be thought about in centrally planned complex societies. Democratic elections could be one way of fixing responsibility for failure of plans imposed from above, but Hayek believes that centralized planning would lead to corruption of democracy itself.[3]

The second claim that Hayek makes is that centralized planning, even if not possible, when imposed from above would require and lead to concentration of power in the hands of certain people, making its coexistence with democracy impossible. In fact, that is the central concern in Hayek's writings. The problem for him was not planning *per se*, but whether centralized planning and political and civil freedoms can coexist.[4] Hayek argues that the only kind of planning possible in a democratic set up is one that includes a regulatory framework for individual choices. Here, planners do not inhibit individual choices but ensure that individual decisions flourish in the right kind of constitutional framework. So, decisions about production and prices are unacceptable since they distort the market-based information system, but regulations about environmental restrictions imposed beforehand on all kinds of productions, are fine.

Let's assume here that Hayek argues for allocation of resources through free market-based mechanisms as the best response to the practical needs of consumers. When the state attempts this allocation from above, through experts, it ends up distorting the market's efficient information mechanism and in the worst scenarios ends up giving state officials enormous amounts of power—a discretionary power that could pave the way to "serfdom."

So, what kind of position does this Hayekian critique of central planning leave us with? In a Hayekian world, it is only in a free market-based system that a society could grow at its own pace and without interference from outside. Further, this free market system, from a Hayekian viewpoint, is less prone to authoritarianism. Is Hayek making a strong empirical claim about incompatibility of central planning and democratic freedoms and the compatibility of free market and democratic freedoms? Has this empirical claim been borne out? Very superficially, yes. The Soviet Union did move toward authoritarianism and the inefficient economic system did collapse there. However, many countries in the west, and countries like India, have successfully experimented with various degrees of governmental control over the economy without ever descending into full-blown authoritarianism. On the other hand, countries like China, Singapore and Vietnam have shown us that states can incorporate a high degree of market economics without embracing freedom in other domains.

The larger point here is that one cannot discover in advance, like rationalists or central planners tend to do, what kind of economic transactions will work for the different contexts. Arguing for a certain kind of empirical economic order for all contexts and cultures is akin to "a plan to resist all planning."[5] Rationalism ought to be repudiated with a different kind of thinking about practical activity, something that does not involve creating a blueprint for practical activities. Hayek's work does tend to speak in the language of a blueprint, and here, it betrays its rationalist roots. A Hayekian worldview ends up celebrating a certain kind of ordering of economic activities without leaving a space for different contextual judgments about the same. A defense against authoritarianism is a laudable goal, but to assume that a free market-based mechanism will protect us against the same, in different contexts, would be a grave simplification of the complexities of practical life. In other words, I am suggesting that Hayek's critique of central planning is limited as a critique of doctrinal rationalist thinking, for it ends up becoming a doctrine itself.

III—James Scott's Critique of High Modernism

James Scott, in *Seeing Like a State*, provides a more nuanced critique of high modernism/rationalism. Instead of locating the threat to human freedoms in a specific kind of economic order, Scott's focus is the larger ideology that pervades modern statecraft, as much in the capitalist west as in the Soviet Russia. I will argue that Scott ends up facing the same problem of trying to impose a general analysis on issues that belong to different contexts and might require varied judgments and analytical lens.

Scott's argument is that a certain kind of high modernist thinking pervades over most of the modern statecraft. High modernist ideology finds complex practices of communities illegible and in turn attempts to make them legible for statecraft. While mostly harmless, under certain circumstances—like where civil society organizations lack the wherewithal to challenge state actors—it could have disastrous consequences. Scott cites examples from different spheres to make his point.[6]

The first chapter of *Seeing Like a State* discusses modern forestry's attempt to grow a "planned" forest, for a natural forest was unamenable to the revenue requirements. Scott argues that while "planning" forests, proponents of scientific forestry missed out on "all those trees, bushes, and plants holding little or no potential for state revenue." Missing from the planners' vision "as well were those parts of trees, even revenue-bearing trees, which might have been useful to the population but whose value could not be converted into fiscal receipts."[7] The planners' focus was only on productive trees useful for timber. The trees were planted in rows with regular distance maintained between them for easy management and the larger organic life of a forest was ignored. The point that Scott is trying to make is that the earlier versions of modern forestry failed to recognize the complex organic world that a forest is and viewed forests only through the lens of revenue-bearing timber. The recognition of the failure of earlier versions of modern forestry, Scott argues, was a recognition of this limited way of looking at forests.

Scott, similarly, discusses at length the limitations of the high modernist urban planning, with its emphasis on segregation between residential and commercial use areas and a fascination for wide roads and high-rise apartments. Through a discussion of Jane Jacob's critique of Le Corbusier's vision of a modern planned city, Scott argues that high modernist architectural plans missed out on various organic practices that make a city livable and safe. Commenting on Jane Jacob's critique, Scott writes,

> The planners conception of a city accorded neither with the actual economic and social functions of an urban area nor with (not unrelated) the individual needs of its inhabitants. There most fundamental error was their entirely aesthetic view of order. This error drove them to the further error of rigidly segregating functions. In their eyes, mixed uses of real estate— say, stores mingled with apartments, small workshops, small restaurants, and public buildings—created a kind of visual disorder and confusion.[8]

Scott's larger point is the same, that a city has to be viewed as complex processes that organically grow out of different kinds of interactions, and the plans that simplify these complexities end up creating urban conglomerations that are unsafe, uninspiring and fail to serve their avowed purposes. Citing the example of modern Brasilia, Scott argues that the planned Brasilia failed to appeal to the new residents because "it lacks the bustle of street life, that it has none of the busy street corners and long stretches of storefront facades that animate a sidewalk for pedestrians."[9]

Scott makes similar arguments about forced villagisation in Tanzania and also about the modern state's attempts to give standardized surnames to their populations. Through all these, Scott wants to point out that states found complex practices unamenable to certain outside interests. Also, the complexity of these practices and, consequently, their usefulness was lost when they were supplanted with the planned order from above.

So far James Scott's analyses looks convincing and it does seem that the modern statecraft's attempt to simplify complex practices has led to a destruction of the contextual pragmatic knowledge. Scott then turns the same lens towards the debate on role of leadership within the Soviet Communist party. He refers to the debate between Vladimir Lenin and Rosa Luxembourg on the role of Marxist intelligentsia while sympathizing with the latter's argument that a revolution cannot be directed from above by the elite leaders. It is not a disciplined party that is led from above, but the active movement with intensive grassroots involvement that could lead to the establishment of a radical progressive society. Scott's larger point again is that even a radical party will succeed in its aims only if it is built up from below.

I want to, here, suggest that Scott's discussion of the question of leadership in a revolutionary party betrays the tendency to push a defense of local and organic processes a step too far. How a movement, democratic nation, or any other kind of organization of people should be lead is a complicated question, and answering this through formulaic answers skeptical of all kinds of direction from above is akin to imposing a singular plan on different contexts and problems. The kind of leadership suitable in a context will depend on the particular conditions prevalent in that situation. Sometimes it might be prudent for a leader to lead their parties and countries in directions that might not be agreed to by everyone.

Dipankar Gupta, in *Revolution from Above*, argues that we have greatly underemphasized the role that leaders and their qualities have played in the establishment of democratic regimes. Focusing on India, Gupta writes that if the leaders of the independent movement in India had gone by the opinion of the lower workers of the party or the larger populace of the country, then we might not have succeeded in enacting a secular constitution in the first place.[10] The point that I want to highlight through Gupta's work is that it is difficult to articulate a specific kind of position on the role of leadership in a party or a political movement. While Scott's larger point, which he makes through Rosa Luxembourg, on the importance of inner party democracy and engagement is well taken, it is doubtful if one can tell in advance which style of leading a party, political movement or a nation will work in different contexts. These are, by definition, practical matters, and an attempt to give a formulaic answer to these questions starts falling on the same analytical side as that of rationalist thinking.

It should be clear that Scott nowhere suggests that he is articulating a clear position of/on what should work in different contexts, though in *Two Cheers for Anarchism* Scott does endorse an anarchist emphasis on the value of unorganized mutuality.[11] In most examples that Scott cites his point is well taken, though it seems difficult if one can think of the unorganized mutual order as the best solution in all the contexts. As Gupta has argued in his book, it is difficult to imagine that certain modern orders would have at all emerged through unorganized mutuality. Scott is certainly not oblivious to these problems, but it is difficult to see what kind of theoretical solutions can Scott's writings provide to someone who wants to go beyond Scott's critique.

The argument in the chapter to this point has been that both Hayek and Scott offer us analytically insightful though, in the end, limited critiques of rationalism. Both of these thinkers, Hayek more than Scott, end up advocating a certain kind of ordering of the world while critiquing rationalism. Even though framed as a critique of plans that are imposed from above, both Hayek and Scott's analysis ends up providing us, even if unintentionally, with a plan for different contexts and situations.

IV—Michael Oakeshott's Philosophical Critique of Rationalism

As discussed above, works of Hayek and Scott could be read as a defense of a certain ordering of practical interactions. In Hayek's work, this leads to a defense of market-based systems, while for Scott it culminates in a defense of the unorganized mutual relations emerging from below. Does Oakeshott also provide us with a defense of a particular way of ordering our interactions? A certain reading of *Rationalism in Politics* can make one believe that Oakeshott is giving a primary place to practical knowledge, knowledge that cannot be learned through principles and doctrines. *Rationalism in Politics* is certainly an attempt to distinguish between two kinds of knowledge, the *technical* and the *practical*, but one would be mistaken to consider this as Oakeshott giving primacy to the "practical" if one places it in the context of his larger philosophy. This chapter will discuss below the wider philosophy that enables Oakeshott to critique rationalist thinking while warning us against the limitations of practical activity.

Understanding the limitations of the practical worldview remains a preoccupation throughout Oakeshott's writings. Oakeshott argues that the practical viewpoint is a certain way of ordering our experience; the practical mode of experience is the experience arranged from the perspective of a desiring self, it is the world ordered to denote its helpfulness or obstructiveness to the purposes of a practical agent.[12] There is certainly no escape from the practical viewpoint, though there are ways of experiencing that cannot be reduced to the practical agent's view. One can look at the same events from different perspectives. For instance, consider the example of buying a shirt at a supermarket, which Bhikhu Parekh uses in his work "The Political Philosophy of Michael Oakeshott."[13] While choosing a shirt, our practical interest is in procuring the best shirt that we can buy. This is an uncomplicated practical task and we have a fairly good understanding of how to go about it. There are factors that one must consider while buying a shirt: The finances involved and whether one can afford a particular shirt; the distance of the supermarket and the time it will take to reach there and whether to go there today or tomorrow, etc.

One can also view the activity of choosing a shirt from a different perspective. One can think about the numerous things that are assumed in this process of choosing a shirt at a supermarket. One can reflect on the very idea of choice and the conditions that make choice possible, e.g., deliberation, availability of different options or a human agent who is going to do the choosing. This second kind of reflection is different from the act of choosing itself, and *vide* Oakeshott we can term this kind of reflection as "theoretical" reflection on choice. Instead of choosing, one is reflecting on what all is assumed in the activity of choosing. The product of this theoretical reflection, if one ends up taking this activity seriously, is a theory of choice.

The point to be noticed in the above example, and a point that Oakeshott makes at various places, is that there is no direct link between a theory of choice and the practical activity of choosing a shirt. The knowledge of a theory of choice will not make us better at choosing a shirt. Choosing a shirt is a practical activity, while a theory of choice dwells upon the conditions that are assumed in choice. For a practitioner, choice is an uncomplicated idea, something we do every day, but for a theoretician, choice is an invitation to think further, a mystery to be understood further, as Oakeshott would say.

In other words, a theory of something and a practical decision to do something are completely different in nature. A practical view assumes things, uncritically, while theory reflects on what all is assumed in these activities. If a practitioner chooses to investigate the assumptions of an activity, it will necessarily take her toward a theory of that activity. Also, while practical activity is about *doing*, and its goal is to achieve something here and now, a theorist's goal is *understanding* something in its completeness. A practitioner's urgency to act necessarily impedes a theoretician's goal of achieving complete understanding of the conditions assumed in that activity. Put differently, while practice is oriented toward doing and consensus, a theorist by nature is oriented toward completeness and criticality.

Oakeshott also separates a practical worldview from other kinds of intellectual activities. Throughout his philosophical writings, history as an intellectual activity remained one of his preoccupations. For Oakeshott, by the logic of her activity an historian is always interested in the past for the past's sake, but because we live in the present and practical worldview is the most dominant perspective, the remnants of the past (a document or an object) are mostly found entangled in, what he calls, "practical-present." All the enquiries begin from the present, but an historical inquiry can only begin by first separating these remnants of the past from the practical-present. The separation of remnants from the past from practical-present requires intellectual training and effort, and though one often fails in achieving this, it remains a necessary condition of any kind of historical inquiry. The separation of practical interest from historical inquiry also bars certain kinds of observation from historical inquiry. "In 'history' no man dies too soon or by 'accident'; there are no successes, and no failures and no illegitimate children. Nothing is approved, there being no desired condition of things in relation to which approval can operate, and nothing is denounced. This past is without the moral, the political or the social structure which the practical man transfers from his present to his past."[14]

The other inference that Oakeshott's draws from his theory of history is that the "historical" past cannot be used for the present purposes. One can certainly draw lessons from the past, and we certainly do that in practical activity, but this usage necessarily changes the character of the historical past. To put it in another way, there is a clear separation between history and a practical person's view of the past, and one can pursue each only while destroying the other.

Science and poetry are the other two intellectual activities that Oakeshott separated from practical activity. Scientific description of the world is the world looked at from the perspective of quantity and full communicability. While practical experience is the experience organized from the perspective of a desiring subject, scientific descriptions are devoid of any subjective viewpoint. Oakeshott explains this through an example:

> If I say: 'It is a hot day', I am still making a statement about the world in relation to myself. Its reference is more extended, but the remark is unmistakably in the practical idiom. If I say: 'The thermometer on the roof of the Air Ministry stood at 90°F. at 12 noon G.M.T.' I may not have emancipated myself completely from the practical attitude, but at least I am capable of being suspected of making a statement, not about the world in relation to myself but about the world in respect of its independence of myself. And when, finally, I say: 'The boiling point of water is 100° Centigrade', I am making a statement which may be recognized to have achieved the idiom of 'science'.[15]

Oakeshott suggests that science, by the logic of its identity, is constituted by statements devoid of subjective markers. Science provides an "objective" account of the world, while the practical account is from the perspective of a desiring self.

Poetic response, in Oakeshott's writings, is associated with a contemplative response to images. Each "going-on" is capable of eliciting two kinds of responses. One is the response we get when what appears in front of us is probed further to reveal what does not appear immediately. This first kind of response is the explanatory response, a response common to history, science, theory and practice. Explanations in the modes of practice, history and science are pursued differently, but at some level, they are all explanatory responses. Every "going-on" is also capable of eliciting a second kind of response, which Oakeshott calls the "contemplative" response. In this second kind of response, we are not driven by the interest to explain what appears in front of us through what doesn't appear, but treat it is a mere "image." "Further, images in contemplation are merely present; they provoke neither speculation nor inquiry about the occasion or conditions of their appearing but only delight in their having appeared."[16] Only the uninitiated would ever ask questions about the factual correctness of poetic images. The questions about fact and (non)-fact are not recognized as valid questions in the activity of poetic imagination.

The above paragraphs provide a brief account of how Oakeshott separates different kinds of intellectual activities from the practical worldview. There is another question that one needs to address, which pertains to Oakeshott's theorization of civil association in *On Human Conduct*. Could one argue that Oakeshott was trying to present civil association as the best form of association? Oakeshott was certainly more inclined toward civil association, but to draw out a recommendation out of his theorization of civil association would go against his larger philosophy.

While theorizing *civil association* Oakeshott is reflecting on a kind of association found in the modern world, another kind of association he calls *enterprise association*. Oakeshott then describes the various conditions of a civil association, e.g., a rule of law, non-purposiveness, etc. A theory of civil association is provided here, a kind of association that already manifests itself in various practices of modern democracies. It would be difficult to argue that Oakeshott meant his theory of association as a recommendation to establish civil associations. A theory of civil association is a reflection on the conditions of civil association, a kind of association that is getting lost in larger public imagination. What one gets here, at best, is a definition and understanding of the postulates of civil association.

Let us get back to the three different critiques of rationalism that have been discussed in this chapter. The larger point that the chapter is trying to put forth is that while it is plausible to imagine what a Hayekian or a Scottian position on practical matters would be—a Hayekian would argue for a free market-based economic system and a Scottian would recommend the unorganized mutual order that emerges from below—it is difficult to imagine what an Oakeshottian position on practical matters would be. Given the fact that Oakeshott specifies and separates the practical worldview from other kinds of activities, it becomes difficult to argue for a certain kind of practical position out of Oakeshott's writing.

A critique of rationalism requires that we should be able to point out the deleterious effects of rational plans and doctrines imposed from above, but these critiques in turn have a tendency to become plans to criticize planning. Oakeshott's critique of rationalism is unique because while on one hand, it provides us with a critique of doctrinal interventions in practical life, on the other, it warns us against the limited practical perspective and separates theory, science, history and poetry from practical activity. An Oakeshottian agent, even if one could get over the paradox in the term itself, is certainly not the one who elevates practicality over other kinds of activities.

NOTES

1. Paul Franco, *Political Philosophy of Michael Oakeshott* (New Haven: Yale University Press, 1990).
2. Friedrich A. Hayek, *The Road to Serfdom* (New York: Routledge, 2001), 51.
3. Ibid., 59–74.
4. Ibid., 91–104.
5. Michael Oakeshott, *Rationalism in Politics and Other Essays* (London: Methuen & Co. Ltd, 1962), 21.
6. James Scott, *Seeing Like a State* (New Haven: Yale University Press, 1998), 3–5.
7. Ibid., 12.
8. Ibid., 133.
9. Ibid., 126.
10. Dipankar Gupta, *Revolution from Above: India's Future and the Citizen Elite* (New Delhi: Rupa, 2013).
11. James Scott, *Two Cheers for Anarchism: Six Easy Pieces on Autonomy, Dignity, and Meaningful Work and Play* (Princeton, NJ: Princeton University Press, 2012).
12. Oakeshott, *Rationalism in Politics*, 207–12.
13. Bhikhu Parekh, "Political Philosophy of Michael Oakeshott," *British Journal of Political Science* 9, no. 4 (1979), 489.
14. Oakeshott, *Rationalism in Politics*, 154.
15. Ibid., 146.
16. Ibid., 217.

INDEX

© The Editor(s) (if applicable) and The Author(s),
under exclusive license to Springer Nature Switzerland AG 2019
E. S. Kos (ed.), *Michael Oakeshott on Authority, Governance,
and the State*, Palgrave Studies in Classical Liberalism,
https://doi.org/10.1007/978-3-030-17455-2

Printed by Printforce, the Netherlands